D1439082

COROMANDEL

COROMANDEL

A personal history of South India

CHARLES ALLEN

Little, Brown

LITTLE, BROWN

First published in Great Britain in 2017 by Little, Brown

1 3 5 7 9 10 8 6 4 2

Copyright © Charles Allen 2017
Maps © John Gilkes

The moral right of the author has been asserted.

All rights reserved.
No part of this publication may be reproduced, stored in a
retrieval system, or transmitted, in any form or by any means, without
the prior permission in writing of the publisher, nor be otherwise circulated
in any form of binding or cover other than that in which it is published
and without a similar condition including this condition
being imposed on the subsequent purchaser.

A CIP catalogue record for this book
is available from the British Library.

ISBN 978-1-4087-0539-1

Typeset in Caslon by M Rules
Printed and bound in India by
Manipal Technologies Limited, Manipal

Papers used by Little, Brown are from well-managed forests
and other responsible sources.

Little, Brown
An imprint of
Little, Brown Book Group
Carmelite House
50 Victoria Embankment
London EC4Y 0DZ

An Hachette UK Company
www.hachette.co.uk

www.littlebrown.co.uk

History would be an excellent thing, if it were only true.

Leo Tolstoy, writing to N. N. Gusev, 1908.

The past is never dead. It's not even past.

William Faulkner, *Requiem for a Nun*, 1951.
Paraphrased by Barack Obama in his presidential nomination speech 'A more perfect union', Philadelphia, 1 March 2008.

CONCANEES or CANNEREENS.

Are the descendents of the brahmins, who came and settled here from Goa and other parts of the country, they are chiefly traders sroffs goldsmiths &c.

Gouache of a Brahmin couple from the Konkan, from an album of 'Native types', c. 1845. The crudely printed caption reads: 'CONCANEES or CANNEREENS are the descendants of the Brahmins, who came and settled here from Goa and other parts of the country, they are chiefly traders sroffs [*shroffs*, or bankers, from Arabic *saraaf*] goldsmiths &c.'

CONTENTS

LIST OF MAPS

The maps depicted in the book are a creation of the author for illustrative purposes only. The maps and the external boundaries of India on the maps have not been authenticated and may not be legally or factually correct.

PREFACE:
A HEALTH WARNING TO THE READER

This book is mostly about South India and aspects of its cultural history that I find particularly fascinating – or challenging. I do not claim for one moment that it is more 'correct' as history than anything else that has been written, only that it is my attempt to make sense of some of the forces and contradictions that have shaped the multifarious culture of the Indian South – hence my subtitle 'a personal history'. Although written for a general readership I very much hope it will also appeal to English-speaking readers in India and to HINAs (Hindus in North America) and HIBs (Hindus in Britain) – hence my health warning.

I write as a secular humanist. Despite my Indian roots, my cultural attitudes have been shaped largely by Britain, which is an increasingly secular society. We British are in general not just irreligious but downright anti-religious. A recent survey carried out by the *Observer* newspaper showed that 61 per cent of the British population thought that religion is 'a negative influence in the world rather than a force for good'. Only 15 per cent disagreed.[1]

On the Indian subcontinent it is very much the other way round. Religion continues to shape South Asian society to a degree unthinkable in most of Europe – although not in the United States of America, where polls suggest that around 42 per cent of Americans believe in Creationism and only 19 per cent in Darwinian evolution.

So reader, if you truly believe that Hanuman and his monkey army helped Rama build a bridge linking the Indian mainland to the island of Lanka in the golden age of the Treta Yuga; or that the Buddha Sakyamuni ascended to the Tushita heaven on a ladder to preach to the mothers of all the Buddhas; or that the Prophets Elijah and Moses appeared before Jesus of Nazareth on a high mountain; or that the Prophet Muhammad rode Al-Buraq, the winged steed, on his night ride from Mecca to Jerusalem; or that when the Guru Nanak visited Mecca the Kaaba moved to be wherever his feet pointed – then please read no further. This is not the book for you and I have no wish to cause you offence.

And you, reader, since your eyes are still on this page – thank you for keeping an open mind.

Charles Allen, London

A NOTE ON NAMES, DATES
AND ILLUSTRATIONS

An illustration from James Forbes, *Oriental Memoirs*, 1813.

In my dating I have employed BCE (Before the Common Era) and CE (Common Era) in preference to the now politically incorrect BC and AD.

Wherever possible I have illustrated my text with black and white drawings and early photographs from yesterday's India. Every effort has been made to obtain clearance for their use, although in some cases it has not been possible to locate a presumed copyright holder. All who supplied photographs or helped me with information and support have, I hope, been named and thanked in my Acknowledgements and Picture Credits. All uncredited contemporary photographs were taken either by me or by my wife, Liz Allen.

The names of many people and places mentioned come in different forms and spellings according to source and language used. For example, the town in Tamil Nadu known as Trichy to the British, and as Trichinopoly to Sanskrit-based language speakers, is better known to Tamil-speakers as Tiruchirappalli (or variations in spelling thereof). Here I am sticking to the best-known version (in this case, Trichy), with the local spelling added in brackets where appropriate.

I have tried wherever possible to avoid that loaded word 'Aryan', with all its negative connotations. The original Vedic term was 'Arya' and I am sticking with that in reference to the Sanskrit-speakers whose distinctive culture first emerged in Northern India about three and a half thousand years ago. Their word for their priestly caste was *Brahmana*. This was shortened to *Brahman* and then anglicised into Brahmin, which is just plain wrong. Even so, Brahmin is now common usage so Brahmin it is here.

The word 'Sanskritist' also requires clarification. In academic terms, a Sanskritist is not simply someone who knows all the *Shastras* by heart but a scholar who studies them as a philologist trained in the structure of language. So Panini, the scholar credited with assembling the first Sanskrit grammar, *Ashtadhyayi*, could be said to be the first Sanskritist, but not the Brahmin priests who assisted him. Similarly, the great philologist Sir William Jones became in time a Sanskritist but, arguably, not so his chief pandit Ramlochan Cantaberna, the man who taught him Sanskrit at what was then the most important centre of Sanskrit learning in Bengal, Nadiya, and who afterwards joined him in Calcutta both as a language teacher and as what we would now call a 'Reader'. This is not to downplay the role of such pandits, who were always to be found at the shoulder of every foreign linguist who ever came to India and who were in many instances extremely erudite. These pandits and munshis (language teachers) could well be described as the unsung heroes of early Indology, rarely given the credit they deserved.

A European imagining of India's Malabar and Coromandel coasts and Ceylon as rich in trade goods, including cloths, ivory, pearls, coconuts, spices and stuffed tigers, and seemingly as much populated by Africans as Indians. This illustration appeared in the Churchill brothers' *Collection of Voyages and Travels*, published in 1744, incorporating an earlier work: *A True and Exact Description of the Most Celebrated East-India Coasts of Malabar and Coromandel*, written by the Catholic missionary Father Philip Baldaeus of Delft in 1672. Employed by the Dutch East India Company, Baldaeus was the first European to give an account of the *Mahabharata* and *Ramayana*. He also proposed that European civilisation had its roots in India.

INTRODUCTION:
SOMETHING ABOUT MYSELF

Arab coasting dhows off the Malabar coast. A watercolour painted by
Lieutenant-Fireworker Thomas Cussans in 1820.

He stood up against the mast, swinging in circles, swoop-
ing from sky to sea, and looking out under his hand. The
rising sun climbed slowly out of the trough of the waves
astern. Ahead the sea stretched to a low dark line which
might be the land. From horizon to horizon, covering
all that sea, the white horses rode westward towards the
doubtful coast.

Jason saw the land harden before his eyes as the ship
rose on a great wave. He shouted, 'Land ho!', and then:
'Coromandel!'

John Masters, *Coromandel!*, 1955

I have called this book *Coromandel* chiefly for sentimental reasons. I first became aware of that sonorous word as a fifteen-year-old schoolboy exiled in England. *Coromandel!* was the title of the third in a series of *Boy's Own*-style adventure stories set in India written by John Masters, an ex-Indian Army officer turned popular novelist. It was all about a West Country lad who sails to India with a map to find the legendary Coromandel and make his fortune. I reread it recently and found it not half as good as I thought it was – but the magic of that word Coromandel has always stayed with me, as the very essence of South India in all its elusiveness and allure. I'm not alone in thinking this. The French fashion-house Chanel markets a perfume it calls Coromandel which, it claims, 'unfurls the enveloping notes of its amber vibrato before giving way to a lingering voluptuous accord'. It lists the perfume's ingredients as frankincense, benzoin and patchouli. If it were up to me, those ingredients would be sandalwood, nutmeg, cinnamon and cloves, with a touch of pepper and cardamom to give it added spice.

Supporters of the late Edward Said, whose book *Orientalism* caused a mighty rumpus when it was published in 1978, would call such sentiments typically Orientalist, but I would refer them to the Bengali writer-in-exile Nirad Chaudhuri, who in his book *The Continent of Circe* (1965) compared Mother India to the Greek sorceress Circe, who seduced men with her enchantments and kept them trapped on her island. That is rather how I feel about India, the land of my birth. Ever since I can remember I have been immersing myself in her muddy waters, getting her dust between my toes. Almost my earliest memory is of lurching on elephant-back through steamy sub-tropical jungle, my father having borrowed a couple of elephants from a local maharaja to go in search of a legendary copper temple lost in the jungles of north-eastern Assam. I remember losing my sola (note spelling!) topee, which in those days was mandatory for any white child in the sun, and the elephant retrieving it from the forest floor and handing it back to me with his trunk, ever so delicately. I have loved these gentle, intelligent giants ever since, and fully understand why the early Buddhists and Emperor Ashoka in particular chose the elephant as a symbol of their faith. I used to be puzzled as to why Hinduism did not follow suit and why the cow was preferred. Now I know better, as a later chapter explains.

Three other particularly vivid images from my Indian childhood have stayed with me. One is of my father dispensing justice on the front verandah of our bungalow. He was then a Political Officer in the North-East Frontier Agency, where he had responsibility for maintaining law and order among the hill tribes bordering India's frontier with Tibet. It was customary for officials like him to make themselves available outside office hours to all and sundry, and this is what I remember him doing, morning and evening, on the verandah, so that there were always queues of people – many of them wild-looking men in rudimentary loincloths armed with bows, spears and short swords – waiting for him to hear their petitions or resolve their quarrels. It left me with a lasting image of my father as the very embodiment of British rule in India, which I grew up believing to be essentially benevolent, even if paternalist. Apparently a majority of British people share those same early views of mine, since a recent YouGov poll found that 43 per cent of the British public are generally proud of colonialism and the British empire, and only 21 per cent regret that it happened.[1]

A second memory comes from that same bungalow. When I was about four my parents went to Calcutta (now Kolkata), leaving me in the care of my father's boss, who was a bachelor. I had a slight fever, which was why I was lying on my bed in the middle of the afternoon. I heard a hiss, and there on the floor by the door was a large cobra. I screamed and went on screaming until a servant ran in with an axe and chopped the cobra in half. Then my father's boss appeared with a shotgun and blew the cobra's head off. He told me it would be better not to say anything about this to my parents, so I never did. But from that day on I have lived in terror of snakes. Just thinking about it as I write these words is enough to make the hairs prickle on my scalp.

It follows that to think of the hooded Indian cobra *Naja naja* as death incarnate seems to me entirely reasonable. Recent research published by the American Society of Tropical Medicine and Hygiene has put the figure of deaths from snake-bite in India at forty-six thousand annually, which is a long way from the Government of India's official estimate of two thousand fatalities. Given such figures, it is easy to see why in India the cobra remains an object of fear – and of worship. Not only does it deliver death, it also disappears underground every summer, only to reappear with a new skin with the monsoon rains, seemingly reborn. So one can understand why it continues to be treated with as much reverence as caution – nowhere more so than among the Nairs in Kerala – and why the three great religions that took shape in early India all incorporated the cobra into their respective faiths.

My third memory is one of the last from my Indian childhood. My family were about to depart for Bombay (Mumbai) to board a troopship bound for Liverpool. On the morning of 31 January 1948 I paid my usual visit to the servants' quarters behind our bungalow, where I found everyone unusually subdued. The cook was crying. I asked why and was told that 'Bapu' had been killed. I had no idea who Bapu was but out of sympathy with the cook I began crying, too. But then I was told that there was no need to cry because Bapu was now sitting on a lotus leaf in Swarga (heaven) in the company of Lord Vishnu. That image of the assassinated Mahatma Gandhi seated on a lotus leaf with his spinning-wheel has stayed with me ever since.

So mine was a privileged upbringing, as a scion of a ruling class, rooted in the fact that six generations of the male members of my family chose to seek their fortunes in India, in occupations as varied as the Indian Civil Service (ICS), the Indian Army, indigo-planting and missionary work. Many were born in India, like myself and my parents before me, and at least a dozen that I know of lie in graves as far apart as Ali Masjid in the Khyber Pass and Colombo. The rest did their best to come Home – always implied with a capital 'H' if not actually spelled that way – to die in Cheltenham or thereabouts on modest pensions.

That elephant ride in the Assam jungle was over seventy years ago. In 1966 I was lucky enough to be posted by Voluntary Service Overseas to Nepal to teach English at a school outside Kathmandu. I'm not sure the boys I taught learned much but I did, because Nepal was then the last surviving Hindu monarchy on the subcontinent, as well as having the last surviving pocket of Mahayana Vajrayana Buddhism. Nepal was also where I met my future wife Liz, and since then she and I have been drawn back to the subcontinent time and time again, to criss-cross the country by whatever means were available to us, which now tends to be a comfy air-conditioned car with driver.

Ever since that first elephantine adventure of my childhood the notion of quest has had me hooked. Without quite knowing why, I have made pilgrimages to Kedarnath and Badrinath, dipped my head under the icy waters of the actual source of the Ganges at Gaumukh and at its legendary source in Lake Manasarovar, and completed *parikarama*s – circuits of holy places – of Mount Kailas and Kawa Karpo in far eastern Tibet, to say nothing of visiting thousands of Hindu *mandir*s and *kovil*s, Jain *basti*s, Sikh *gurdwara*s and Buddhist *stupa*s, *vihara*s and rock-cut *chaitya*s. I can even claim to have completed the *char dham yatra* – pilgrimage to the four holiest abodes, of Badrinath, Dwaraka, Puri and

Rameshwaram – though more by chance than religious intent. The mysteries of the unknown and the unexplored have led me to search for yetis in the Himalayas and for the lost land of Shambhala in far western Tibet, to trace the footsteps of the Chinese pilgrims Faxian and Xuanzang and, more recently, to track down the minor and major rock edicts and pillar edicts of the great emperor Ashoka, scattered far and wide across India, Pakistan and Afghanistan.

This travelling was never about gaining merit or the absolution of sins. It was always the journey that mattered, and what these travels could tell me about the country and its history – a history so alluring, so epic as to keep drawing me back. There is so damn much of it, and so much still unexamined, still disputed, still buried and waiting to be brought back into the light.

So it has gone on for half a century. In the process I have been drawn ever deeper into Indian India, to which I'd like to think I have learned to expose my inner self as much as the twenty-year-old Rudyard Kipling did when he began his night walks into Indian Lahore in the 1880s, of which he wrote in a letter to a friend:

> I am now deeply involved with the people of the land. I hunt and rummage among 'em, knowing Lahore City – that wonderful, dirty, mysterious ant hill – blind-fold, and wandering through it like Haroon-Al-Rashid in search of strange things. India is now my own place, where I find heat and smells of oil and spices, and puffs of temple incense, and sweat and darkness, and dirt and lust and cruelty, and, above all, things wonderful. I am in love with the country and would sooner write about her than anything else.[2]

I, too, love the land of my birth, and have been lucky enough to be allowed to write about her these past forty years. However, the fact is that I know far more about North India than I do about the South, which is partly why I set myself the task of researching and writing this book, which concentrates on the country south of the Narmada, the river that takes its name from the Sanskrit for 'Giver of Pleasure', and which the British, for no reason that I can establish, called the Nerbudda.

The Narmada runs east to west along a rift in the Earth's crust that forms a natural 800-mile ditch across the country. This, by ancient tradition, marks the divide between North and South India, and with good reason, since the Narmada is banked on both sides by mountain ranges: the Vindhyas to the north, the Satpuras on its south bank. In geological terms the Vindhyas and Satpuras are part of a whole, the so-called Vindhyan supergroup, made up of layer upon layer of loose rock strata piled one upon another. Taken together, the ditch and its palisades create a formidable barrier, and one that the early chroniclers of the Arya were quick to designate the southern limits of their primary homeland, drawing on a word from the Prakrit or common tongue, *Dakhina*, to name the unknown country beyond in their more refined Sanskrit *Dakshina*, the 'south country', subsequently smoothed out into the word Deccan.

In the days of the British Raj this country south of the Narmada River was widely known as the 'sloth belt', the idea being that it was a more provincial sort of place than the North, with its own slower pace of doing things, and so a social, cultural and political backwater which ambitious civil servants and military officers tried to avoid. It wasn't, of course, but the tendency has always been to equate India with the North and to treat the South as an adjunct.

There is some justification for this, because before the supremacy of European sea-power India's identity was largely shaped by waves of migrants emerging out of the mixing bowls of Eurasia by way of what is now Iran and Afghanistan. It meant that the political spotlight was always on the Indus, the river basin of the Punjab, and the Doab – the fertile alluvial plain lying between the Ganges and the Jumna. Three and a half millennia ago this became Aryavarta, the heartland of Arya culture, where two social groups – Brahmin priests and thinkers, and Kshatriya warriors and rulers – locked together in symbiotic alliance. This unique nexus gave Aryavarta-Bharat-Hind-India the stabilising continuity that made it possible for Mahatma Gandhi to speak in the 1920s of 'the beauty of the caste system', because, for him, it was caste that had saved Hindu India from disintegration: 'I believe that if Hindu society has been able to stand, it is because it is founded on the caste system.'[3]

In later years Gandhi's contacts with the Dalit social reformer Dr Bhimrao Ambedkar led him to modify what we would now consider to be his reactionary views. But Gandhi's point stands. That Brahmin–Kshatriya alliance was the *stambha*, the central column or backbone, around which Hindu society in the North revolved, even through what many would regard as the darkest days of Sultans Mahmud of Ghazni and Ala-ud-Din, Emperor Aurangzeb (who did more to sow division between his subjects than any of his Mughal predecessors) and Lord Lytton (who, as Viceroy, not only refused to implement available relief measures during the catastrophic Great Famine in South India in 1876-8, but ensured that record amounts of grain were exported to Britain at the same time).

But how much of this applied south of the Narmada River, to the Deccan and, in particular, to the deeper South and the country that many of its inhabitants would prefer to speak of as *Tamilakam*, 'the land of the Tamil people' (the ancient heartland corresponding to the present-day states of Kerala and Tamil Nadu but extending northwards to include Andhra Pradesh and

Telangana as well as parts of Karnataka and Odisha)? The earliest recorded appearance of that word 'Tamil' can be seen on King Kharavela's inscription on the Hathigumpha rock cave outside Bhubaneshwar, inscribed in about 150 BCE, where he speaks of a *tamira samghatta* or 'Tamil confederacy', although in its earliest form the word was *dravida*, which much later gave rise to 'Dravidian', the term now used to describe the family group of languages widely, but by no means exclusively, spoken south of the Narmada (see Map 1 on page 11).

We are, in essence, talking about two distinct peoples and cultures. Consider and contrast, for example, the two key states of Uttar Pradesh (UP) in the north and Tamil Nadu (TN) in the south. Both play hugely important roles within their respective regions as social, political and religious hubs but are utterly different in so many ways. The present population of the state of UP (roughly the size of the United Kingdom) is well over two hundred million, which is nearly three times that of TN (roughly the size of England). According to the 2011 National Census the female literacy rate in UP is 59 per cent as compared to TN's 74 per cent; the mortality rate for females between birth and twelve months is 87 per 1000 in UP and 54 per 1000 in TN; the sex ratio is 91 females per 100 males in UP and 100 females per 100 males in TN. In terms of social make-up, one fifth of the population of both states is made up of persons classed as belonging to the Scheduled Castes, also known as Dalits and formerly known as Untouchables, and in both states the so-called Scheduled Tribes, formerly known as Tribals, make up just 1 per cent of the population. However, in other respects the two states are markedly different: Muslims make up 19 per cent of the population in UP and 6 per cent in TN, which also has a 6 per cent Christian population; Brahmins make up 11 per cent of the population in UP but only 4[4] per cent in TN; high-caste Thakurs and Vaishyas make up 10 per cent of the UP population, but in TN this designation breaks down entirely because of the absence of established higher-caste categories. One other statistic which I find significant is that of seven Nobel Prize winners of Indian origin, three have been Tamil Brahmins, all of them scientists.

These two Indias may form a political whole, but in cultural terms they are chalk and cheese, old and new, volcanic and alluvial, *shakti* and *shiva*, rice and wheat, *todi* (think toddy) and soma (the mysterious intoxicant drunk by the early Arya), *dosa* (rice pancake) and chapatti (unleavened flatbread), water buffalo and cow, Dravida and Arya. This North–South difference is neatly epitomised in the current leaders of these two states. In UP the newly installed Chief Minister at the time of writing is a Hindu nationalist belonging to the Bharatiya Janata Party (BJP) – the lean, shaven-headed, saffron-clad Rajput firebrand Yogi Adityanath, the *mahant* (head) of the Goraknath *math* (monastic order) at Gorakhpur. In TN it is the stocky, moustachioed figure of Edappadi Palaniswami, drawn from the dominant Gounder or Kongu Vellalar agriculturalist and landowning community, and a stalwart of the All-India Anna Dravida Munnetra Party, which until her recent death was dominated for years by the matriarch Jayalalithaa, known to her devotees as Amma (mother) or *Thanga tharagai*, the 'golden girl'.

But perhaps the greatest difference of all is in language. The further you travel south of the Narmada River the stronger that sense of Dravidian or Tamil identity becomes – and the louder that liquid, bubbling, melodic sound of spoken Tamil and its variants.

This division between North and South is at its most obvious when the major language groups spoken on the Indian subcontinent are plotted on a map (see Map 1). Today almost 94 per cent of first languages spoken in India belong to one or other of the two dominant language families: Indo-Aryan, spoken by about 74 per cent of Indians, and Dravidian, spoken by about 24 per cent. So three-quarters of India's present-day population speak one or other of the Sanskrit-based Indo-Aryan languages such as Hindi, Gujarati, Marathi and Punjabi; just less than a quarter speak languages that are Tamil-based in origin, whether Tamil, Telugu, Malayalam, Kannada or Tulu. The remaining 2 per cent is divided between the so-called Austro-Asiatic group and the Tibeto-Burman group of languages spoken along India's borders abutting Tibet and Burma.

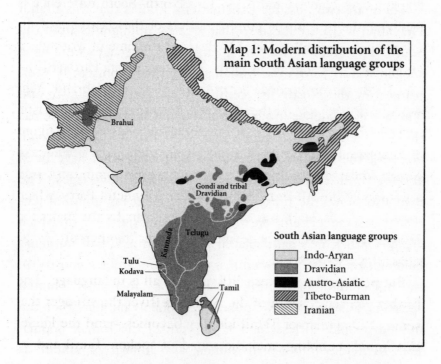

Map 1: Modern distribution of the main South Asian language groups

South Asian language groups

- Indo-Aryan
- Dravidian
- Austro-Asiatic
- Tibeto-Burman
- Iranian

The modern distribution of the two main South Asian language groups – Indo-Aryan and Dravidian-Tamil – along with three smaller groups: Austro-Asiatic, now spoken only in small pockets in central and eastern India; Tibeto-Burman, spoken along the Indian sub-continent's pre-1947 Himalayan and eastern borders; and Iranian, spoken on the western borders of Pakistan. (Adapted from 'Language families and branches', in *A Historical Atlas of South India*, OUP, 1992.)

Packed into one solid triangle in the deep south are the Dravidian language speakers, just as you would expect, with scattered
pockets of outriders extending along the Vindhyan supergroup,
plus one isolated pocket far over to the west, which marks the
location of the Brahui language speakers, now entirely surrounded
by Baluchi-speakers who form part of the Iranian language group,
itself descended from Proto-Indo-Iranian. But what on earth is
that pocket doing there, you might well ask, so isolated from the
nearest Dravidian-speaking population by more than 800 miles
(1300 kilometres)?

There are two possible explanations. One is that this Brahui
Dravidian was introduced to that area by immigrants from the
South. The other is that Dravidian-based languages were once
spoken widely across the Indian subcontinent, only to be sup-
planted in the North and centre by speakers of Indo-Aryan.
There is no evidence in support of the first explanation, whereas
there is considerable supporting evidence for the second,
not least the number of Dravidian loan words that have been
absorbed into Hindi and other Sanskrit-based languages. The
map also shows the presence of a third language group of particular relevance here: Austro-Asiatic, the speakers of which
are now stuck in small isolated pockets in a sort of no-man's
land between the two dominant language groups, mostly in
the hill country of central India. These are mainly Munda-
speakers, a language now spoken by probably no more than ten
million people, so less than 1 per cent of the Indian population. It divides into North Munda, also known as Santali, as
spoken in the plateau country of Jharkhand, Chhattisgarh and
parts of West Bengal; and South Munda, spoken in the hills of
Odisha and Andhra Pradesh. Traces of Munda are also found
in a number of mixed languages spoken all the way along the
foothills of the Himalayas, all of which points to it being much

more widely spoken in South Asia in the distant past, and, in all probability, pre-dating Dravidian.

This, by inference, is the prime language of those often spoken of as *vanavasi*, 'forest people', *girijan*, 'hill people', or simply aboriginals or tribals. Now classified for official purposes as Scheduled Tribes, they are now increasingly referred to as Adivasi, or 'first people' – as they will be here.

These two non-Sanskrit peoples, Dravidian and Adivasi, are very much the chief focus of this book, but be warned that what I have written is partial in both senses of that word: partial in that it is incomplete, and partial in only considering aspects of South Indian history that I find particularly intriguing.

The structure of my book is roughly chronological, in that I begin with prehistory and end in India in the twenty-first century, but in between I have hopped about a bit. I have written mostly about the Dravidian South but I have included parts of the middle ground between the two major language groups. This includes what was the ancient pre-Sanskrit kingdom of Kalinga but became Orissa and is now Odisha State, where Odiya (formerly Oriya) is the predominant language. Although part of the Indo-Aryan language group and so quite distinct from the Dravidian group, Odiya is derived from the spoken Prakrit of Eastern India, which is the primary language of the earliest written Jain texts, suggesting that it came with early Jain immigrants from the North and overwhelmed the many local tribal Munda languages then being spoken. I have also made a brief diversion into what was for centuries Maratha country and is now Maharashtra, chiefly so that I can enlarge on that important but still largely unknown ruling dynasty the Satavahanas.

I have also found it impossible to ignore early historical events north of the Narmada boundary wall-and-ditch. One cannot consider the impact of Brahminical culture on South India without writing about the Arya and where they came from – which in turn means at least touching on that extraordinary and still barely understood culture that preceded the Arya, initially called the Indus Civilisation, then the Harappan Civilisation and now, in some circles (but not here), the Saraswati Civilisation or even Meluhha. So that means saying something about the controversial issue of origins, about which a great deal of chauvinist nonsense is now being promoted in some quarters.

I have also explored the religious impulse in its main manifestations, ranging from the religion of the Vedas through to the revolutionary heterodoxies of Buddhism and Jainism and on by way of bhakti through to the impact of sea-borne monotheism first introduced by early Christian missionaries and subsequently by Arab traders and their missionaries, and what came after in the form of Western colonialism.

None of those forebears of mine I mentioned earlier who were part of that colonial process in India consciously saw themselves as instruments of imperialism, but that is what they were. The British Raj was not, as Lord Curzon once argued, 'the greatest force for good the world has ever seen'. Nor was it, as the nineteenth-century Bengali philosopher Keshab Chandra Sen liked to say, the coming together of 'parted cousins'. For all the good intentions of men like my father – and there were of plenty of them on the ground – British imperialism was very good for Britain but very bad for India, even if it was never the vast satanic mill that some make it out to have been.[5] Like the curate's bad egg in the old *Punch* joke, 'parts of it are excellent', and there is a case for preserving those same parts from historical oblivion, particularly with regard to the Orientalist movement of the late eighteenth and early nineteenth centuries and its role both in the recovery of India's past and in helping to kick-start the Bengal Renaissance. Just as the munshis and pandits who taught them were not given their due in the nineteenth century, so today the tendency is to overlook the pioneering role of the Orientalists themselves. Readers who know something of my earlier work will not be surprised that I have more to say on this subject, not to extol their superiority but simply for the record.

In all these areas I have set out to counter what I consider to be bogus history – in Trumpian language, 'alternative facts' – by offering what I believe to be a more reasoned alternative. But at the end of the day it is up to you, dear reader, to judge for yourself whether what I have written is any more valid. Here you might like to consider the wise words of one of India's most distinguished contemporary historians. 'Remember, of course, to be very cynical,' declared Professor Romila Thapar in a speech made to fellow academics back in 1999. 'All historians when they put out theories have an axe to grind and have a political message. So always ask yourself, what is the political message of this historian that you might be reading?'[6]

A Kani or Kanikkar forest-dweller from the mountains of southern
Kerala and western Tamil Nadu, from a photograph taken by Edgar
Thurston's colleague Kadambi Rangachari, published in Thurston's
Castes and Tribes of Southern India, 1909.

I

THE INDIAN PLATE

'View of Cape Comorin, the Kumla Kumari Pagoda, and islands –
from a point 1.25 miles N.E. of the Cape.' Detail of a pen-and-ink
and wash drawing of Cape Comorin by Robert Bruce Foote in 1860.

I can only begin at the end, by which I mean at the very tip of
India, where the mainland ends and the waters begin – waters
that until recent times were known throughout India as the *kala
pani*, which can be translated either as 'black water' or 'waters of
death'. To those Hindus who took their religion very seriously,
as most did and many still do, those waters were taboo. To sail
upon them or even to swim in them was to be fatally polluted. So
the ocean effectively marked the limits of Hinduism, which may
help to explain why India was never a seafaring nation or, indeed,
why Indians were never – apart from one brief but significant

foray into South East Asia by the Imperial Cholas in the eleventh century – colonisers.

That is one way of looking at it. A more prosaic approach would be to say that I have come to Kanyakumari, better known outside India as Cape Comorin, to stand on the very tip of that geophysical marvel the Indian Plate, overlooking the confluence of three great watery deeps: the Bay of Bengal, the Arabian Sea and the Indian Ocean.

I am, to be quite honest, a tad disappointed. With so much drama in its making I had expected Kanyakumari to be more special. Perhaps I expected it to resemble the pen-and-ink and wash drawing (see page 17) executed by the geologist Robert Bruce Foote shortly after his arrival in India in 1860 to join the newly established Geological Survey of India. Foote is one of those undervalued pioneers who helped lay the groundwork for what we take for granted today; in his case, Indian geology and Indian prehistory, which earned him the title of 'father of Indian prehistory'. On 30 May 1863 Foote recognised a Palaeolithic hand-axe lying on the parade-ground at Pallavaram cantonment, just outside Madras, for what it was. He went on to discover many more Stone Age tools and settlements in South India, so beginning the first systematic research into early human history in India.

Over the course of five decades of geological surveying in South India Foote located and identified something close to four hundred prehistoric sites. After his official retirement in 1903 he continued to write and publish up to the end of his life in 1912. His ashes lie in Holy Trinity Church in the little hill-station of Yercaud, in Tamil Nadu's Shevaroy Hills.

Foote's vast collection of palaeoliths and other Stone Age artefacts laid the foundations for the early history department in the Chennai Museum. But Foote was primarily a geologist, and his drawing makes the point very nicely: the rocks were there first.

In 1912, the year in which Foote died, the German geologist Alfred Wegener published *The Origin of Continents and Oceans*, which was in its own field as radical as Darwin's *On the Origin of Species*. Wegener argued that hundreds of millions of years ago the Earth's outer shell had formed one huge land-mass which had then broken apart: the theory of continental drift. For the better part of half a century his theory remained just that, for want of proof – until the discovery in the 1950s that the ocean sea-floors were expanding, giving rise to the concept of tectonic plate movement.

The most spectacular example of continental drift and tectonic plate movement has to be the Indian Plate, a triangle of geomorphic crust which aeons ago broke away from the single supercontinent of Gondwanaland to drift north-eastwards across the globe. As it slid so it scraped over magmatic hotspots, releasing stupendous amounts of volcanic gases and lava – a catastrophic venting that may well have contributed towards the extinction of the greater dinosaurs but most certainly created the layers of thick lava topped by granite boulders that make up much of the triangular tableland known as the Indian Plate, which the Arya (of whom I have a lot more to say in a later chapter) named the Deccan (derived from the Sanskrit *dakshina*, 'south country').

This triangular tableland is the first India, the original. Northern India came after, only taking shape after the Indian Plate had collided with the Eurasian Plate. By a process of subduction this still ongoing collision first undermined and lifted what is now the Tibetan Plateau and then buckled, giving rise to the Himalayas. As the waters drained off this new plateau in one vast proto-Ganges so the great trough between the two land-masses filled with sediment 6 miles deep, to become the Gangetic and Indus plains.

So you could say that the Deccan was born out of fire, Northern

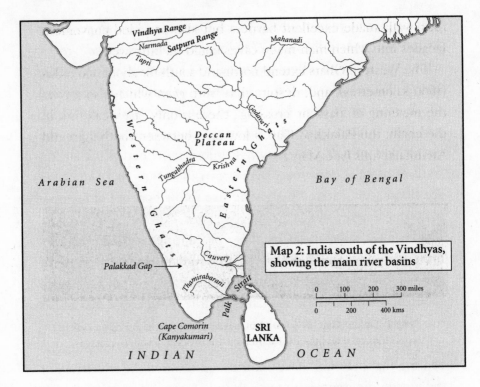

Map 2: India south of the Vindhyas, showing the main river basins

India out of water. The further north you travel the more unstable the land becomes, and vice versa. The only earthquakes in the South are the political ones.

But the Deccan is also a tilted tableland, with its highest elevation on the west, where a formidable mountain range extends north and south, rising in a series of *ghat*s or 'steps' from which it takes its name: the Western Ghats. Somewhat confusingly, they are referred to in Indian classical literature as 'Malaya', from the Tamil and Malayalam word for mountain, *malai*. 'These hills,' wrote one of the first British surveyors to explore them with a scientific eye, 'are in terraces formed of horizontal strata of green-stone, amygdaloids, waskes and basalt. The most compact strata do not readily decompose, and their lateral planes present a per-pendicular wall.'[1] William Sykes went on to point out how these rock walls made excellent barriers but also provided convenient facades into which man-made caves could be burrowed.

The Western Ghats extend north and south for about 990 miles (1600 kilometres), and, despite that word *ghat*, which also carries the meaning of 'pass' or 'crossing', there is only one weak link in the chain: the Palakkad Gap, a low pass between the Nilgiri and Anaimalai hills (see Map 2).

The Palakkad Gap, as painted in watercolours across two pages of an album of drawings by Lieutenant-Fireworker Thomas Cussans in 1820.

Until the building of the railways in the nineteenth century the Palakkad Gap provided the only significant east–west corridor though the mountains. As such, it was almost certainly the main portal through which early humans, having hitherto stuck to the coastal strips that had made possible the eastward migration of *Homo sapiens* out of East Africa, first penetrated into the Deccan interior. They did so by following the Nila River (also known as the Punnani or Bharathappuzha) upstream. Proof of this drive inland comes from the extraordinary number of megalithic burial sites, in the form of granite slab cists, stone-lined burial chambers, urn burials and worked stone tools, found beside the Nila and its main tributaries.

But the Palakkad Gap also provided a crossing point in both directions, so it later became increasingly important strategically as trade routes began to develop in historical times. From about 300 BCE onwards it gave the Chera rulers of Karur – known to the Greek scholar Ptolemy as Korevora, a once-flourishing town on a side tributary of the Cauvery (Kaveri) River – access to the sea-coast, leading to their initial control of the profitable sea-trade with Arabia and the Mediterranean world. Many centuries later it gave the Tamil Brahmins access to Malabar. Later still it served as a gateway for the Perso-Afghan general Hyder Ali and his son Tipu Sultan in their numerous assaults on Malabar.

The Western Ghats rise to no more than 8760 feet (2670 metres) at their highest point, but that is enough to catch the full force of the South-West Monsoon. This has kept the western shoreline thoroughly well-watered, creating lush tropical rain-forests wonderfully rich in their biodiversity. On the Roman *Tabula Peutingeriana* map in Vienna (of which more in Chapter 3) the Western Ghats are shown as 'Mons Lymodus', with an accompanying inscription which reads *In hic locis elephanti nasciunter*: 'In this place elephants are born'. Today those same forests constitute the last viable sanctuaries for the wild elephant in India, even though these sanctuaries are now divided by forest encroachment into eight separated populations. The Indian wild elephant has had a hard time of it in South India, in the past because of its use as a weapon of war – the ancient equivalent of the panzer tank – but in more recent centuries because of its servitude as a so-called temple elephant. Today Elephant Family, set up by the late Mark Shand, is just one of a number of charities working in partnership with the Wildlife Trust of India and local forest departments to create corridors between the fragmented sanctuaries in Kerala and Karnataka.

The Western Ghats have also created a rain-shadow, leaving the central plateau starved of rainfall. That means its rich volcanic soil can offer only limited forest cover in the form of sub-tropical dry forest and scrubland, providing poor grazing and poorer harvests. What saves this interior from becoming a desert is India's North-East Monsoon, when the south-westerly winds turn about in the autumn and start blowing from the north-east. These winds pick up moisture as they cross the Bay of Bengal, some of which falls on the eastern flanks of the southern section of the Western Ghats. This rainfall drains into a series of extended river systems that follow the gentle slope of the land all the way across the peninsula to empty into the Bay of Bengal.

Once the first hominids and the modern humans who followed them had rounded the tip of the Indian peninsula these rivers gave them access to the interior – most obviously the Godavari and the Krishna, which constitute two of the four largest rivers in India in terms of water inflow, each with numerous tributaries. In the case of the Krishna, one of its longest tributaries is the Tungabhadra, which joins it just west of Kurnool in the very centre of the Indian peninsula. Here the Tungabhadra forms the northern boundary of the Bellary District (now Ballari in Karnataka). In 1872 the geologist Robert Foote was contacted by the engineer in charge of public works in Bellary who wanted him to take a look at a ridge just to the north-east of Bellary town known locally in the Kannada language as Hiregudda ('big hill').

A prominent peak on the ridge, known from its shape as Kappagallu, or 'Peacock Hill', was found by Foote to be strewn with worked stone tools 'in all the several states from the roughest beginning to the most polished and highly finished axe, adze or chisel'. So busy was Foote exploring what he afterwards described as 'this celt factory' that he had no time to fully explore Peacock Hill and, in particular, its northern slopes. However, following reports of 'very interesting graffiti' on that side of the hill Foote returned to Bellary in 1903 to find the vertical surfaces of its larger

(Above) Robert Bruce Foote in old age. (Right) Some of the 180 Palaeolithic celts (stone implements with cutting edges) found by Foote on Kappagallu or 'Peacock Hill', near Bellary.

(Above, left and right) Two of the many rock faces on Kappagallu Hill, near Bellary, covered in Neolithic petroglyphs showing domestic cattle being herded and sacrificed, as well as scenes depicting long lines of dancers.

rocks covered in what he termed 'rock-bruisings' but now known as petroglyphs – images hammered or picked into rock surfaces – many showing long-horned, hump-backed cattle along with their herders. These he described, somewhat dismissively, as 'very rough sketches of human beings in groups and singly, and many figures of birds and beasts of various degrees of merit'.

What Foote found at Bellary proved to be 'the most important Neolithic settlement in the country . . . most prolific in implements of all kinds and in all stages of manufacture . . . the site of the largest Neolithic manufacturing industry as yet met with in any part of India'.[2] But that was not all. At the foot of Peacock Hill was a huge mound entirely made up of what appeared to be petrified ash. Similar mounds had earlier been spotted in the Bellary area and at half a dozen other sites on the Deccan. Since they appeared to have a glassy surface and gave out a hollow sound when struck they were assumed to be volcanic. However, as reported by Thomas Newbold, a young officer in the Madras Infantry with an unusually enquiring mind, the local view was that these mounds were organic, being 'the burnt bones of enormous giants or *Rakshas* [demons] of old, immolated during the demi-fabulous periods of the *Mahabharata*. All were agreed as to their great antiquity.'[3]

Back in the 1840s Newbold had examined one of these mysterious mounds and compared the contents with ashes found in Hindu funeral pyres. Newbold had concluded that the mounds were entirely composed of bones burned in 'continuous and long continued fires', the result of mass cremations of either cattle, 'the remains of great sacrificial holocausts performed by the *Rishis* [Hindu sages] of old', or humans, the outcomes of 'the bloody struggles that took place between the early Brahminical settlers in Southern India and the savage aboriginals, handed down in the records of the former as *Rakshasas*, giants and demons'.

Foote took a more scientific approach and his researches

showed that the great mounds were the outcome of repeated
firings of huge piles of cow-dung, produced by generations of
cattle-herding pastoralists during the Neolithic period and after.
He speculated that these great pyres must have played an important part in the religious rituals of these cattle-herding peoples.

Foote's theories were subsequently proved correct by the
field-work begun by Raymond Allchin and others in the 1960s.[4]
Their excavations revealed post-holes for tethered cattle as well as
earthworks in the form of great corrals in which cattle, buffalo and
pigs were kept. More recent researches by the palaeoclimatologist
Dr Dorian Fuller, Dr Ravi Korisettar, Professor of Archaeology at
Karnatak University, and Dr P. C. Venkatasubbiah of Dravidian
University have further refined Allchin's findings by showing that
heavy monsoon rainfall during the Mid-Holocene warm period
had greatly encouraged forest growth in the Deccan but had
begun to ease off from about 3000 BCE onwards. This had made
it possible for nomadic pastoralists to flourish on the Deccan for
the first time, soon followed by settled village life and the planned
cultivation of crops from about 2400 BCE onwards.[5]

What had further helped determine the later human settlement
of the South Indian peninsula was the slowing of the eastward
flow of its rivers by the Eastern Ghats. These are more hills than
mountains but their elevation is enough to cause the rivers flowing through them to slow, meander and divide, so providing the
perfect nurseries for the farming of rice, wheat and pulses.

One of the first to grasp the significance of this drainage system
was a remarkable man of many parts named Robert Caldwell,
an Ulster Scots Presbyterian whose remains lie beside those of
his wife Eliza in the church they and their congregation built
at Idaiyangudi, some 30 miles east of Cape Comorin. Caldwell
arrived there in 1841, having walked all the way from Madras, and
he died there in 1891, after stamping his mark in many other fields

beside mission work, including anthropology, archaeology and linguistics. His numerous writings have been called 'pejorative, outrageous, and somewhat paternalistic' by one Indian historian, while another has described his contribution to both the spread of Christianity in South India and the cultural awakening of the region as 'unmatched during the last two hundred years'. He also has a good claim to be remembered as a social reformer and 'pioneering champion of the downtrodden'.[6]

Caldwell made his home in the district of Tirunelveli (known to the British as Tinnevelly) on the banks of the Thamirabarani (known to the British as the Tamraparni) River, the most southerly of the country's great rice-bowls. Caldwell saw the Thamirabarani as the region's life force, and in his *Political and general history of the district of Tinnevelly* he wrote that: 'If the history of the dawn of a higher civilisation in Tinnevelly could be brought to light, I have no doubt that the Tamraparni, the great river of Tinnevelly, would be found to occupy the most prominent place in the picture. It must have been the facilities afforded by this stream for the cultivation of rice which attracted to its banks family after family of settlers from the north.'[7]

What makes the Thamirabarani exceptional is that it is fed by both summer and winter monsoons, and so comes into full flood twice a year. This is because it has its source in the last outcrops of the Western Ghats, at the foot of a 'noble conical mountain' known variously as Pothigai, Pothiyam, or Pothiya-ma-malai, all meaning 'a place of concealment', but also as Agastya Malai, or 'the hill of Agastya', arising, as Caldwell explained, 'from the tradition that the great *rishi* Agastya, when he retired from the world after civilising the south, took up his abode in its inaccessible recesses. It is long supposed by all Natives to be inaccessible, on account of the force of the charms with which Agastya had fenced in his retreat.'

Rishi Agastya and his sacred mountain sanctuary come under

deeper scrutiny in the next chapter, but the point that Caldwell wanted to make was that this twice-yearly run-off from Pothigai Malai was what made rice cultivation possible. The annual rainfall on its summit was found to amount to 300 inches by a certain Dr Broun, astronomer to the Maharaja of Travancore, who had ignored local prohibitions to make his way to the top and set up a meteorological observatory there. This enabled Caldwell to state that rainfall there was twelve times more than what it was in the Tirunelveli plains: 'Here we see the reason why it is that, though the plains of Tinnevelly are so parched and dry, and though the rainfall is so insignificant, the Tamraparni rolls to the sea its full flood of fertilising waters twice every year, and twice every year enriches the beautiful valley through which it flows with abundant crops.'

Fed by these distant rains, the farmers of Tirunelveli were able to plant and harvest twice a year, so that only the Cauvery River to the north produced greater yields. 'Such a river would necessarily prove an attraction to settlers,' Caldwell continues, 'if not from the very first, yet at least from the first appearance in the district of a people systematically practising agriculture and acquainted with the cultivation of rice by irrigation.'

It was here in these silt-rich plains laced with numerous channels that the South's first farming communities settled and prospered, leading to the first urban centres. Until the railways came along, long-distance movement between these population centres was chiefly by boat, up and down the coast and along the major river channels, giving rise to numerous ports along the coast and inland beside the rivers. Good roads were never a priority during British rule and it remained that way until after Independence in 1947, by which time population growth had put such a strain on the railway infrastructure that state governments were forced into major road-building programmes.

The creation of what are now South India's well-managed and very profitable rice-bowls was the end result of the so-called Neolithic Revolution, which saw the transition from mobile hunter-gathering to the domestication of livestock and stock-breeding, and the planting and harvesting of cereal crops, accompanied by the storing of produce in granaries, and so homesteads, villages and towns. There is as yet no convincing archaeological evidence to challenge the standard theory that this farming revolution began in the Levant and the so-called Fertile Crescent (Lower Egypt and Mesopotamia) in about 9000 BCE and spread eastwards by way of Iran and Central Asia, reaching South Asia in about 7500 BCE, after which it spread through the river valleys of the Indus and the Punjab and on across the Gangetic plain. There is not a trace of Neolithic farming south of the Vindhyas before about 3000 BCE, which was about the time that domestic rice cultivation became established both in India and China. It seems that the Neolithic Revolution and all the advances that went with it came late to South India.

Robert Caldwell's posting as a missionary to the little village of Idaiyangudi, south of Tirunelveli and just a few miles up the coast from Cape Comorin, was his first. Here he won many converts from among the local Nadars, known to him as 'Shanars', whose hereditary occupation was, in his words, 'that of cultivating and climbing the Palmyra palm, the juice of which they boil into a coarse sugar'. These toddy-collecting Shanars became the subject of Caldwell's first anthropological study, a pamphlet entitled *The Tinnevelly Shanars*, published in 1849. They were the largest of several communities in his area condemned by Brahminical edict to languish among the lowest rungs of the caste ladder, which helped to explain why they also made up the largest numbers of Christian converts. Kanyakumari District, in which Idaiyangudi falls, remains to this day the most Christianised district in Tamil Nadu.

(Above, left) A toddy-tapper at work, with his wife and child. A miniature from an album of forty-five gouaches from Tanjore known as the
Boileau Album, drawn by a local artist for John Peter Boileau, a member
of the Madras Civil Service from 1765 to 1785. (Above, right) A Paraiyar
couple from an album of sketches of South Indian costumes, 1843.

But the Nadars or Shanars were by no means at the bottom of
the social scale, because below them, and considered by them
to be vastly inferior, were a community known to Caldwell as
'Pareiyas and Pullers [more correctly, Mallas], the hereditary slaves
of the wealthier classes'.

The name of this unfortunate underclass – spelled by Caldwell
and others in a variety of ways, but let us stick with 'Paraiyar' –
had already by Caldwell's time become synonymous with
'outcaste' in the word 'pariah'. This most unfair branding goes
right back to the days of Francis Day of the East India Company

(EICo), who in 1639 bought an unprofitable 3-mile strip of the Coromandel coast from a local Nayak ruler and 'improved' the local name of *nari medu*, or 'jackal's mound', into Madras.[8] Since Day and his fellow traders were themselves viewed locally as unclean and without caste they were obliged to employ local Paraiyars as their servants, since Paraiyars had no caste to be polluted. One of the earliest accounts of British travellers in India, published in 1613, describes them as 'the abhorred Piriawes', who acted as public executioners and were considered 'the basest, most stinking, ill-favoured people'.[9]

Yet even the Paraiyars regarded themselves as socially superior to those whose status was so low as to be right off the social scale altogether, as Caldwell describes:

> Though the Pareiyas themselves will admit that they belong – or, as they would prefer to say, that they belong at present – to the lowest division of castes ... they are, equally with the higher castes, filled with that compound of pride of birth, exclusiveness, and jealousy, called 'caste feeling'. Whenever they have an opportunity, the Pareiyas deal out the very same treatment to other castes which are inferior to them.

But Caldwell was wrong in speaking of 'other castes', for these were more properly those without caste rather than outcaste. In his *History of Tinnevelly* Caldwell describes them peremptorily as 'the rude, black aborigines'. For the most part, these were forest-dwellers, living their own lives outside society in small, isolated jungle or mountain communities.

On two of those extraordinary edict rocks inscribed by order of the great emperor Ashoka in central and south Odisha in about 258 BCE, we find him warning the peoples on the southern borders of his newly conquered territory to behave themselves.

MALAY WADERS.

(Left) A couple described as 'Malay Waders' but more correctly Malai Vedans, a tribe of hunter-gatherers inhabiting the mountains of north Kerala and western Tamil Nadu. The caption describes them as 'A class of savage people, who never appear in Towns, they are not permitted to wear cloths [sic] but large leaves, their chattering speaking very difficil [sic] to understood [sic]'. Today they number some seventeen thousand, equally divided between the two states. (Below) Two Kanikkar men demonstrate their fire-lighting skills.

He terms them 'Atavikas', or 'forest-dwellers'. Similarly, in the remarkable book on statesmanship and political economy known as the *Arthashastra*, written by the Brahmin Chanakya, who acted as counsellor to Emperor Ashoka's father and grandfather, these same Atavikas are described as 'living in their own territory, many in number and brave, who fight openly, seize and ruin countries, having the same characteristics as kings'. Formerly known as tribals, today we have come to recognise them as India's 'first people', to whom the term *adivasi* ('original people') was awarded by social reformers in the 1930s as an improvement on the politically loaded term *dalit*, meaning 'oppressed' or 'ground down' – a term first employed by the Maharashtrian political activist Jyotirao Phule in the 1880s but subsequently picked up and applied to greater effect by Dr B. R. Ambedkar.

Included among Caldwell's 'rude, black aborigines' were a tribe living in the mountains who called themselves Kanikkar, literally 'landowners'. In Caldwell's time these Kanikkar tribals could be found throughout the mountain forests of the most southerly section of the Western Ghats. According to the 1981 Census, today their descendants are reduced to fourteen thousand in number, most of them living in or near the four designated wildlife sanctuaries of the Agastya Malai hills between Thiruvananthapuram in Kerala and Kanyakumari and Tirunelveli in Tamil Nadu.

'The jungle Kanikars have no permanent abode, but shift about from one part of the forest to another. They live together in small communities under a *Muttakai* or headman, who presides over tribal council meetings, at which all social questions are discussed and settled. Their settlements, composed of lowly huts built of bamboo and reeds, are abandoned when they suffer from fever, or are harassed by wild beasts, or when the soil ceases to be productive.'[10] So wrote the pioneer ethnographer Dr Edgar Thurston, superintendent of the Madras Museum, in his monumental seven-volume *Castes and Tribes of Southern India*, published in 1909, compiled with the help of his two colleagues L. K. Ananthakrishna Iyer and N. Subramania Iyer, working in Cochin and Travancore respectively.

The Kanikkar tribe's farming practices were rudimentary: 'The Kanikars first clear a patch of forest and set fire to it. The ground is sown with hardly any tillage. When after two or three years the land diminishes in productiveness, they move onto another part of the forest.' This was the classic shifting agriculture known as 'slash-and-burn', practised by tropical and semi-tropical forest-dwellers throughout the world. Although the Kanikkar grew cereals, pulses, tapioca and sweet potatoes, they saw themselves primarily as hunters and foragers: 'The Kanikars wander all over the hills in search of honey. Other occupations are trapping, capturing or killing elephants, tigers or wild pigs, and making wickerwork articles of bamboo or rattan. They are employed by the Government to collect honey, wax, ginger, cardamoms, *dammar* [a resin used for varnish] and elephant tusks.'

Like so many peoples in South and central India now classed as Scheduled Tribes, the Kanikkar considered themselves to be dispossessed, even going so far as to describe themselves as *thankam*, or hereditary landowners. And like many such communities, they were essentially egalitarian. A century ago they were respected by all who came into contact with them, being described as 'straightforward, honest and truthful'. Much the same can be said for their present-day descendants, despite the pressures placed on them and their fast-shrinking homelands. Their language is today classified as a Malayalamoid sub-group, with no clear identity of its own.

The Kanikkars' ancestors were most probably among the many 'first Indians' who entered India over the course of multiple eastward migrations extending over many thousands of years.[11] Their prime concerns would have altered very little over that extended period: survival, food and the fertility of both themselves and those elements of their surroundings that kept them fed. Fertility is crucial to the survival of the tribe, so the earliest representations of the human form in modelled clay took the form of fecund women with exaggerated female parts. These concerns would have been coupled with fear of the known, such as snakes, tigers and other mortal enemies, and even greater fear of the unknown, in the form of ghosts, evil spirits and the ancestral dead. This gave rise to various forms of pantheism, animism or totemism, all involving worship or propitiation through offerings and sacrifices of the elemental forces present in nature, such as animal-spirits, tree-spirits and water-spirits. This is the core religion of the hunter-gatherer.

Today most of the Kanikkar follow identifiably Hindu religious customs but a century ago they still had their own forest deities, worshipped at jungle gatherings beside streams. These were presided over by the tribe's shaman, chosen not by heredity but by his or even her special ability 'to invoke the deity and who sometimes becomes inspired and gives expression to oracular utterances'. Their rituals involved simple offerings, including the sacrifice of a cock, and a great deal of drumming, chanting and dancing which culminated in the participants becoming possessed and falling into trances. The Kanikkar buried rather than cremated their dead, and to ensure that their spirits could not return to harm the living, they planted a coconut palm over their graves.

In short, the Kanikkar of the Agastya Malai were typical hunter-gatherers, living close to nature and very much on the edge. Like their ancestors before them, these tribes took only what they needed from their forest surrounds, and when the rains came on they retreated to rock-shelters, where their previously unconsidered wall paintings and petroglyphs are now being rediscovered all over the Indian hinterland. Their descendants remain a marginalised underclass still shamefully looked down upon by India's urbanites. All the same, they and others like them constitute India's most senior citizens.

So now to the question of origins. Where did hunter-gatherers akin to the Kanikkar come from? The first thing to be said is that much of what you and I learned at school or college is already out of date, irrespective of when you left school, so fast are such new sciences as archaeogenetics developing alongside new theories such as that of the 'Aquatic Ape'. That theory, first put forward by the marine biologist Sir Alister Hardy in 1960, argues that early humans did not learn to stand upright as hunters on the wide open spaces of the African savannah, as stated in virtually every biology textbook written in the twentieth century, but by living alongside water and coastal strips, and by foraging for food such as mussels and shellfish in the shallows – a process that led to their bodies adapting to make the best of their watery environment.[12]

Archaeogenetics is still in its infancy yet already advanced enough to tell us that those of us without recent African ancestry are descendants of a handful of fertile women who were part of a prehistoric eastward migration out of East Africa. These women carried in their mitochondrial DNA (mtDNA) the Haplogroup L (a haplogroup being a population group sharing a common ancestor through either the matrilineal or patrilineal line). For reasons unknown, these Haplogroup L-bearers crossed into the Arabian peninsula, most probably by way of the Horn of Africa at a time when the oceans were significantly lower and the coastal corridors much wider than today as a consequence of ice age glaciation. Their female descendants subsequently mutated to form two major lines, one carrying Haplogroup N, the other carrying Haplogroup M.

These two haplogroups N and M together define the 'Out of Africa' thesis. This argues that the female ancestors of those modern humans carrying Haplogroup M kept on moving eastward, supplanting and replacing (and to some degree inter-breeding with) earlier humanoid species as they spread. Their descendants are now spread across most of the globe – but not in Western Eurasia in any significant numbers. Some 60 per cent of the modern inhabitants of the Indian subcontinent carry Haplogroup M, with the heaviest concentrations in the south, the east and along the west coast.

Meanwhile, the carriers of Haplogroup N had spread along the eastern shores of the Mediterranean and the southern fringes of the Black Sea and the Caspian Sea. Only in comparatively recent times did they move into Western and Northern Europe, where they remain the predominant haplogroup. But like all haplogroups, this Haplogroup N mutated and further divided into a number of lesser haplogroups, one of which is Haplogroup R – which is found in the remaining 40 per cent of South Asians.

How long ago these human migrations first began is disputed, but there is general agreement that our ancestors were preceded out of Africa by at least three species closely related to ourselves, including the Neanderthals and Denisovans. This is where Hardy's Aquatic Ape hypothesis comes in, since these watery humanoids were exceptionally well placed to take advantage of those phases during the Late Pleistocene epoch, which ended some 12,000 years ago, when glaciation lowered ocean levels and exposed wider shorelines. These provided a natural corridor for hominids like *Homo sapiens* who had adapted to foraging in a waterside environment. At the height of the so-called Last Glacial Maximum some 22,000 years ago sea levels were almost 400 feet (120 metres) lower than they are today.[13] This exposed a broad shelf all the way along the coast of India, most notably

off what is now the Gulf of Cambay, where the Narmada and
Tapti rivers flow in from the east to debouch into the Arabian
Sea – both giving easy access into the interior. Further south
this exposed shelf allowed access to the islands of Lanka,
Lakshadweep and the Maldives. But ocean levels also rose
during the interglacials, so migration along the shorelines would
have been in distinct waves, with long gaps in between. Some
fifteen thousand years ago a new phase of deglaciation began,
with a corresponding rise in sea levels, stabilising some 2500
years ago with our present shorelines.

There is evidence that this rise was accompanied by occasional surges, so-called meltwater pulses when the collapse of
ice-sheets released huge amounts of melted ice, resulting in
tsunami-like inundations of coastal areas newly colonised by
plants, animals and, of course, humans.

There is also general agreement that the massive eruption
and fallout from the Mount Toba volcano in Sumatra seventy-
four thousand years ago caused an ecological disaster, with thick
layers of volcanic ash being deposited all over the whole of South
and East Asia. According to one theory, *Homo sapiens* had already
begun to move east out of East Africa before the Toba event.
The alternative and predominant view is that this migration only
began after Toba but then spread very rapidly, enabling the first
true humans to reach India by some sixty thousand years ago.

An important contribution to this debate comes from the
Jwalapuram site, a dry river-bed with a deep deposit of river
sediment in the Jurreru River valley in Kurnool District, Andhra
Pradesh. Remarkably few early human remains have been found
in India, for which the Indian porcupine's fondness for chewing
old bones may be partly responsible, but a decade ago fragments of burnt human bone and one tooth from the Pleistocene
era were uncovered by an international team led by Michael

Petraglia, Chris Clarkson and Ravi Korisettar while excavating the floor of a rock-shelter at the base of a large boulder known as Jwalapuram Locality 9.[14] The proliferation of microliths (worked stone flakes used as tools or weapon heads), beads and worked bone showed that the site had been in more or less continuous occupation since about thirty-five thousand years ago. When the river-bed itself was dug into at a number of points a thick layer of volcanic ash was found, beginning some 7 feet under the ground surface: the fallout from the Toba volcano. At two of these sites microliths were uncovered both above and below the ash, which led the authors of the subsequent reports to conclude that this was evidence of human occupation in India prior to the Toba eruption – conclusions since challenged by another team of archaeologists, who have shown (to me, very convincingly) that the microliths uncovered below the ash belt at Jwalapuram are far cruder than those above, which are strikingly similar to well-worked microliths found in South African sites dating from sixty-five thousand years ago and after. This suggests that the cruder microliths found under the ash layer were the work of archaic hominid species such as *Homo erectus*, and the more refined microliths above the ash the work of the first fully human migrants out of Africa.[15]

Jwalapuram is exceptional in containing perhaps the oldest and most enduring microlithic sequence yet found in India but it is only one of a number of sites that are now beginning to reveal the secrets of early human migration in India. Rivers provided the easiest access into the interior from the coast, among them the Narmada, with its distinctive mountain ramparts on both banks – the so-called Vindhyan supergroup. A by-product of these Vindhyan rock formations and the Deccan 'traps' further inland is the presence of rock overhangs which provide perfect shelters for man and beast. From the 1860s onwards

archaeologists became increasingly aware that such rock-shelters
had served as rainy-season retreats for all sorts of ascetics, but
Jains and Buddhists in particular. One of those archaeologists,
Archibald Carllyle of the Archaeological Survey of India (ASI),
went on to discover that many of these same rock-shelters had
also housed much earlier human inhabitants, who had left
paintings on the walls, 'all evidently of great age, done in red
colour ... to illustrate in a very stiff and archaic manner scenes
in the life of the ancient stone chippers'. Sadly for poor Carllyle,
he became increasingly irrational and even violent, leading to his
dismissal before he could take his discoveries further.

A few years ago, while visiting an early Buddhist monastic
complex near the village of Panguraria, sited on a spur of the
Vindhyas overlooking the Narmada River west of the town of
Obaidullaganj, I found time to explore an extended line of rock-
shelters. Some had crude bed-platforms cut into their floors by
their Buddhist occupants but nearly all showed signs of much
earlier human habitation in the form of simple paintings on the
walls or overhangs. Often these were no more than the classic
'hand impressions' found in caves and rock-shelters all over the
world, but others showed animals being hunted by men armed
with bows and arrows. More recent paintings, using a white
lime-based paint rather than the red ochre found in the earlier
wall paintings, were of men mounted on horses, armed with
swords and spears.

Those particular rock-shelter paintings at Panguraria had
first been spotted in 1970 by a team of archaeologists from
the Nagpur Circle of the ASI looking for signs of early human
settlement. They in turn had been inspired by the pioneering
work of the late Dr Vishnu Wakankar, who has been called
'the father of Indian rock art'. Dr Wakankar had spent several
years studying early rock art in Europe, Egypt and the United

(Above) A typical rock-shelter at Panguraria, overlooking the Narmada River.

(Above, left and right) Hand impressions and armed horsemen painted on the ceiling and walls of the same cave, the latter probably dating from about 800 BCE.

States before returning to redraw the map of prehistoric rock art in India, his greatest coup coming in 1956 when he identified more than two hundred cave paintings contained within a large sandstone outcrop on the northern flank of the Vindhya range south of Bhopal, known to the local people as Bhimbetka, the 'seat of Bhim' – the mighty Bhima being one of the heroes of the *Mahabharata*. Supporting evidence in the form of microliths and simple petroglyphs (rock carvings) led Dr Wakankar to claim that some of the rock-shelters had initially been inhabited by *Homo erectus* at least a hundred thousand years ago and by *Homo sapiens* from thirty thousand years ago. Something approaching a thousand rock-shelters with paintings have since been discovered at the Bhimbetka complex, which in 2003 was declared a World Heritage Site.

Dr Wakankar and his colleagues identified five stages in the development of this rock art, beginning with simple representations of bison, rhinoceroses, tigers and elephants in green and red pigment, moving on to hunting and domestic scenes such as dancing, and ending with the appearance of horsemen armed with swords and spears drawn in white or yellow pigment. Extravagant claims have been made for the dating of Bhimbetka, but I shall stick with the line taken by UNESCO, which states that its rock-shelters contain paintings 'that appear to date from the Mesolithic period right through to the historical period'.

That term Mesolithic refers to the period between the Palaeolithic, when humans were purely hunter-gatherers using chipped stone tools, and the Neolithic, when they first began to plant crops, herd animals and use polished stone tools, so its dating varies from place to place. Very few characteristically Mesolithic sites have so far been found in India, although we should bear in mind that many sites along coastal plains would have been lost to the sea after the ending of the last ice age.

Even so, this paucity rather suggests that the majority human population inhabiting India remained locked in the hunter-gathering phase until comparatively recent times. Yet when that transition to the Neolithic phase began it did so with one mighty bang – although none of it was in the South.

Brahmin priests conduct their ancient rites over a fire in the corridor of a South Indian temple, following rituals that were first established many millennia ago.

2

THE KNOWLEDGE

STONE
SEAL

Alexander Cunningham's mysterious stone seal from Harappa.

It may strike the reader as perverse that I should now devote an entire chapter to early developments north of the Narmada. But the fact is that much of what shaped or influenced the culture of the Indian South had roots in the North. So bear with me, dear reader, if I begin by writing about what, for the sake of simplicity and to avoid raising hackles, I shall call the Harappan Civilisation,[1] taking its name from the place where its archaeological potential was first spotted by an army deserter, an eccentric Englishman named James Price who chose to reinvent himself as 'Charles Masson, an American gentleman from Kentucky'.

In 1826 Masson was crossing the Punjab on his way to Afghanistan when he made camp at a small village he called Haripah,
beside a dried-up watercourse in what is now Pakistan: 'Behind
us was a large circular mound, or eminence, and to the west was
an irregular rocky height, crowned with the remains of buildings,
in fragments of walls, with niches, after the eastern manner ...
Tradition affirms the existence here of a city ... destroyed by a
particular visitation of Providence, brought down by the lust and
crimes of the sovereign.'[2]

Half a century later, when General Alexander Cunningham,
founding father of the Archaeological Survey of India (ASI),
came to examine the mound at Harappa he found it devastated
by contractors who had used its bricks to lay the track for the
Lahore–Multan railway line. He moved on, believing that there
was little left to find. But he later got his hands on a 'most curious
seal' from that same site (see illustration above), engraved with the
figure of a bull, above which was 'an inscription in six characters,
which are quite unknown to me. They are certainly not Indian
letters ... I conclude that the seal is foreign to India.'

Cunningham was wrong, but never lived to see *how* wrong.
Another half century passed before the moment when the
archaeologist Rakaldas Banerji, while excavating a two-thousand-
year-old Buddhist stupa on the summit of a large mound known
locally as Mohenjo-Daro, or 'hill of the dead men', in Sind west of
the Indus River, realised that its foundations rested on the bricks
of much older and far more extensive buildings.[3] The then director of the ASI, Sir John Marshall, came to see for himself, and
what he saw there led to the first chapter of India's history having
to be totally rewritten. 'Hitherto India had been almost univer-
sally regarded as one of the younger countries of the world. No
monuments were known to exist of an earlier date than the third
century BC,' wrote Marshall.

Now, at a single bound, we have taken back our knowledge of Indian civilisation some 3,000 years earlier and have established the fact that in the third millennium before Christ, and even before then, the peoples of the Punjab and Sind were living in well-built cities and were in possession of a relatively mature culture with a high standard of art and craftsmanship and a developed system of pictographic writing.[4]

Since Marshall wrote those historic words scores of Harappan Civilisation sites, large and small, have been excavated on India's side of its border with Pakistan. With one major exception, virtually all the major settlements were located on the alluvial plains of the Indus and along its tributaries in the Punjab. The outstanding characteristic of this Harappan Civilisation was its extensive urbanisation, involving a score or so of city-states or nucleus cities each with satellite towns and villages, and with trading ports dotted along the coast, covering a territory larger than the farmed lands of ancient Mesopotamia and Egypt combined.[5] A combination of seeming stability and self-sufficiency provided the platform for advances in ceramics, handicrafts, metallurgy and other trades. Thanks to their fondness for toys modelled out of clay, we know that they used several types of bullock-drawn carts with solid wheels but not the light horse-drawn chariot. Similarly, there are numerous depictions on Harappan seals of bulls, elephants, rhinos, water buffalo, lions, tigers, supposed unicorns and other creatures, but not a single depiction of a horse or a horse-drawn chariot.[6]

Some two thousand of these stone seals or sealings have so far come to light and they provide revealing insights into what the Harappans may have thought and believed. Most show one or more animals or human figures accompanied by a row of very distinctive pictographs, logographs or written characters.

Ever since Cunningham took note of this 'pictographic writing' scores of well-qualified philologists and hundreds of enthusiastic amateurs have tried to make some sense of it. Their difficulty lies in the fact that very few seals carry more than four or five of these 'characters' and none more than twenty-four, which is in marked contrast to the extensively inscribed cuneiform tablets of Mesopotamia, for example. This suggests that this Harappan 'script' is not a written language at all but more in the nature of symbols identifying goods, amounts, places, ownership and so on. In recent years much-publicised claims have been made that purport to prove links with either the Dravidian or Sanskrit language families, but the fact is that despite all the industry of such acknowledged experts as the indefatigable Tamil scholar Dr Iravatham Mahadevan (whose pioneering work on the identification and deciphering of Tamil-Brahmi is described in a later chapter) and the Finnish scholar Asko Parpola, the deciphering of the Harappan 'script' is still a work in progress.

What offer a far more profitable line of enquiry are the images on the seals, of which the most famous is Seal 420, uncovered in 1928 from Mohenjo-Daro (see illustration on page 49). It shows a figure seated on a platform, facing forward in a yoga-like *padmasana* or 'lotus-position' posture. His arms are covered in bangles and he wears an elaborate headdress in the form of a pair of curved horns with a plant-like object in the centre. His head is ill-defined – not surprising, when you consider that the seal measures barely one inch (2.7 centimetres) square and is damaged – but with some squinting and a little imagination it can be seen as three faces, one facing forward and two in profile. Sir John Marshall had no hesitation in calling this horned man a 'proto-Siva', or early form of Lord Shiva. 'In the first place,' he wrote, 'the figure has three faces and that Siva was portrayed with three as well as with more usual five faces, there are abundant examples to prove. Secondly, the head is crowned with the horns of a bull and the *trisula* [trident] are characteristic emblems of Siva. Thirdly, the figure is in a typical yoga attitude, and Siva was, and still is, regarded as a *mahayogi* – the prince of yogis. Fourthly, he is surrounded by animals, and Siva is par excellence the "Lord of Animals", *Pashupati*.[7] Reasons of delicacy may have led Marshall to make no mention of another feature: the figure's erect member.

Since Marshall's pronouncement several more proto-Shiva-as-Pashupati seals and tablets have been uncovered, four at Mohenjo-Daro and one at Harappa. What Marshall saw as the three-pronged trident of Lord Shiva is now seen to be a pair of horns with a branched plant or tree growing up between them, a feature found on a number of other seals. This did not prevent that much-respected husband-and-wife team of archaeologists and historians Raymond and Bridget Allchin from declaring in 1997 that here was clear evidence of Shiva worship at the centre of the Harappan Civilisation.[8]

Two examples of horned figures on seals. (Above, left) John Marshall's damaged 'proto-Siva' seal as found in 1928. (Above, right) A sealing from 1938 showing a simpler version of a totemic horned figure, with the sapling between the horns more clearly defined.

But Shiva has never been a horned god. To my mind, the key element here is nature-worship. What many of the other human figures portrayed on the seals have in common with many of the animals also shown are horns. As the distinguished archaeologist Jonathan M. Kenoyer has remarked in connection with the 'Shiva-as-Pashupati' seal, 'Large horns could represent the power, strength, and virility of the animal; by analogy whoever wore a headdress with the horns would possess similar attributes. The anthropomorphic figures with these headdresses may depict powerful hunters or shamans, or even some form of water buffalo or cattle deity.'[9]

Everything we know about the Harappan Civilisation shows that it was a farming culture that depended on the summer monsoon and the melting of the Himalayan snows combining annually to flood its fields with a rich layer of silt. Initially there was too much of both monsoon rain and snow-melt, leading to widespread inundation, but from about 3000 BCE onwards a steady easing-off of monsoon rainfall meant a decrease in flooding, which greatly encouraged farming and urban settlement. But as the monsoon continued to decline, providing less summer precipitation, so the flow of those rivers most dependent on this source was reduced. Consequently, this highly developed urban civilisation went into decline from about 2100 BCE onwards, characterised by a withdrawal from the big city centres and a shift towards the edges of the Harappan heartland, with a marked build-up of settlements in the region covered by today's Punjab and Haryana states, and a smaller concentration on the Kathiawar peninsula. What followed has been described as a 'collapse', with many factors besides reduced rainfall playing their part, including earthquakes and river capture.[10]

By about 1800 BCE the great urban centres of the Harappans had been all but abandoned as the lower Punjab experienced something similar to what occurred in Britain after the collapse of the Roman empire. The Romans left behind well-made roads, walled cities, temples and villas built of stone, brick and plaster, and nothing like them was seen again in Britain until after the Norman conquest seven centuries later. Similarly, in Northern India the urban brick-based culture that defined the Harappans was not to be seen again until the Indo-Iranian city of Taxila was laid out under Darius the Great in about 500 BCE.

What happened between those two dates remains to this day the most controversial question in Indian history.

In 1974 some Bhil peasant farmers from the village of Daimabad, sited on the Maharashtrian plateau some 45 kilometres north of Aurangabad, were digging up the roots of a dead tree for firewood when they made a remarkable find: a hoard of four cast bronzes. Three were in the form of animals standing on wheeled platforms: a rhinoceros, water buffalo and elephant. But it was the fourth item that caused all the excitement: a two-wheeled chariot drawn by a pair of yoked oxen complete with horns and exaggerated humps but with otherwise very equine bodies. Standing on the central pole is a small dog, and on the chariot itself is a naked man with a shaven head, holding a whip or reins. He stands just over 6 inches (16 centimetres) high and is portrayed realistically in every respect but one: his genital member (or possibly a sheath covering it) is erect and its tip divided to form a four-headed cobra. The Daimabad Charioteer very quickly became the subject of heated debate in academic circles.

The four bronzes had been uncovered beside a large mound on the left bank of an upper tributary of the Godavari River. The site had previously been excavated by the ASI but was immediately re-examined in an attempt to date the bronzes, which led to their being assigned to 'the earliest phase of the Malwa occupation of this site' (i.e. c. 1600-1400 BCE). This has not prevented the authorities at the National Museum in New Delhi from listing the bronzes as dating from 2000 BCE, which seems a little on the wishful side.

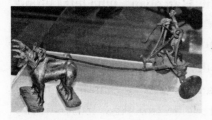

The Daimabad Charioteer (with detail), part of a cache of four bronzes unearthed outside the village of Daimabad in Maharashtra in 1974, now in the National Museum in New Delhi. The man is ithyphallic, or in a state of sexual arousal. The oxen have horns and humps but also horse-like features.

If the Daimabad bronzes are indeed from the early Malwa phase – and even that is a big if, since they could well date from much later – then they are very special indeed, because nothing like them has so far emerged from any post-Harappan site. Rhinos, buffalo and elephants are all well represented on Harappan seals and as terracotta toys, but not so the friendly dog, which is a crucial tool in the hunter's and the herdsman's portfolio. Then there is that chariot, a vehicle unknown on Harappan art. It has been suggested that what is represented here is bull-racing, a traditional post-harvest sport known as *khurak* that still takes place in some rural areas of Maharashtra. But this takes no account of the charioteer with his bizarre cobra-head erection. He is no toy, nor is he an ordinary mortal, which suggests that he represents a priapic god. He may well represent a key moment of transition between two very different cultures:

the old settled urban culture of the Harappans, who left behind a mass of evidence in the form of buildings, terracotta artefacts and seals, and a new, shifting culture that left virtually nothing tangible other than firepits, wooden post-holes, potsherds and just enough in the way of arrow- and spear-heads and slag heaps to show that its people had entered the Iron Age. It is as if the people who made them had better or more important things to think about.[11]

So strikingly different are these two cultures, the old and the new, that it is as if there were two quite different peoples. But that is not how some people see it. They are the proponents of the 'out of India' theory, which argues that there never was a collapse in the Harappan Civilisation, only a decline followed by a resurgence that developed into a new culture, dominated by people who called themselves Arya and who revered sacred texts they called the Vedas, chanted in a sacerdotal language called Sanskrit. There was no inward migration, this theory further maintains, but there was an outward migration, during which the Arya exported their language westwards, so that it is quite correct to call this now widespread language group 'Indo-European' – because it began in India and spread to Europe.

Such revisionism flies in the face of all the evidence – archaeogenetic, archaeological, linguistic, zoological, botanical, geographical and theological – but so seriously is it being promoted that it has to be challenged, albeit as succinctly as I can.

In the previous chapter I referred to mitochondrial DNA and the presence of the two Haplogroups M and N in the DNA of most Indian women. But haplogroups also occur in the male Y chromosome. For example, the Y chromosome Haplogroup H is believed to have originated in India some forty thousand years ago and is still prevalent there.[12] But within this same Y chromosome is Haplogroup R, one particular branch (or subclade) of which,

known as Haplogroup R1a1a, is far more widespread than the other
subclades. Its highest concentrations are found among Eastern
Europeans but also in Western Mongolia, Tajikistan, Southern
Uzbekistan, Eastern Iran, Afghanistan and Pakistan, here particularly among the Pashtuns, Sindhis, Baltis and Kashmiris. Within
modern India, high percentages of Subclade R1a1a are found
among West Bengal Brahmins, Konkanastha Brahmins and Iyengar
Brahmins, but also among the Khatris of the Punjab – Punjabi traders who have always claimed superior caste status as Kshatriyas, all
the Sikh gurus being Khatris – and among the Madeshis on both
sides of the India–Nepal border (see Map 3).[13]

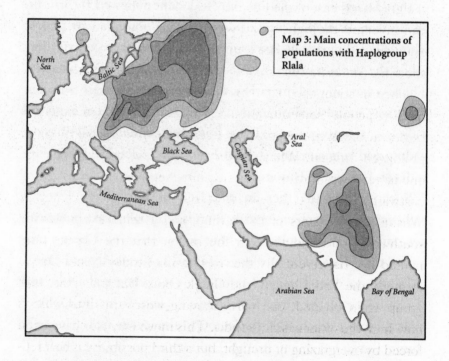

Map 3: Main concentrations of
populations with Haplogroup
R1a1a

The modern distribution of population groups with the Y chromosome
Haplogroup R1a1a supporting the 'out of the Eurasian steppes' theory.
(Adapted by Hxseek from Underhill et al, 2009).

All these carriers share a common male ancestry, which leads to the question: where did this Haplogroup R1a1a originate?

According to the latest research, the most likely explanation is that Haplogroup R1a1a mutated out of Haplogroup R1a in the Eurasian steppe about fourteen thousand years ago.[14] This is a crucial piece of evidence in support of the 'out of the Eurasian steppe' theory, which argues that this is where a Proto-Indo-European language first began to be spoken, making it the *Urheimat*, or 'original homeland', of the Indo-European language family. About ten thousand years ago significant numbers of this Subclade R1a1a detached themselves from their parent group and moved south to seek a new home for themselves as pastoralists in the grasslands east of the Caspian Sea. Here they tamed the horse and invented the light spoke-wheeled and horse-drawn chariot, as evidenced in the chariot burial sites of the Proto-Indo-Iranian-speaking Sintashta culture of the Northern Eurasian steppes.

Then in about 1900 BCE this horse-riding and cattle- and goat-herding people (sometimes referred to as the Androvono culture) began to break up, possibly as a consequence of overgrazing or prolonged drought. Whatever the cause, these nomads split up, one large group moving westwards into Anatolia, another moving eastwards into what is now Western Mongolia to become the Wusun ('descendants of the raven'), and a third group moving southwards into and through the region that the Greeks later named Bactria, essentially the river basin of today's Amu Darya, formerly the Vedic Vaksu, the Greek Oxus. But then this third group again divided, one party moving westwards into what is now Iran, the other east into India. This move may also have been forced by overgrazing or drought, but a third possibility is that religious differences had grown that were too serious to be resolved, such as the emergence of proto-Zoroastrianism, with its worship of a sole creator, Ahura Mazda, 'lord of wisdom'.

Whatever the reasons, from about 1500 BCE onwards a distinctly new form of society began to appear in the western Punjab, dominated by a vigorous and mobile people whose preferred mode of transport was the *asva*, or horse, and whose secret weapon was the fast-moving horse-drawn *ratha*, from *rotho*, or 'wheel'.

During excavations carried out at Mohenjo-Daro in 1950 by the charismatic Sir Mortimer Wheeler, the last British archaeologist to head the ASI, a number of skeletons were uncovered which Wheeler declared to be victims of a massacre: Harappans killed by Arya invaders. Wheeler's theory of violent invasion has since been disproved by more solid archaeological evidence, which points to the arrival of a predominantly pastoralist people by degrees and over an extended period. But these were a people habituated by centuries of nomadic living to an austere way of life. They built no temples to their gods, only fire-altars, fire-pits and sacrificial posts – and even here there is astonishingly little archaeological evidence. We know that *yajna*, or animal sacrifice, played a hugely important role in the Arya's religious rites, and that complex *vedi*s, or fire-altars, had to be constructed employing various patterns of bricks depending on the sacrifice involved, and that each time a sacrifice was repeated the fire-altar had to be enlarged. Yet, for all these requirements, no such fire-altars have ever been found. It is quite possible that they were destroyed after use, because this was a culture entirely unconcerned with the material or permanent settlement – initially, at least.

But above all, the Arya saw themselves as a people invested in knowledge, encapsulated in a single word: *veda*. To my mind, no one has put it better than the Italian publisher and philosopher Roberto Calasso as to what made the Arya so special. 'It was the civilization in which the invisible prevailed over the visible,' he has written.

There is no point looking for help from historical events, since there is no trace of them. Only texts remain: the *Veda*, the Knowledge, consisting of hymns, invocations, incantations in verse, of ritual formulas and prescriptions in prose ... Their minds teemed with images. Perhaps this was also why they had no interest in fashioning and sculpting figures of the gods. As if, already surrounded by them, they felt no need to add others ... There are very few tangible remains of the Vedic period – no buildings survive, no ruins or traces of buildings. At most, a few meagre fragments on show in various museums. Instead, they built a Parthenon of words: the Sanskrit language, since *sam skṛta* means 'perfect'.[15]

The Arya's everyday spoken language was an early form of Prakrit, meaning 'original' or 'vernacular', out of which there emerged the more refined, hieratic and priestly Sanskrit, the language of the *Vedas*. These *Vedas* were originally spoken of as *shruti*, or 'that which is heard', composed to be chanted as hymns. They consisted of four collections in total, assembled over the course of some thousand years from about 1500 BCE onwards. They were too sacred to be sung by anyone other than the priests, so they were committed to memory and passed on by oral transmission within the priestly community. Only many centuries later were they set down in writing as the first of the sacred texts of what we now call Hinduism – unless, of course, you believe that the language these Arya spoke was first written in the pictographic characters of the civilisation they replaced, in which case you have to account for the gap of more than a thousand years between the last Harappan pictographs being made and the first appearance of Brahmi script in the third century BCE.

The *Vedas* chart the eastward progress of a people made up of five tribes who were never overwhelming in terms of numbers

but whose better organisation and more advanced technology –
characterised in the horse and the chariot – gave them the edge,
leading to their assuming authority over the host population. The
history of India is replete with similar but better documented
examples, from Alexander the Great and his highly disciplined
Macedonian troops in the fourth century BCE to Major Stringer
Lawrence's creation of a modern Indian army based on the
Prussian model in Madrasapatnam in the 1750s.

The earliest and most important of the four works that make up
the *Vedas* is the *Rig-Veda* (*R-V*), which can be loosely translated as
'Let knowledge shine'. In the form that has come down to us it is
made up of 1028 *suktas*, or hymns, organised into ten books. Every
hymn is directed at a named god – not the gods of Hinduism as
we know them today but two kinds of deities: benevolent *devas*,
who were entirely abstract; and the often hostile gods they called
asuras, who were elemental. Many of these deities they shared
with their first- and second-cousins further to the west. A tablet
from central Turkey carries the names of the gods Indra, Mitra
and Varuna as guarantors of a peace treaty drawn up between
the Hittites and the Egyptians in about 1400 BCE. All three are
among the most powerful of the Vedic gods: the *deva* Mitra is the
binder of contracts and social order, as well as being a sun-god; the
asura Varuna began as the most powerful of the elemental gods,
associated with water and rain, but was gradually eclipsed by his
rival Indra, the thunderbolt-wielding lord of heaven, to whom a
quarter of the hymns of the *R-V* (289 in number) are directed.
Next in popularity comes Agni, god of fire, to whom 218 hymns
are directed.

Vishnu and Shiva, so dominant in later centuries, are all but
insignificant to the early Arya. Vishnu merits six hymns in the
R-V while Shiva is entirely absent under that name, although part
of his multifarious character lurks there as Rudra, 'the howler',

god of wind. What is also apparent is that the composers of the *R-V* had no time for the worship of Shiva in his prime form, the linga, since linga-worship is unequivocally condemned in the *R-V*.[16] This injunction points to linga-worship already being an established local practice, seemingly as shocking to the Arya as it appeared to the Victorians three thousand years later.

The *R-V* is a compilation of hymns assembled over centuries, with additions and interpolations. The earliest are identifiable by their more archaic language – an archaism that has obvious linguistic links with the sacred texts of Iranian Zoroastrianism, the Avesta, and its language, Early Iranian. There are also many cultural similarities which point to these two languages having a common source in Proto-Indo-Iranian.[17] Indeed, it was these close language affinities that led the eighteenth-century jurist and philologist Sir William 'Oriental' Jones to the revelation that the Sanskrit he had begun to study in Bengal in 1783 was not only born out of a shared Proto-Indo-Iranian parentage but was also part of a much wider and older language family with relatives extending far beyond Asia. That same link subsequently led the Indologist Max Müller to coin that now heavily loaded word 'Aryan', and to enthuse about 'our nearest intellectual relatives, the Aryans of India, the framers of the most wonderful language of Sanskrit, the fellow workers in the construction of our most fundamental concepts, the fathers of the most natural of natural religions'.

To understand the huge cultural gulf between the Harappans and the Arya you have only to consider what is and is not to be found in the *R-V*. Why, for example, does the *R-V* contain no reference to the unicorn-like creature that features so prominently in the Harappan seals, or to the rhinoceros, the elephant or the tiger? The early Arya had no words for them because they were unknown to them before they entered India.

Consider also the cow. The Arya's domesticated cattle were almost as much interlopers as they themselves, being of taurine stock (*Bos taurus taurus*) rather than the humped Indian zebu (*Bos indicus*), sometimes known as the Brahmini. These cattle were the Arya's lifeblood, glorified along with their horses as symbols of their moveable wealth and the basis of their sustenance. It followed that the most important of the Arya's rituals were the sacrifices of what was most precious to them: their horses and their cows. When the Sanskritist Horace Wilson, for many years Secretary of the Asiatic Society in Calcutta before leaving in 1833 to take up the first chair in Sanskrit at Oxford, began to translate the *R-V* into English he was astonished to find references to the killing and eating of cattle. For example, in Wilson's pioneering translation *R-V* 10.86.14 reads: 'The worshippers dress for me fifteen (and) twenty bulls: I eat them and (become) fat, they fill both sides of my belly.'

Since Wilson's time scores of Sanskritists, from Wilson's protégé Rajendralal Mitra all the way down through the generations to the present distinguished (and much vilified) historian D. N. Jha, author of *The Myth of the Holy Cow* (2001), have come to the same inescapable conclusion: that the *Vedas* contain frequent references to the sacrifice and eating of cattle. As that well-known historian the late D. D. Kosambi put it: 'Vedic Brahmins had fattened upon a steady diet of sacrificed beef'.[18]

Conversely, I can find no dogs portrayed on Harappan seals.[19] The domesticated dog, *Canis familiaris*, is believed to have first established links with hunters in central Eurasia some twenty-five thousand years ago. The *R-V* tells us that the Arya saw dogs as companions and protectors.[20] So when, for example, the god Indra has some cattle stolen, he is helped to find them by a female spirit of the clouds named Sarama, also known as *devashuni*, 'the divine bitch'. She is the mother of all dogs and gives birth to two four-eyed brindle dogs, who become the watch-dogs of the god of death, Yama.[21]

Snakes are absent from the *R-V* other than an evil python-like creature called Vritra, 'the squeezer', the personification of drought and the opponent of the rain-bearing god Indra. But this Vritra is also described as a *dasa*, the pejorative epithet that came to be applied by the Arya to the non-Arya people of the Indian plains. If the Arya of the *R-V* had never seen a snake, imagine what terror a first encounter with a 3-metre-long King Cobra must have inspired. I can remember as a child seeing one of these fearsome reptiles – black with distinctive yellow chevron patterns down its back – streaking across the road ahead of our car, so long that its body extended all the way across the road, leaving us all stricken with horror. By the time the last of the four Vedas, the *Atharva-Veda*, had been composed in about 800 BCE, its authors knew all about snakes and lived in terror of them; consequently it devotes whole chapters to charms for the exorcism of black, white and striped snakes from dwellings. Only later did the Arya reach a true accommodation with snakes, so that by the time the domestic rituals known as the *Grihya Sutras* had been assembled in about 400 BCE the snake was becoming akin to a god. Now householders are required to put out a special bowl in a special place, and fill it with clean water with the invocation 'Honour to the divine serpents'. The words *Naag* and *Nagas*, referring both to the cobra and to a race of quasi-divine half-man, half-snake beings of the underworld, have also started to appear in sacred texts and mythology.

The first of the two great Indian epics, the *Mahabharata*, is filled with stories of snakes both as quasi-gods and as people, usually presented as hostiles who are converted to become protectors and allies of humanity. The most disturbing of these tales is the *Mahabharata*'s account of a pogrom which almost brings about the extermination of the snake race. This starts with the burning of the ancient forest of Khandava, west of the Jumna (Yamuna) River

in what is now the Delhi region, which is the abode of 'the enemies of the gods', who are Nagas led by the snake-king Takshaka.
The snake-hating Arya king Janamejaya drives the snake-people
out of the forest by fire and executes their leaders in a *sarpa satra*
or snake sacrifice. A boy sage named Astika, who is the offspring
of a Brahmin father and a Naga mother, then calls on Janamejaya
to stop the killing and to set Takshaka free – and from this time
onwards the Nagas and the Arya live together in peace.

We can read into this a transformation into myth of the subduing of the snake-worshipping peoples of the Haryana plain by
the advancing Arya. From about 400 BCE onwards these indigenous
Naga snake-gods were brought into the Arya fold to become allies
and protectors – not only in Brahminical Hinduism, but also in
Jainism and Buddhism. To this day, a number of peoples of the

(Above, left) A bas-relief from a Buddhist stupa excavated at Nagarjunakonda by
Arthur Longhurst showing the subduing of a Naga snake-king. (Above, right) One
of four Jain images of uncertain date carved on the four sides of a 7-metre-high
standing stone at Thirakoil, north of Tellar in Tamil Nadu. It shows the Naga
snake-king Dharanendra protecting with his hoods the 23rd Jain tirthankara
('ford-crosser') Parshvanath from storm clouds sent by his enemy the cloud deity
Samvara, with his queen Padmavati also holding an umbrella.

Indian subcontinent declare themselves to be Nagavanshi or 'of Naga descent', most notably the Nairs and Bunts of Kerala and Tamil Nadu (of whom more in the next chapter) and the Nagavanshi Rajputs of the mountain country of Kalahandi in Odisha.

The same test can be applied to flora as to fauna – for example, to the soma plant. The *R-V* devotes no fewer than 123 hymns to the sacred soma, as indeed does the Avesta. This was some form of still unidentified vine the juice of which was distilled and drunk as part of a hugely important life-conferring ritual and may possibly have contained a psychoactive substance. The older books of the *R-V* make constant allusions to soma drinking but over time the ritual loses its importance, to the point where soma ceases to be an elixir and becomes a moon-god, also known as Chandra. The inference has to be that the soma vine was no longer available in the plains of the Punjab.

By contrast, the sacred *tulasi* or tulsi plant (basil) today occupies a very special place in every Hindu household as a manifestation of Vishnu's consort Lakshmi, having undergone an elevation from obscurity in the Vedas to centre stage in the Puranas.

Lastly, to Vedic geography and what it tells us about roots.

I have described the Narmada River as the boundary between the two Indias. Today it is firmly entrenched in Hindu tradition as one of the *Saptasindhu*, the seven sacred rivers of India. Devotional hymns to these seven rivers, also known as the *Saptapunyanadi* or 'seven auspicious rivers', are a feature of daily worship for a great many Hindus, with no doubts as to which these seven rivers are. Three of the seven – the Ganges (Ganga), the Jumna (Yamuna) and the Indus (Sindhu) – water the North; two – the Godavari and the Kaveri – water the South; and the Narmada waters the middle. The seventh river is that most beguiling and mysterious of rivers, the Saraswati.

No river receives more adulation in the *R-V* than the Saraswati,

A Vaishnava Brahmin and his wife water the sacred tulsi plant in the courtyard of their home as part of their morning rituals. A goauche from the Boileau Album, probably drawn by an artist working in the Company style in Tanjore in about 1780.

where she is described as 'best mother, best river, best goddess', and as 'surpassing in majesty and might all other rivers, pure in her course from the mountains to the ocean'. Book 6 of the *R-V* is considered among the earliest and it includes the hymn known as the *Saraswati Sukta*, full of praises for the river's power and virtues. 'Most dear amid dear streams, seven-sistered, graciously inclined, Sarasvati hath earned our praise,' reads part of Ralph Griffith's translation. She is described as 'sprung from threefold source', 'the Five Tribes' prosperer', and 'marked out by majesty among the Mighty Ones, in glory swifter than the other rapid streams'. So patently, the Saraswati was a river of huge significance to the authors of *R-V* 6 – and with good cause, because we are told that it was on her banks that the sacred language of Sanskrit was received from the gods and where the first hymns to the gods were composed. Indeed, the Saraswati River defined the very heartland of the Arya as Brahmavarta, the 'land of Brahma's people'.

So where is this sacred Saraswati River, since no such river appears on any modern map? And why should Saraswati be best known today as the benign and beloved goddess of learning and the arts, the consort of Brahma no less, most often portrayed seated on a lotus flower and strumming the sitar-like instrument known as a *vina*? Her riverine origins barely get a look-in – except in those circles where the Saraswati River plays a central role in the 'out of India' thesis.

One of the last of the books of the *R-V* to be composed is Book 10, by which time it is the Indus River, under its ancient name of Sindhu, that is being celebrated as the mightiest of all rivers. The Saraswati is now just one of ten lesser rivers and its qualities have greatly diminished. And as the centuries pass so the Saraswati's manifestations continue to diminish. By the time the *Panchvimsha Brahmana* in the *Sama-Veda* has been composed, in about 800 BCE, the Saraswati is no longer able to hold up the heavens and consequently has gone underground.[22] And when the great epic of the *Mahabharata* first began to be assembled soon after that date the river is described as fragmented, disappearing and reappearing, having been commanded by a sage named Utatha to disappear into the sands and to desert the land.

And yet all the while the Saraswati continues to be honoured as the fountainhead of the Arya's homeland, and in the code of laws known as the *Manusmriti*, or 'Laws of Manu', written no earlier than the third century BCE, this homeland is declared to be bordered by the Saraswati on one side and by a second river known as the Drishadwati on the other.

One of the first Western scholars to attempt to locate this homeland was Horace Wilson. In the introduction to his translation of the *Vishnu Purana* Wilson identified the Saraswati and Drishadwati as two minor rivers of the Punjab. 'The holy land of Manu,' he wrote, 'lies between the Drishadwati and Saraswati rivers: the Caggar [Ghaggar] and Sursuti [Sarsuti] of our barbarous maps.'[23]

The present-day Sarsuti River is little more than a stream that rises in the Siwalik foothills just east of Ambala in Haryana. As it flows south-west it is joined by another stream before merging with the Ghaggar River, which itself is a pretty insignificant river, except in the immediate aftermath of the monsoon. However, the former course of the Ghaggar survives in the form of an extensive dried-up river-bed. Modern satellite imagery confirms the existence of just such a palaeo-channel, in the form of a dried-up river course that extends westwards deep into the Rajasthan desert and continues all the way to the coast. So there was once a river here that ran all the way from the mountains to the sea. Yet all the scientific evidence shows that it ceased to flow to the sea several thousand years *before* the first of the Arya ever set foot in India. This was largely as a consequence of reduced monsoon rainfall combined with tectonic activity in the Himalayan foothills that redirected the Ghaggar's upper reaches into the Jumna River. Reduced seasonal rainfall and snow-melt continued to fill its upper channels but its lower course simply disappeared in the sand.

So how could this dried-up river-bed ever have been the site of the celebrated Saraswati of old?

The answer is that the Punjabi Sarsuti-Ghaggar was not the original Saraswati. That word derives from the Proto-Indo-Iranian word *saras-vat-i*, referring to pools, marshes or still water. It has the same linguistic derivation as the Avestan *Haraxvati* and the Old Persian *Harauvati*, these being the ancient names of a river today known as the Harut in south-western Afghanistan. The Harut has its source in three streams that rise in the mountains south-east of Herat. It then flows south for some 250 miles before ending in the salt-marshes of Hamun-i-Helmand, a shallow lake also fed by the more impressive Helmand River (referred to in the Avesta as the 'Haetumant' – see Map 4). This Harauvati River was sacred to the Zoroastrians as the home of the river goddess Surta Anahitya, the 'mighty and pure one', the divinity of the waters who nurtured cattle and crops and was associated with fertility,

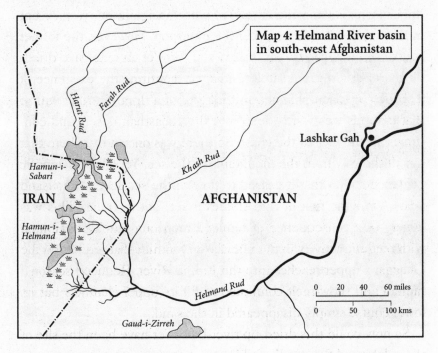

The Helmand River basin in south-west Afghanistan, showing the Harut River ('Harut Rud', top left on the map) with its three sources flowing into the marshlands of Hamun-i-Helmand from the north. This was the original Saraswati River and thus the original Arya homeland of Brahmavarta.

healing and wisdom. Surta Anahitya is not so much the goddess Saraswati's twin-sister as herself by another name. Here, then, is the real Saraswati River and the original Arya homeland.

Five thousand years ago this first Brahmavarta of the Arya was significantly less hostile than it is today. But the same decline in the south-west monsoon that affected the Harappan Civilisation also made itself felt in the south-western corner of Afghanistan. The rich pasturelands became incapable of sustaining large herds and flocks, so the local pastoralists moved on. Some chose to migrate eastwards with their horses, chariots and livestock – and as they moved so the sacred river of their fathers moved with them, but now just as a pious memory, to be replanted in the upper Punjab along the course of what was already a largely but

(Above, left) The Zoroastrian goddess Anahita incised on a fourth-century Sassanian seal. (Above, right) The goddess Saraswati in the homely form in which she is portrayed today, with a sitar-like *vina* in one pair of hands while her other hands hold a stylus and a palm-leaf manuscript. Detail of a gouache painting from Mysore c. 1835.

not yet entirely dried-up river-bed. But soon even this substitute Saraswati River became incapable of nurturing their cattle and crops, so that its decline had to be accounted for in pious fables. The river goddess was then transformed into the much-loved Hindu deity that she is today, the wife of Lord Brahma, goddess of wisdom and patron of knowledge, learning, music and the arts.

The *Mahabharata* transforms into magnificent myth the quarrels and conquests of the five Arya tribes as they pushed on into the Doab country between the Ganga and Yamuna rivers and then across the great Gangetic plain. As they advanced they subdivided into rival clans, each led by chieftains bent on establishing their own *janapada*s (literally 'people's feet', so footholds). The more warlike of the clans expanded by conquest into *mahajanapada*s or city-states, and their clan leaders now increasingly became hereditary rajas as kingship acquired a new sanctity.

The sacred space of the Aryavarta expanded into the more mundane geography of Bharatavarsam, 'the continent of Bharat', nominally referring to a legendary king from the *R-V* named Bharata but a word that can equally be read as 'the continent maintained by fire', suggesting the clearance of the jungle by the most basic form of farming – slash-and-burn. The hymns of the *Atharva-Veda*, the last of the four Vedas, reflects this settling-down process. Most of its hymns are a mix of flattery directed at one or other of the deities, coupled with demands for divine help, often in the form of spells and invocations.

Nowhere is this combination of flattery and demand more apparent than in the best known of all the hymns of the *Atharva-Veda*: Book 12, known as the *Prithvi Sukta*, in which the composer heaps praise on the earth-goddess Prithvi but also calls on her to give to the new settlers all that she has to offer. The *Prithvi Sukta* is frequently cited as the earliest example of human environmental responsibility, but modern translations seem to have moved a long way from the first renderings of the *Prithvi Sukta* into English by the industrious Sanskritist Ralph Griffith.[24] Griffith's translation of the *Prithvi Sukta* makes it clear that the Arya are asking the earth to work for them – as, for example, in Verse 4:

> *She who is Lady of the earth's four regions, in whom our food*
> *and our corn-lands had their being,*
> *Nurse in each place of living, moving creatures, this Earth,*
> *vouchsafe us kine [cattle] with milk that fails not.*[25]

So it goes on. But Prithvi is also called upon again and again to give the Arya protection from their foes, more specifically those known collectively to the Arya as Dasas or Dasyus, described as the 'God-blaspheming Dasyus ... on whom the men of old before us battled'.

The numerous references in the Vedas to these same Dasas as demonic enemies to be fought and subdued suggest that the Arya occupation of the land was by no means peaceful. One can imagine a situation akin to that faced by the Protestant settlers of New England in the seventeenth century, who initially had to rely on the Native American tribes for help to survive the harsh winters but then found themselves increasingly unwelcome as they expanded deeper into the interior. As in North America, so in Northern India, where the autochthonous peoples were also demonised as savages, so that the word *dasa* came to mean 'slave' or, more kindly, 'servant', but accompanied by such slighting epithets as *amanusah* ('sub-human'), *adhara* ('inferior'), *avratahas* ('without religious rites'), *krishnatvac* ('dark-skinned') and *anas* ('noseless', i.e. flat-nosed).

The Vedic religion was now evolving into a corpus of beliefs nowadays increasingly referred to as Vedanta, meaning 'the conclusion of the Vedas'. This was formalised from about 700 BCE onwards with the addition of a further tranche of spoken texts going under the generic term Dharmashastra, 'scriptures of universal order'. It was these later texts rather than the Vedas that laid the parameters of what we might now call Brahminical Hinduism. They also set out new ground rules for the proper ordering of society, enshrining into sacred law the born superiority of the ruling elite, taking their cue from four lines of verse in what is perhaps the most famous – or is it notorious? – hymn known as the *Purusha Sukta*, from *Rig-Veda* Book 10, which describes the division of the superman Purusha into four orders of men:

V. 11. *When they divided Purusha how many portions did*
        they make?
        What do they call his mouth and arms? What do
        they call his thighs and feet?
V. 12. *The Brahman was his mouth; of both his arms was*
        the Rajanya [Kshatriyas] made.
        His thighs became the Vaishya; from his feet the
        Shudra was produced.[26]

These much-quoted lines to all intents sanctified the Brahmins, the priests of the Arya, as the mouth-piece of Brahma, through whom the Arya received their God-given laws, along with the God-given social order known as *varna*, a vexatious word which, thanks to the Portuguese, is usually translated as 'caste', although it can equally be interpreted as 'race', 'class of men' or even 'colour'. On the second rung of the *varna* ladder were those named in the *Purusha Sukta* as Rajanyas, or 'those who rule', better known as Kshatriyas, destined by birth to rule and fight. Below them, but also considered worthy to undergo the *upanayana samskara*, the sacred thread ceremony that proclaimed them as 'twice-born', were the Vaishyas, the merchants and agriculturalists. Lastly, the Shudras, who made up the Arya labour force. But even they shared the birth privilege of *varna*, perhaps reflecting shared origins outside India. All the rest of humankind were *avarna*, or 'non-*varna*', destined always to be outsiders and outcastes.

So the Dasas remained outside the law, with no prospect of ever being accepted into the fold. We can assume that many had no option but to bend the knee and accept their fate. But others, we can equally assume, withdrew deeper into the forests and high-lands, including those who migrated south across the Narmada. As far as the Arya were concerned, what lay beyond the Narmada, the Dakshina, was still unknown country, wild and hostile, and dominated by demons and demon armies.

There is so much to marvel at in the complexities of the Vedas and Vedanta. But we should also bear in mind that this was all the work of Brahmin priests and thinkers – created out of piety, certainly, but very much to their advantage. The Brahmin caste remains to this day the oldest and longest-lasting closed shop in history. For all the abuse that has been heaped upon them in recent years – and particularly in the Tamil-speaking regions – the Brahmins were, and still are, a quite astonishing phenomenon: a self-perpetuating elite of intellectuals who came up with specu-lations about time and the cosmos that were centuries ahead of any such thinking elsewhere. At some early point in their his-tory this minority priestly elite had the good sense to form an alliance with a group of warriors to whom they gave good advice in return for their protection. There is a hint, in allusions to an epic struggle between the Brahmins and the Kshatriya warrior caste that ended with the destruction of all the latter, that in their rise to pre-eminence the Brahmins had to fight for survival. The outcome was the formation of a Brahmin–Kshatriya alliance, an axis of thinkers and warriors, that gave these two parties such an advantage that it survived almost intact right up to the twentieth century.

Quite apart from their religious duties, the intellectual and political skills of the Brahmins served generations of rulers extremely well, including foreign rulers just as much as native Rajputs, so much so that a British official writing in the 1870s could feel moved to describe the Brahmins he worked with in the Madras Presidency as 'so much more intelligent, learned, supple and pleasant to deal with than the common people that almost all writers [on India] have confined themselves to Brahminical life and have led people to imagine that India is what Brahmins are'.[27]

An illustration from the Tamil *Ramavataram*, showing Rama firing Vishnu's bow gifted to him by the sage Agathya at the demon king Ravana, supported by his ally Hanuman and his monkey army. One of a set of eight gouaches probably painted in Tanjore in about 1800.

3
AGASTYA'S COUNTRY

The stone colossus of the Tamil sage Thiruvalluvar facing
Kanyakumari and the walls of the *kovil*.

Stepping out of the car at Kanyakumari I find myself in the
market-place of a very ordinary, dusty, noisy Indian town, its
main street crowded with holidaymakers doubling as pilgrims –
or is it vice versa?

What they have come to see lies immediately offshore: two
islets side by side, but not quite as drawn by the geologist Robert
Foote back in 1860 (as shown at the start of Chapter 1). One
carries a neat stone temple, topped by half a dozen pink Indo-
Saracenic domes. This was built in 1970 in the face of vociferous

objections from environmentalists, who thought the rock was
best left untouched, and from the local Christian community,
who declared the islet to be St Xavier's Rock.

But it is what was built on the second island that draws all
eyes. It was entirely funded by the state government of Tamil
Nadu, took ten years to construct and was completed in the
last days of 1999. It takes the form of a 133-feet-high statue in
granite of a standing human male figure. He is thickly bearded,
formidable in appearance and faces inland, his right hand raised
in the three-fingered salute familiar to every Boy Scout. What
is so unusual about this statue in the Indian context is that it
represents neither a deity, nor a ruler, nor a recently deceased
politician. The statue is of the Tamil moral philosopher and
poet Thiruvalluvar, and each of its 133 feet is said to represent
a chapter of his literary masterpiece: the two-thousand-year-old
Thirukkural, or 'Revered couplets'. His three raised fingers sig-
nify the three major themes expounded in that writing: *Aram*,
Porul and *Inbam* – respectively, 'morals', 'public ethics' and
'love'.

Cynics who read Thiruvalluvar's *Thirukkural* in translation
might be inclined to dismiss it as a collection of platitudes delivered in rhyming couplets. The poet has also been criticised for
his patriarchal view of women, and even that great champion of
Tamil culture Robert Caldwell felt able to satirise his verse in
a spoof poem he wrote in his *Chutney Lyrics*, published anony-
mously in 1871, which begins:

> *Cursed is the man, whatever his worth,*
> *Who is poor in purse and low in birth.*

> *The unity of the Tamilian nation*
> *Is cemented by caste and litigation.*

To cook for man, woman was chiefly meant.
Ignorance is her best ornament.

But Thiruvalluvar deserves better, even if it means reading him in English – as in the first English translation of the *Thirukkural* by Francis Whyte Ellis, a Madras civil servant who has had the rare accolade of having recently had a district in Madurai named after him: Ellis Nagar. Here below are three of Ellis's couplets from Chapter VIII, on the subject of married love:

78. *As in a barren soil a sapless tree,*
    So flourish those in wedded bliss, whose souls
    Know not the sweets of love.

79. *What though the body each perfection own,*
    If in the breast, the beauty of the mind,
    Exist not.

80. *That breast alone contains a living soul,*
    Which love inspires; void of this genial warmth,
    'Tis bone o'erlaid with skin.

This unfinished work was enough to inspire the French scholar Edouard-Simon Ariel to work on his own French translation, declaring in a letter to his eminent colleague Eugène Burnouf that what was so wonderful about these verses was that 'its author addresses himself, without regard to castes, peoples, or beliefs, to the whole community of mankind; the fact that he formulates sovereign morality and absolute reason; the fact that he proclaims in this very essence, in their eternal abstractness, virtue and truth ... the tenderest emotions of the heart'.[1]

That sums it up very succinctly. No wonder, then, that for a

great many South Indians the *Thirukkural* symbolises their *ulaga
podhmarai* or 'common creed', as well as offering a guide to the
good life lived in harmony with humanity and nature. At the very
least, the *Thirukkural*'s 1330 melodious couplets, ten to each chapter, are easy to remember and full of good sense.

The statue of Thiruvalluvar outside the School of Oriental and
African Studies in London, unveiled in 1996 with the Indian High
Commissioner in attendance.

Thiruvalluvar first entered my consciousness as a larger-than-
life-size grey painted statue seated cross-legged on the lawn
outside the library of the School of Oriental and African Studies
in London. Its erection there in 1996 was first and last a political
statement, as is that much larger representation off Kanyakumari.
Both are expressions of Tamil India's growing self-assertion. When

Chief Minister Dr K. Karunanidhi allocated funds for the Indian statue in 1990 he was cocking a snook at Northern India on behalf of the South and his own regionalist political party, the Dravida Munnetra Kazhagam (DMK) or 'Dravidian Progress Federation'. Much the same goes for the SOAS statue. But what both statues also celebrate are Thiruvalluvar's humble origins, which is why he is such a hero to the common man, and why his bearded image can be seen on the dashboards of buses and lorries all over South India.

So who exactly was Thiruvalluvar?

His name is made up of two Tamil words. *Thiru* is the local equivalent of the Sanskrit honorific *sri*, and with the same added implication of 'holy'. However, *Valluvar* refers to a tribe of astrologers, astronomers and medicine men who were said to have acted as priests to the Pandya rulers in Madurai long before the arrival in South India of the first Brahmin priests, after which the Valluvar were relegated to the lowest rung on the Hindu social ladder. Most accounts describe Thiruvalluvar as born of a Brahmin father by an outcaste Paraiyar mother. So Thiruvalluvar is very much a symbol of the emergence of the oppressed underclasses after centuries of oppression by the higher castes.

No one knows for certain when Thiruvalluvar lived, or where he lived, and some question if he ever lived, and perhaps it doesn't matter. Popular tradition has it that he was a weaver by occupation who lived with his dutiful wife in Mylapore (now swallowed up by Chennai), where his supposed house is now a temple with its own statue akin to that on the SOAS lawn. However, in 2005 this widely accepted version was challenged by the Kanyakumari Historical and Cultural Research Centre, which announced that it had established Thiruvalluvar's true origins. A name inscribed on a tenth-century copper plate had led them to the most southerly section of the Western Ghats, known in British days as the

Tinnevelly Range but carrying a variety of far older names, including Pothigai Malai, Pothiyam Malai, Agastya Malai and Mahendra Giri.

This is the same thickly forested mountain country that constitutes the homeland of the semi-nomadic hunter-gatherers known as the Kanikkar mentioned in Chapter 1. It seems that when the oldest member of the Kanikkar, said to be 105 years old, was questioned by researchers he declared that his people knew these mountains as Thiruvana Malai because they had been named after one of their own, the poet-saint Thiruvalluvar. According to the old man, Thiruvalluvar had been born there and had ruled the area as its king, frequently roaming through the hills with his wife in search of honey. After his death the Kanikkar people had added Thiruvalluvar to their gods and continued to worship him to the present day.

But then other South Indian communities also claim Thiruvalluvar as one of theirs, including Jains, Buddhists and Shaivas. These claims make the point that Thiruvalluvar stands for Tamil and Dravidian identity. He is the South's champion in the face of advancing Sanskritisation from the North.

Here Thiruvalluvar's first English translator, Francis Ellis, deserves a further mention. Ellis's career as a civil servant got off to a disastrous start when as a young judge and magistrate in Thanjavur (known to the British as Tanjore) in 1805 he attempted to arrest a servant of the Raja of Tanjore who was alleged to have tortured a plaintiff by putting crushed chillies in his eyes. The enraged raja's protest to the government led to Ellis being posted to Masulipatnam in Telugu-speaking country, where he had the good fortune to meet the Telugu scholar Mamadi Venkayya, who directed him towards Telugu and Tamil literature. He is also said to have adopted local customs, including the wearing of 'native' dress.

In 1810 Ellis was forgiven and made Collector of Madras, where he was instrumental in setting up the College of Fort St George. This was in emulation of the East India Company's (EICo's) College of Fort William in Calcutta, where local pandits taught the vernacular languages to newly appointed civil servants very much to the benefit of both parties. Ellis was insistent that every newly arrived Company employee should learn Tamil, having recognised that here was the basic structure for all the South Indian languages. This argument, which he called his 'Dravidian Proof', was first set out in his introduction to his colleague Duncan Campbell's *Grammar of the Teloogoo Language*, published in 1816.[2] What made that publication possible was Ellis's gift to the College of a printing press together with Tamil types, enabling the first accessible Tamil grammar to be printed in 1813.[3] Other publications in Kannada, Telugu, Malayalam and Arabic followed.

Ellis died of cholera in Ramanathapuram in 1819 before his translation of the *Thirukkural* could be completed, so that only eighteen translated chapters were ever published. We will never know how much else he had already translated because after his sudden death all his papers fell, by a bizarre twist of fate, into the hands of a notorious character named Rous Peter, whose cook used them as firelighters in his kitchen (more of the appalling Peter in a later chapter).

What we do know is that Ellis greatly admired Thiruvalluvar's work. In 1818 the EICo's Madras Presidency suffered a severe drought, which led Ellis to order the digging of twenty-seven new wells in the worst-affected area. One of these new wells was dug in the grounds of the little Periyapalayathamman temple at Royapettah (now swallowed up into Chennai). Its surrounding wall carries a long inscription by Ellis in which he uses a couplet from the *Thirukkural* to explain his actions during the drought.

So Francis Ellis deserves his due as the first European to

suggest in print that the South Indian languages had a common root that was not Sanskrit, and the first to name that common source 'Dravidian'. His death at the age of forty-two meant that the credit went to the missionary scholar Robert Caldwell.

For all his good works, Caldwell was a man of his time, a firm believer in the combined blessings of the Pax Britannica and Protestant Christianity. But that should not obscure the wide-ranging nature of his scholarship, not least his pioneering study of the Tamil language and its origins. Taking up from where Ellis had left off, Caldwell recognised that the four main spoken languages of the South – Tamil, Malayalam, Kannada and Telugu – formed a distinct language family of their own, which he, too, proposed to call 'Dravidian'. 'The word I have chosen is "Dravidian", from *Drāviḍa*,' wrote Caldwell in the introduction to his ground-breaking *Comparative Grammar of the Dravidian or South Indian Family of Languages*, published in 1856. 'It is a term which has already been used more or less distinctively by Sanskrit philologists, as a generic appellation for the South Indian people and their languages, and it is the only single term they ever seem to have used in this manner. I have, therefore, no doubt of the propriety of adopting it.'

This Dravidian language family, he argued, was quite distinct from Sanskrit, with which it had nothing in common other than loan words: 'My own theory is that the Dravidian languages occupy a position of their own between the languages of the Indo-European family and those of the Turanian or Scythina group – not quite a midway position, but one considerably nearer the latter than the former.'

In challenging the accepted view of the time that Sanskrit was the only significant source of India's language and culture, Caldwell helped to draw attention to the unique cultural identity of the Dravidian peoples of South India. It was the Brahmins, he argued, who had introduced what he termed 'idol-worship' to the South, together with 'the Puranic system of religion' and the Brahminical concept of caste which had reduced former rulers, warriors and farmers to the status of Shudras. Above all, it was the Brahmins who had undermined and reduced the status of Tamil literature by replacing it with Sanskrit. Paternalistic and imperialistic Caldwell may have been, but his championing of Dravidian combined with his church's work in raising the status of lower-caste Christians and in establishing mission schools undoubtedly helped kindle what has been called variously the Dravidian Movement or the Tamil Renaissance.

Today philologists tend to divide the Dravidian family group into four main branches: Northern, Central (Kolami-Parji), South-Central (Telugu-Kui) and South (Tamil-Malayalam-Tulu-Kannada). There is also a growing preference among some South Indians for the dropping of those Sanskrit words Dravidian (as a language group) and Dravidians (as a people) in favour of Tamil and *Tamilakam*, 'the homeland of Tamil'. But that does not go down well with the speakers of other languages that also have a proto-Dravidian origin. This same determination to mark out their own identity gave rise to the agitation among Telugu-speakers that led to the formation of India's newest state of Telangana, formed in June 2014 with Hyderabad as its capital. Not wishing to offend speakers of Malayalam, Telugu or Kannada, I shall stick with 'Dravidian', except when speaking specifically of Tamil country, which is essentially Tamil Nadu (TN) state as it is today.

But Thiruvalluvar's recent elevation off Kanyakumari has come at a price, because his statue quite literally overshadows an even older symbol of the Dravidian South. Robert Foote's drawing from 1860 shows just one solid structure on shore, a low building with red and white striped walls surrounded by a half a dozen mud and palm-leaf huts. This is the ancient shrine of the virgin goddess Devi Kanyakumari, protector of ascetics. The town was her dwelling place long, long before Thiruvalluvar, which explains why Cape Comorin's proper name is Kanyakumari and has been so for at least two thousand years.

In the primordial past, so the Puranas tell us – and Hindu mythology does a far better job in seeking to comprehend the temporal parameters of the cosmos than do the holy books of the three main monotheistic religions – the Devas were assailed by their demonic rivals the Asuras, who wreaked havoc on earth. It was known among the gods that only a pure virgin girl could defeat them so Bhumi Devi, Mother Earth, appealed to Parashakti, the Divine Mother, to intercede on her behalf. The Devas performed a *yajna*, or fire sacrifice, and out of the fire pit emerged a young virgin. She then travelled to the southern tip of India and settled there, hence the name Kanyakumari, or 'virgin adolescent girl'.

At this point the great god of yogis Lord Shiva appeared on the scene, saw the virgin goddess, fell in love and determined to marry her. A marriage was arranged, to take place at midnight at the close of a particularly auspicious day. But a divine sage then realised that the Asuras could be destroyed only if Kanyakumari remained a virgin. He therefore intervened by assuming the form of a rooster and crowing as Lord Shiva approached just before the midnight hour. Hearing the cock crow at what he mistook for the approaching dawn, Shiva concluded that he had come too late and had missed his chance. So Shiva returned to his abode in the Himalayas, and Kanyakumari, believing that she had been jilted, was plunged into grief. She tore her hair, broke her bracelets and anklets and scattered what was to have been their wedding feast far and wide – particles of which make up the multi-coloured sands and pebbles found along the south-ern seashore. She then became an ascetic, vowing to perform austerities until such time as Lord Shiva returned for her. Hence

Devi Kanyakumari's exalted position as patroness of yogis and ascetics.

Delightful as this story is, it is just one of many variations on the theme of local female deities being absorbed into the Shaiva canon. Devi Kanyakumari goes back a lot further than her failed alliance with the Great God Shiva. Despite her virginity, she is part of a much older form of religious expression: the cult of the Mother Goddess, known in the South as Amman (Mother) or Aatha (Mother), Mariamman (Mother Mari), or simply Mari, which means 'rain'. Mariamman's prime attribute is as the bringer of rain and, by extension, fertility. She is also the goddess who wards off all the so-called 'heat diseases' such as rashes and smallpox, and she has her fierce aspect, in which capacity she is worshipped as Angala-amman, the 'Mother Protector', a fearful apparition with wild, unkempt hair and blood dripping from extended fangs who guards the village from ghosts and demons and accepts blood sacrifices.

Northern India has comparatively few shrines devoted exclusively to the Mother Goddess, chiefly because she has been more thoroughly absorbed into the person of Shiva's *shakti*, his consort in the form of Durga Mata or Kali. In the South shrines of the Mother Goddess are seen in virtually every village, often sited close to one or more anthills, the favourite haunt of cobras. Here the goddess is found in her most basic forms, often as no more than an approximation of the female form modelled out of sand and clay or even as a slab of granite with a sharp tip at the top not unlike a spear-head, frequently seen garlanded with flowers. One such Amman shrine is the Angala Parameshwari temple at Putlur, now swallowed up in the north-western suburbs of Chennai, where the goddess takes the frankly unprepossessing form of a large anthill supposedly resembling a pregnant woman sleeping with her mouth wide open. Hence the name of the village, Putlur, from the Tamil word *putru*, 'snake hole'.

(Above) A clay image of the goddess Amman from a village near Salem in Tamil Nadu. (Right) A non-Brahmin priest at the Samayapuram Mariamman temple near Trichy making an offering to a *murti* (image) of the goddess made of sand and clay.

Besides these simple country shrines, the Mother Goddess also has a number of major temples devoted to her worship in Tamil Nadu, one of them being the Punainallur Mariamman temple in Thanjavur, built by a Maratha ruler in the 1680s following a dream in which Mariamman appeared to him and told him to look in a particular grove outside the city. There the raja found the deity in the form of a white anthill, around which he built the temple. As an unbeliever, I have to say that it was a disappointment after the architectural marvels I had earlier seen in Thanjavur itself, and much less interesting than another temple just across the road, which had been built in the shape of a giant stone linga and yoni. But perhaps the true real significance of the Punainallur Mariamman temple lies in the fact that large numbers of childless couples come here to pray for fertility, and if successful return to hang small cradles from the branches of the temple's tree. Sufferers in search of cures also come here to leave small effigies in clay showing the part of the body they believe to be affected. Here, as in all Amman temples, most of the worshippers are women drawn from the lower castes. They make offerings to the goddess in the traditional form of *mavilakku* – a sweet dish made of unrefined molasses, rice flour and separated butter – or *pongal*, a mix of rice and lentil cooked in terracotta pots. Brahmin priests may be in attendance but the actual rites themselves are said to be performed by laymen from the lower castes. To me and to other sceptics here is evidence that the worship of the Mother Goddess pre-dated the arrival of Brahminical Hinduism in the South.

As for Devi Kanyakumari, her extreme antiquity is vouched for by the unknown Greek or Roman author of *Periplus Maris Erythraei*, or 'Voyage round the Erythraean [i.e. Arabian] Sea'. This guide to the coastal regions of the Red Sea, Yemen, the Persian Gulf and India's western and eastern seaboards was written in the first century CE at a time when trading links between the Graeco-Roman and Indian worlds were at their peak. Its author appears to have been a very experienced trader or seafarer who had been there and done it all. After describing the various features of the Deccan's eastern seaboard he goes on to describe the cape itself, his words proving that even two thousand years ago it was linked both to a goddess and to asceticism:

> Next to this is another place called Komar, where is the cape of the same name and a haven. Those who wish to conse-crate the closing part of their lives to religion come hither to bathe and engage themselves in celibacy. This is also done by women, since it is related that the goddess once on a time resided at the place and bathed. From Komarei towards the south [*sic* – east] the country extends as far as Kolkhoi, where the fishing for pearls is carried out. Condemned criminals are employed in this service. King Pandion [i.e. Pandya] is the owner of the fishery.[4]

The famous *Tabula Peutingeriana* map of the Roman world, now housed in the National Library of Austria in Vienna, also has its origins in the first century with later additions, although what survives today is a medieval copy. The last folio of the map (discussed in detail in Chapter 6) shows India, with its southernmost cape marked as 'Comara'. The 'Comara', 'Komar' or 'Komarei' of the Romans is, of course, the 'Kumari' of the Indians, and from there it is only a short step to the Portuguese 'Cumerin' and on to the Comorin of our day.

So the goddess Kumari and her sisters most certainly pre-date the arrival of Brahminical Hinduism in what may be called the deep south. And here one name stands pre-eminent, head and shoulders above all others: Agastya. He is the rishi, or sage, credited with bringing the Sanskrit language to the South – and yet, paradoxically, this same sage Agastya is also claimed to be the man responsible for bringing the gift of the Tamil language.

A few miles north of Kanyakumari the very last of the peaks of the Western Ghats rise out of the plain. They are part of that same thickly forested mountain redoubt mentioned earlier that goes go by such names as the Tinnevelly Range, Pothigai Malai, Pothiyam Malai, Agastya Malai and Mahendra Giri, 'the hill of Mahendra'. This last has a particularly honoured place in Hindu tradition, taking its name from *maha*, 'great', and *Indra*, the Vedic rain god who has his home on Mount Meru, the primordial mountain at the centre of the cosmos. In the human world its geographical location shifts from place to place and it looms particularly large in the second of the great epics of Hinduism, the *Ramayana*.

Laid out in twenty-four thousand couplets, 'Rama's journey' is built around the person of the god-king Rama and his epic struggle with Ravana, the demon king of Lanka. I have been assured that Prince Rama himself was born on 4 December 7323 BCE. Even so, the widespread consensus among modern scholars is that his story was composed in two phases, with the book's five middle sections probably assembled no earlier than the fourth century BCE and the first and last sections added in about the first century BCE. Central to the story is Rama's portrayal as an incarnation of Lord Vishnu, who begins his spectacular rise to prominence at this same time. What is also apparent from the story is that the author or authors of the *Ramayana* were very much at home with the geography of Bharat north of the Narmada, but knew little about what lay beyond, even if its main rivers had been given names.

For many Hindus, there is only one version of Rama's journey and that is Valmiki's *Ramayana*, written in Sanskrit, although many Tamil-speakers would be quick to argue that their version – Kamban's *Ramayanam*, also known as *Ramavataram* – is far superior, being the work of a thirteenth-century court poet from Thanjavur, and first read out by him in the precincts of the vast Sri Ranganathaswamy Vishnu temple on the outskirts of Trichy.[5] This makes the point that there are in fact several hundred extant versions and variations of the tale. Not only does every region in India have its own form of the *Ramayana* story but so, too, do a number of Hindu sects, each with its own take.[6] Even the Buddhists and the Jains have their versions, in which no deities are involved and no mention is made of what one would think of as the highlight of Valmiki's *Ramayana*, which is the kidnapping of Rama's wife Sita by the demon Ravana and her subsequent rescue from the island of Lanka with the aid of the monkey warrior Hanuman and his army of monkeys.

Nevertheless, at the core of most versions are the events which helped to inspire Valmiki and others with the concept of an epic battle between good and evil: a sea-borne military expedition from Bengal that went all the way south as far as the island of Lanka, leading to conflict with one or more local rulers and ending in an alliance with the local king – an invasion that is unlikely to have taken place before the fifth century BCE.

The first English translation of Valmiki's *Ramayana* was made by two missionaries very much in the same mould as Robert Caldwell, William Carey and Joshua Marshman. It was printed at their Baptist Mission Press in Serampore between 1806 and 1808 as part of the declared objective of the Orientalist movement in Bengal not only to study India 'in all its aspects' but also to make India's culture accessible to all. So the *Ramayana* became the first of a series of publications of Sanskrit classics funded by the subscriptions of members of the Asiatic Society of Bengal and the College of Fort William in Calcutta, 'being desirous of promoting the knowledge of the Literature of India, and, at the same time, of disclosing to the Learned of Europe the stores which lie hid in the Ancient Languages of India'.[7]

That first English version of the *Ramayana* makes for heavy reading today and has been superseded by far better translations by modern Indian scholars. However, I have to admit to still having a soft spot for the version published in rhyming couplets in the 1870s by … who else but my hero Ralph Griffith, written in his retirement in the Nilgiri Hills. In the following excerpt Rama's ally, King Sugriva, orders an army of 'ten thousand of our race' to cross the Vindhyas and search the South for the kidnapped Sita, which means crossing all the major rivers until they arrive at the southern sea:

> *'Go forth,' he cried, 'with all this host*
> *Exploring to the southern coast:*
> *The thousand peaks that Vindhya shows*
> *Where every tree and creeper grows:*
> *Where Narmada's sweet waters run,*
> *And serpents bask them in the sun:*
> *Where Krishnaveni's currents flee,*
> *And sparkles fair Godavari …*
> *Search well his forests where the breeze*
> *Blows fragrant from the sandal trees.*
> *Then will you see Kaveri's stream*
> *Whose pleasant waters glance and gleam,*
> *And to the lovely banks entice*
> *The sportive maids of Paradise.*
> *High on the top of Malaya's hill,*
> *In holy musing, calm and still,*
> *Sits, radiant as the Lord of Light,*
> *Agastya, noblest anchorite.*
> *Soon as that lofty-thoughted lord*

His high permission shall accord,
Pass Tamrapaní's flood whose isles
Are loved by basking crocodiles.
The sandal woods that fringe her side
Those islets and her waters hide;
While, like an amorous matron, she
Speeds to her own dear lord the sea.
Thence hasting on your way behold
The Pandyas' gates of pearl and gold.
Then, with your task maturely planned,
On ocean's shore your feet will stand.
Where, by Agastya's high decree,
Mahendra, planted in the sea,[8]
With tinted peaks against the tide
Rises in solitary pride,
And glorious in his golden glow
Spurns back the waves that beat below.[9]

So here we find the sage Agastya, the 'noblest anchorite', seated 'high on the top of Malaya's hill' on the Mahendra mountain, beside the sea.

But Agastya is no ordinary rishi. Long before Sita's abduction she and her exiled husband Rama visit a succession of sages in their hermitages, but none as important as Agastya. They find the sage settled on his mountain top, surrounded by the shrines of Vishnu and all the major gods but one – the notable absentee being Lord Vishnu's rival, Shiva.

Agastya immediately recognises Rama as the incarnation of Vishnu and acknowledges his importance in the cosmic scheme of things by worshipping him as king of all three worlds. He then presents him with Vishnu's bow and arrows, which Rama later uses to defeat his mortal enemy, the demon Ravana. Agastya also intervenes in that final battle by praying to Brahma to come in on Rama's side. So Agastya plays a crucial role in Rama's final defeat of Ravana, which does not explain why he should be held in such high esteem in the Tamil world.

The sage Agastya has many names, one of them being *kuru-muni*, the 'short ascetic', because by all accounts he was so dwarfish as to be unable to walk comfortably. And that is how he is usually portrayed: as a short, stumpy-legged fellow with a beard and a pronounced pot-belly, holding a yogi's beads in one hand and a water-pot in the other. Even his proper name takes two forms, one Sanskrit and one Tamil. The etymology of his Sanskrit name is open to debate but the most logical theory is that it derives from *aga*, 'mountain', and *asti*, 'thrower', because he is the overthrower of mountains. This is how he first appears in the *Rig-Veda* (*R-V*), as one of the *Saptarishi*s, seven sages with quasi-divine powers, and credited as the composer of twenty-seven of the hymns in the first and earliest of the *R-V*'s ten books. He has been fathered by two early Vedic gods, Mitra and Varuna, who after being sexually aroused by the sight of a celestial nymph deposit their seed in a clay pitcher. This is found floating in the River Ganges by a rishi who names the boy born out of the pot *kumbhasambhava*, or 'jar-born'. So Agastya has very solid Vedic credentials.

Agastya's next major appearance is in the *Mahabharata*, where we learn that the Dakshina is filled with demons and, in particular, cruel snake-like creatures called Kaleyas or Kalakeyas, who hate the gods. They are destroying the Brahmins by night, leaving the earth so filled with their corpses, 'like piled-up conch shells', that very few Brahmins are left alive to study and make sacrifices to the gods. Whenever the Kshatriyas fight back to help save the Brahmins the demons hide in the oceans. So the gods call in the sage Agastya to help. But to get to the Kaleyas

Agastya has first to cross the Vindhya mountain range, which in its pride has grown so high as to block the rounds of the sun and the moon. Agastya orders the Vindhyas to bow down low enough to allow him and his wife Lopamudra to cross, and to remain bowed until he returns – which he never does, so leaving the Vindhya prostrate and humbled. By this means Agastya opens a route into the Dakshina. He then drinks up the southern ocean, so enabling the gods to destroy the exposed demons, who have nowhere left to hide. He then makes his home in a series of ashrams, each one set that bit further south. Crucially, he brings with him to the Dakshina a great gift: the sacred language of Sanskrit.

So here is Agastya as the very personification of the Arya, Vedic, Brahmin and Sanskrit penetration of the Dravidian South. And he is also a devotee of Lord Vishnu – a Vaishnava.

But the Tamils know a rather different sage. To them he is Agathya or Agattiyam, the latter name implying someone who is inward-looking, from *agam*, 'inside', and *iyar*, 'belong to'. But he is still dwarf-like, and he shares other features with the Vedic Agastya, such as his origins in a pitcher and his crossing of the Vindhyas from north to south. However, from the Tamil point of view, the main reason for the sage's journey south is to restore cosmic balance. Lord Shiva's wedding to his *shakti* Parvati at his abode on Mount Kailas attracts so many deities that the Himalayas begin to sink, causing the (flat) Earth to tip towards the north. The gods ask Agathya to go south to restore the balance, which he does. But he also takes with him a pitcher of water from the goddess Ganga that contains the Cauvery River. He and his wife Lopamudra then cross the Vindhyas and with the help of the waters of the Cauvery they make the land fertile and habitable by man.

Crucially, in this account Agathya is the bringer not of Sanskrit but the gift of the Tamil language, which Lord Shiva

(Above) Male devotees anoint the statue of Agathya on the summit of his mountain, Pothigai Malai or Agathya Malai. (Right) The pot-bellied dwarf-like sage known to some as Agastya, bringer of Sanskrit and Vedic culture to the South, and to others as Agathya, father of the Tamil language and Tamil culture. This tenth-century carving in volcanic tufa comes from central Java, where the cult of Agastya became widespread following the Chola expansion into South East Asia.

has presented to him to give to the world. He goes on to found and preside over the first Sangam (Cankam), a literary academy or assembly where scholars and poets gather to produce Tamil literature. To this end, he produces the first Tamil grammar, a work entitled *Agathiyam* which is subsequently lost in a great flood which inundates much of the original Tamil country. Agathya is also acknowledged as the founder of Tamil medical studies and martial arts.

In sum, Agathya is *Tamilakam's* founding father. He is also a devotee of Lord Vishnu's great rival, Lord Shiva, which makes him a Shaiva or Shaivite.

So which is the 'real' rishi? The Sanskrit Agastya or the Tamil Agathya?

The oldest surviving grammar of the Tamil language is the *Tolkappiyam*, or 'ancient literature', a work that is regarded as the earliest example of Tamil literature. It is credited to a scholar named Tholkappiyar, who is said to have lived in the Kanyakumari country at the time of the great flood and to have based his *Tolkappiyam* on Agathya's lost grammar. It is further said that Tholkappiyar was one of Agathya's twelve disciples, although nowhere in his grammar does he mention the name of his supposed guru.

However, much of what we know about the Tamil Agathya actually comes from a commentary on the *Tolkappiyam* written by a celebrated fourteenth-century Tamil scholar named Nachinarkiniyar.[10] In this commentary Nachinarkiniyar sets out the now familiar story of Shiva's wedding, the tilting of the world and Agathya's journey south at Shiva's request. But he also provides some additional details, presumed to be from earlier lost sources, which describe how on his way south from the Himalayas Agathya visited a place called Tuvarapati, which our commentator identifies as the coastal city of Dwaraka in Gujarat, one of

India's *sapta puri* or 'seven holy cities', but also a city famously linked to its founder, Lord Krishna. One of the later avatars or manifestations of Lord Vishnu, Krishna takes his name from the Sanskrit *krsna*, meaning 'dark' or 'black', hence his standard depiction as blue-skinned. Krishna gets no mention in the Vedas, but comes into his own in the *Mahabharata*, which is where we first hear about his city of Dwaraka – as a mighty city lost to the sea in a great inundation. 'On the same day that Krishna departed from the earth,' declares the *Vishnu Purana*, 'the oceans rose and submerged the whole of Dwaraka.' Nachinarkiniyar makes no mention of a flood but tells us that at Dwaraka our sage Agathya collected the descendants of Netu-muti-annal, who could be Krishna but could equally be some other ancestral leader. These descendants included eighteen kings and eighteen families 'of the *Velir* and the *Aruvalar*'. He then leads these migrants to settle the South, where they clear the forests and cultivate the land.

The Velirs were historically the members of a royal clan of dynastic kings who were mostly vassals of the more powerful great dynasties of Tamil kings, the Cholas, Cheras and Pandyas, with whom they intermarried over many centuries. There is less certainty over the Aruvalar. According to the late historian K. R. Subramanian, their name was derived from *aruval* or 'bill-hook' and they were pastoralists who made their homeland in Tondai Nadu or Tondaimallam in what is now northern Tamil Nadu. They appear also to have been known as Aruvar, which Subramanian equated with the Tamil word for Nagas, suggesting that they may have been snake-worshippers. Ptolemy the Elder mentions the Aravarnoi, who had in their country the emporium of Malanga where their king Basaronages resided, neither yet successfully identified.[11] However, another theory equates the Aruvalar with the Vellalars, taking their name from the Tamil *vellam*, 'flood', relating to the flooding of the rice-fields, because these Vellalars were farmers who rose to become a dominant landowning class in early Tamil society, second only in status to the kings, who married their daughters. Today found throughout Tamil Nadu, southern Kerala and Sri Lanka, Vellalars such as the Pillais still play an important role in Tamil society – and still speak of themselves as Gangeyas, or 'children of Mother Ganga', as if they had their origins in the North. Both these groups identify themselves with the Kshatriya warrior caste and with Shaivism.

Having settled these immigrants in the South, the sage Agathya retreats to his hilltop hermitage in the mountains – no longer named Mahendra by this account, but now Pothigai or Pothiyil, quintessentially Tamil words meaning 'a meeting place of knowledge or awakening'. However, Agathya still has more blessings to confer on the Tamil people, because on the way to his Pothigai hermitage he encounters Lord Shiva's son Murugan in the guise of an old man, who teaches him various arts that subsequently become integral to Tamil culture: astronomy, healing and harming – the last becoming the Keralan martial art of *kalarippayattu*, said (by Keralans) to be the 'mother of all martial arts'.

This sounds very much like a Tamil version of the Biblical story of Moses leading the children of Israel to the promised land – and there may well be something in that parallel.

The first Western scholar to attempt to reconcile these two versions of Agastya/Agathya was, of course, Robert Caldwell. He has subsequently been castigated for dating Tholkappiyar's *Tolkappiyam* grammar to the tenth century, but the point he wanted to make was that the Tamil Agastya appears on the literary scene long after the Sanskrit Agastya. Caldwell went on to suggest that the latter was essentially a Tamil response to the intrusion of Sanskrit culture on the South and that he may not have been a living person but more likely Tamil culture's 'mythological embodiment'.

Caldwell had a very high opinion of Tamils as 'the least super-stitious and the most enterprising and persevering race of Hindus' and he spoke highly of their culture. Even so, he had no hesitation in stating that what he called the Tamil people's 'higher civilisa-tion' was derived from the Sanskrit North, more specifically from 'a succession of small colonies of Aryans, chiefly Brahmins, from Upper India, who were probably attracted to the South by the report of the fertility of the rich alluvial plains watered by the Kaveri, the Thamirabarani, and the other peninsula rivers'.

These views soon came under attack. One of Caldwell's most outspoken opponents was a former student of a Christian college named Arumuka Navalar, a non-Brahmin born into a literary Pillai family and brought up in the Tamil-dominated Jaffna peninsula in Ceylon. Navalar had helped translate the Bible into Tamil but came to realise that the combination of British rule and Christian missionary activity was undermining both Dravidian culture and his own high-caste Shaivism. In 1850 he set up his own vernacular Tamil printing press to counter what he saw as the anti-Hindu propaganda of the missionaries, as well as establishing Tamil-medium schools in imitation of the mission schools. But Navalar's reforming zeal was marred by his prejudices. His aggressive promotion of high-caste Shaivism and his support for the privileges enjoyed by those same castes made him as many enemies as friends. Even so, that same zeal inspired many young Tamils with such giveaway South Indian high-caste names as Aiyer, Iyengar, Mudaliar and Pillai to take up Tamil cultural studies, many of them as graduates of Jesuit colleges and Madras University.

One such scholar was Mu Raghava Iyengar, born a year before Navalar's death in 1879. As a leading member of what was named the 4th Madurai Tamil Sangam, set up in 1901 in imitation of

Two very different promoters of Tamil culture. (Above, left) The Christian missionary Bishop Robert Caldwell, who was commemorated in a stamp issued by India Post in 2010. (Above, right) An image based on a photograph said to be of the ardent Shaiva reformer Arumuka Navalar, who died in 1879.

the legendary Sangams of the distant past, Iyengar specialised in the study of early Tamil literary sources, inscriptions and place names, in the course of which he discovered that the tradition of a southern migration and ancestral origins in a pitcher was also to be found among other Tamil-language-based communities, most notably the Kannada-speaking Chalukyas, who had ruled over much of the western Deccan between the tenth and twelfth centuries, and the Hoysalas, who had followed them in what is now Karnataka. Both these groups claimed descent from a cattle-herding people called Yadavas with their ancestral home in Dwaraka, from which they had been dispersed after the death of Lord Krishna. Here was further confirmation of a migration south, with or without the sage Agastya.

This mainly Brahmin-led scholarship did not go long unchallenged. Other dissenting voices began to be heard, now representing the underclasses. They found their chief spokesman in the social activist Erode Venkata Ramasamy, affectionately known to his followers as Periyar, from the Tamil word for 'elder' or 'respected person'. Periyar came from the Balija trading community in Erode and became actively involved in nationalist politics in the wake of the horrific Jallianwala Bagh massacre in Amritsar in 1919. He joined the Indian National Congress, only to resign six years later after concluding that it was intent on promoting a caste-ridden Brahminical Indo-Aryan political agenda at the expense of non-Brahmins and the Dravidian peoples of South India. He went on to found what he called the Self-Respect Movement, arguing that the concept of *suya mariyadai* or 'self-respect', based on social equality, was unique to Tamil culture and could be traced back to the Sangam Age. He further held Brahmin ideology to be responsible for the oppression of the lower castes, and led a series of what were intended to be non-violent protests against discriminatory caste laws and practices (of which more in a later chapter).

Accompanying this growing distrust of what was now increasingly viewed as Brahminical propaganda was the desire to restore Tamil culture to its pre-Arya state of supposed perfection. In 1909 an article entitled 'The Morality of the Ramayana' was published in the *Malabar Quarterly Review*, based on the work of a recently deceased scholar and Tamil playwright, Sundaram Pillai, who attacked Valmiki's *Ramayana* as being written 'to proclaim the powers of the Aryans, and to represent their rivals and enemies the Dravidians, who had attained a high degree of civilisation at that period, in the worst possible colour'.[12] This was eagerly seized upon by Periyar, who for the remainder of his long political struggle used it as an example of Arya oppression, culminating in his placing a garland of slippers on a portrait of

Rama and then burning it in public. His book *The Ramayana: A True Reading*, published in 1959, is still banned in the northern state of Uttar Pradesh.

A further by-product of this Tamil revivalism was the promotion of the sage Agathya as the father of the Tamil nation, despite the protests of a number of Tamil intellectuals who recognised it as pure fiction. One such critic was the historiographer K. N. Sivaraja Pillai, a lecturer at the University of Madras. Pillai examined all the evidence relating to Agastya and published his findings in two monographs published in the early 1930s, *Agastya in the Tamil Land* and *The Chronology of the Early Tamils*, texts that I would recommend to any Tamil who sees Agathya as anything more than a symbolic manifestation of Tamil culture.

'Here,' wrote Pillai, 'we find the extraordinary phenomenon of almost the entire Tamil race of the present day enthroning Agastya, an Aryan Rishi, in a rank little removed from that of divinity and paying him homage as to one of their own kith and kin ... The whole extent of Tamil Classical literature has not one word to say about Agastya, or his literary labours ... The only possible explanation for this phenomenon of general silence is that at that time there did not exist even a scrap of the Agastya tradition.'[13]

Since Pillai wrote those words nothing has appeared by way of evidence to challenge his argument that the Tamil Agathya is a product of wishful thinking. As for the Sanskrit Agastya, he remains firmly established at his hermitage on Mahendra Giri or Pothigai Malai – or, as it is much better known today, Agastya Malai. His squat statue is now enshrined on the summit of the highest peak in the range and is an object of pilgrimage, accessible only by three days of hard climbing. Women are not allowed near Agastya mountain, for fear of polluting it.

This Agastya represents the arrival of Sanskritic culture in the

South in the persons of Brahmins with their Vedic gods – quite
possibly under a religious leader named Agastya but not necessarily so. But underlying it is another less obvious story, about
an earlier migration of pre-Arya or post-Harappan peoples from
the North. Some of them might well have been refugees from
a catastrophic inundation on the Kathiawar coast. Either way,
they brought with them their non-Sanskrit languages and their
deities: chiefly mother figures, but also one priapic fertility god
of many aspects, as a lord of yogis, as a hunter and as a lord of all
creatures.

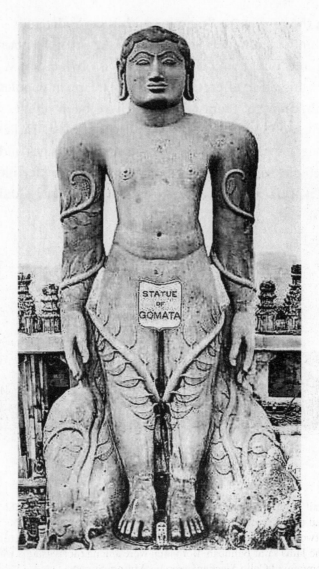

The colossus of Sravana Belgola, for a thousand years the tallest free-standing statue in India, commissioned in about 985 CE by a minister of the Western Ganga king Rachamalla IV. It shows the Jain saint Bahubali in standing meditation with vines growing up his limbs, having renounced his kingdom to seek enlightenment. When Benjamin Rice included a photograph of the statue in his book *Mysore and Coorg from the Inscriptions* in 1909, shown here, he added his own version of a fig-leaf.

4

JAINS AND SANGAMS

North View of the Hill of Sravana — Bellagoola

Detail from a watercolour by John Newman dated August 1806, based on a drawing by Lieutenant Benjamin Ward, showing one of the two great rocks at Sravana Belgola, dominated by the giant statue of the Jaina saint Bahubali. Both men were among the assistants who accompanied Colin Mackenzie on his Mysore Survey.

Wherever you travel in Tamil Nadu or Kerala in December you are bound to meet groups of wild-looking men on the move, in trains or buses or on the roads. They are instantly recognisable as well as unavoidable: barefoot, unshaven, some with painted faces, clad in blue, black or saffron *lungi*s (lengths of cotton cloth worn as loincloths) and little else besides necklaces of tulsi beads. At first sight they can look alarming. You could even mistake them for rowdies who have had too much country liquor, because they are invariably in high spirits, chanting, dancing and banging drums as they go. However, far from being drunk, they are actually undergoing a forty-one-day period of fasting, during which they abstain from alcohol, meat, tobacco and sex. Their unmistakable good cheer identifies them as devotees of Lord Ayyappan. These pilgrims are all heading either to or from the Ayyappan temple of Sabarimala.

Until quite recently the Sabarimala temple was one of the most isolated shrines in Kerala, located deep in the forests of the Western Ghats some 100 kilometres inland from Alleppey (or Alappuzha, as it is now known). For years it was accessible only by two days' walking along forest tracks and so received few pilgrims. But following the elections of a series of left-wing governments from the late 1960s onwards a tarmac road (now National Highway 220) was driven through the mountains to connect Kollam in Kerala with Theni in Tamil Nadu. Today the Sabarimala temple claims to receive a staggering thirty million pilgrims a year. A more realistic estimate would be about five million – which is still a phenomenal figure that places Sabarimala at the top of South India's pilgrimage league.

What makes these statistics even more staggering is that these devotees are almost entirely made up of men, since no woman between the ages of ten and fifty is allowed to mount the sacred *pathinettampady*, a stairway of eighteen steps that gives access to the main platform of the temple. This is on the grounds that women have menstrual cycles and are thus impure. The Sabarimala temple board even claims to have introduced a scanning machine that detects any menstruating woman, and is supported in this by the Travancore Devaswom Board, which argues that banning menstruating women is a centuries-old religious practice – an argument which in April 2016 was declared discriminatory and thus unconstitutional by the Indian Supreme Court.

Ask who Lord Ayyappan is and you will get conflicting answers. By the most popular account, he is the adopted son of a raja who grew up to become a great warrior and protector but then chose to retire to the forest, after asking the king to build a temple at Sabarimala and install his image there. Another account makes him the son of the god Harihara, a fused form of Vishnu and Shiva, whose image first appeared in stone in the sixth century at the cave-temples of Badami, the capital of the Chalukya rulers of Karnataka. A third explanation is that he is an ancient personification of nature, while a fourth equates him with Ayyanar, the guardian protector deity whose fierce life-size terracotta images can be seen, most often mounted on a horse or an elephant, on the outskirts of many villages in Tamil Nadu. This last would seem the most plausible – but there is also a fifth explanation, which begins with the clue that in Kerala Ayyappan also goes by the name of Dharmashasta, 'teacher of the Dharma'.

This blurring of origins matters not a jot to Lord Ayyappan's cheerful devotees, many drawn from the poorer sections of society. Yet I suspect they might be surprised to learn that some of their ancestors might well have been Buddhists, or that Sabarimala may have begun as a Buddhist shrine, that the name of the god they worship as Shasta or Dharmashasta was formerly applied to the Buddha, and that the mantra they chant – *Swamiye saranam Ayyappa!*, 'I take refuge in Lord Ayyappan' – could have had its origins in the Buddhist profession of faith *Buddham saranam gacchami*, 'I take refuge in the Buddha'.

A terracotta and brick statue of the warrior protector deity Ayyanar near Salem. Similar images can be seen on the outskirts of many rural villages in Tamil Nadu.

The Ayyappa cult may well be one of many instances of the appropriation of earlier folk and heterodox practices by Hinduism. Not only Sabarimala but some of the best-known Hindu temples in Kerala and elsewhere are believed to have Buddhist or Jain origins. 'In Travancore...' wrote the author of the *1931 Census Report of Travancore*, 'most of the appurtenances of modern Hinduism such as temples, worship of images, *utsavams* [religious festivals] and religious festivals were all borrowed from the Buddhists... The famous *Sastha* temples now existing in Sabarimala, Thakkala and other places in Travancore were originally none other than temples dedicated to Buddha. Besides these temples, several remains of Buddhist *viharas* and *chaityas* are still seen in different parts of this country. These are indications of Buddhism having been once the common religion in Travancore.'

The author of this report was not some British official but a Telugu Brahmin, Nagam Aiya, author of the three-volume *Travancore State Manual*, published in 1906. Nor was Aiya the only Brahmin to hold such scandalous views. Fifty years earlier one of Aiya's Brahmin predecessors in Travancore State had noted in another report that the Hindu temple of Chitharal, near Nagercoil, had originally been Buddhist, to which the ruler of Travancore, Maharaja Visakham Thirunal, had added his own comment: 'Your description is correct. The Brahmins have appropriated and adapted this Buddhist temple as they have done with many others. What you call *muni* is nothing but the figure of Buddha Gautama.'[1]

But the maharaja was only partly correct. The Chitharal temple he was referring to stands isolated on a rocky ridge above a bend in the Thamirabarani or Kathayar River as it winds south out of the Western Ghats to empty itself into the sea west of Nagercoil. The oldest part of the temple stands on a platform just below the summit, and at first glance it looks very like a classical Greek temple. But whatever the *Travancore State Manual* and Maharaja Visakham Thirumal had to say, this was never Buddhist. It was originally a Jain retreat in the form of a rock-shelter which was then built up into a Jain temple, only to be converted centuries later to the worship of the Hindu goddess Lakshmi.

The Hindu takeover of the Jain temple at Chitharal, whether by lapse or appropriation, was part of a process that happened all over South India over the course of some five hundred years, beginning in the seventh century. In some areas the Jain religion continued to be practised but by the twelfth century Buddhism had been all but extinguished throughout the subcontinent. So

(Above) The former Jain temple of Chitharal with
a Hindu gopuram above, as photographed in about
1900 by the Travancore State artist and photographer
C. Neelakanta Pillai. (Below) Chitharal temple as it is
today after restoration by the ASI.

complete was the triumph of Vaishnavism and Shaivism that to
say today that Jainism and Buddhism were both once widespread
throughout much of South India is to be greeted with polite
disbelief. The historians who accompanied the Arab, Turkic and
Mongol invasions reported the existence of only one 'infidel'
religion in India, and the Portuguese and the Dutch followed suit.
It was not until Sir William Jones and his fellow Orientalists began
their enquiries in the 1780s that this veil over the past began to
be lifted.

The recovery of these lost chapters in India's history began in
the aftermath of what are now known as the four Anglo-Mysore
Wars, fought over the last three decades of the eighteenth century
between the East India Company (EICo) and its local Indian allies
on the one side and the armies of Mysore on the other, led by two
exceptional military commanders: the usurpers Hyder Ali Sultan
and his son Tipu Sultan (whose last years are recounted in a later
chapter). War by war, the EICo gained more and more territory,
which then had to be surveyed to establish what revenue returns
the Company could expect. Two surveyors were appointed, both
Scots: one a surgeon turned botanist; the other a military engineer
in the EICo's Madras Army.

The first was Dr Francis Buchanan (whose name change to
Hamilton in later years has caused much confusion among historians), the second Captain Colin Mackenzie. Both were instructed
to make 'a statistical account of the whole country', but were given
insufficient funding to do it properly – a handicap Mackenzie
resolved by taking on as many assistants as he needed and paying
them out of his own pocket. Thanks to the extensive records he
left behind, we know a lot about Mackenzie, and it is impossible
not to warm to him. He had the luck to meet at the start of his
surveying an eighteen-year-old named Kavali Venkata Boriah
who came from a remarkable family of Telugu Niyogi Brahmin

brothers and was fluent in Tamil, Telugu, Kannada and Sanskrit. Boriah became Mackenzie's main translator and information-gatherer, and came to be regarded by him more as a son than an employee. 'The connection then formed with one person,' Mackenzie later wrote in a letter to a friend, 'then almost a youth of the quickest genius and disposition, possessing that conciliatory turn of mind that soon reconciled all sects and all tribes ... was the first step of my introduction into the portal of Indian knowledge. Devoid of any knowledge of the languages myself, I owe to the happy genius of this individual the encouragement and the means of obtaining what I had so long sought ... A new avenue to Hindoo knowledge was opened.'[2]

This was written after Boriah's sudden death in 1803, which hit Mackenzie hard. However, by then no fewer than four of Boriah's brothers had joined Mackenzie's team, one of whom, Kavali Venkata Laksmiah, stepped into Boriah's shoes. When Mackenzie himself died in 1821 it was Laksmiah who worked with the appointed executor to compile an inventory of Mackenzie's vast collection. Laksmiah was the first Indian to be accepted as a member of the Madras Literary Society and the first to be made an honorary member of the Royal Asiatic Society in Britain.

This closeness to his Brahmin assistants may explain why it took Mackenzie so long to realise that Jainism was a separate religion from Hinduism. His first recorded encounter with the Jain religion came on 24 February 1797 while he was engaged in surveying what the British knew then as Canara country, south of Hyderabad. He had camped at a hamlet called Ibrahimpatnam – now an ugly industrial town – and was working his way along the north bank of the Krishna River when his eye was caught by 'a round temple of blue stone, with a portico of four pillars'. Inside was 'a figure, sitting cross-legged, naked, his head covered with curls, like the figure of Buddh'; the nose was defaced,

Colin Mackenzie flanked by three of his South Indian assistants. The man on his immediate right is his senior assistant Kavali Venkata Laksmiah, while the man holding the telescope is his peon, Kistnaji. A Jain pandit, most probably Durmiah, holds a palm-leaf manuscript. Detail from an oil painting by William Hickey c. 1816, with the monumental Jain statue of Gomateshvara at Karkala in the background.

and a fracture ran through the figure. A woman passer-by told Mackenzie it was 'the figure of *Chindeo* or *Jain-deo*'.[3]

Having never encountered Jains, Mackenzie took little note of it, other than having a drawing made. But he had earlier received news of some unusual bas-reliefs unearthed further upriver by a minor ruler recently ousted by the EICo from his chiefdom who was building himself a new capital at a place called Amresvaram – now better known as Amaravati. They reached Amresvaram to find the raja supervising the extraction of bricks from an enormous mound which had originally been encircled with large stone slabs decorated with intricately carved bas-reliefs. 'If the whole of the circle were faced with these slabs,' conjectured Mackenzie, 'it is to be regretted that this treasure of antiquity did not fall into better hands.'

Mackenzie had no idea what this 'treasure of antiquity' repre-sented, although it was suggested to him that it was the remains of a Jain temple. As luck would have it, his official duties prevented him from returning to Amaravati until almost twenty years had passed, by which time most of the carved marble slabs that had at one time decorated what Mackenzie now knew to be a vast Buddhist stupa had vanished, along with most of the hemispheri-cal mound that they had adorned – broken up and burned for lime or recycled as building material. Fearing for the survival of what remained, Mackenzie set his draughtsmen to make as many drawings as they could, while arranging for a number of slabs to be moved to the port of Masulipatnam, for onward transportation to Calcutta. However, the local Collector in Masulipatnam had other ideas and incorporated the slabs into a monument in the market-place that he named after himself 'Robertson's Mound'. These were subsequently rescued in the 1850s, some going to the Madras Museum and some going to London, where they eventually found a home in the British Museum as the misnamed Amaravati Marbles.

By 1816 Mackenzie had been set right not only about Amaravati but also about the Jains, having been forced to rethink his views by his surveyor colleague Dr Buchanan, who in 1807 had published an account of his travels under the title of *A Journey from Madras through the countries of Mysore, Canara, and Malabar*.[4]

While on the way back to Madras from Mangalore on the last stage of his survey Dr Buchanan had halted at the town of Moodabidri, which turned out to be a major Jain settlement, adorned with some eighteen Jain temples, popularly known as *basti*s. The inhabitants had explained to Buchanan that the entire country thereabouts had at one time been ruled by the Jain rajas of Tuluva but that they were now having to suffer the 'ill-will' of the Brahmins, who regarded them as 'detestable heretics'.

A Jain elder in Moodabidri by the name of Pandit Acharya Swami had then provided Buchanan with what became the first published account of Jainism – even though Buchanan remained under the impression that it was simply a sect within Hinduism. 'The proper name of the sect is *Arhita* (worthy) [more correctly, *arihant*, 'conqueror'],' Buchanan wrote.

They acknowledge that they are one of the twenty-one sects who were considered by Shankara Acharya as heretical ... The *Vedas*, and the eighteen *Puranas* of the Brahmins, the *Arhita* reject as heretical ... The gods of the *Arhita* are the spirits of perfect men who, owing to their great virtue, have become exempt from all change and misfortune, and are all of equal rank and power. These *Siddha* (the holy) reside in a heaven called Mocsha, and it is by their worship only that happiness is attained.

According to Buchanan's informant, Jainism had once been widespread throughout India: 'They allege that formerly they extended over the whole of *Arya* or *Bharata-Khande*, and that all those

who ever had just pretensions to be of Kshatri descent were of
their sect. It appears that until the time of Rama Anuja Acharya
[Ramanuja, eleventh-century Vaishnava theologian and famous
enemy of Jainism] many powerful princes of the south of India
were their followers.'

Buchanan also learned that the centre of Jainism in South India
was not Moodabidri but further inland at Sravana Belgola, near the
fortress-town of Seringapatam (Srirangapatnam). He subsequently
visited Sravana Belgola in May 1801 but was confined to his tent
by an eye-infection which prevented him from seeing for himself
the huge statue that dominates one of the two great hemispheres
of exposed rock that flank the little village of Sravana Belgola. So
painful did this infection become that Buchanan was forced to
break off his enquiries and head back to Seringapatam for medical
attention.

Buchanan's loss was Mackenzie's gain. After reading Buchanan's
published account Mackenzie hurried to Sravana Belgola, his band
of pandits and artists now strengthened by the inclusion of a Jain
pandit named Durmiah from Mysore, who was not only able to
assist with inscriptions written in Halegannada or 'Old Kannada'
script, but also provided Mackenzie with more information about
Jain history – some of it wildly inaccurate, such as the notion that
the Jains were refugees from Mecca. The outcome was Mackenzie's
Account of the Jains, published in 1807 in the ninth volume of the
Asiatic Society of Bengal's august journal *Asiatick Researches*.

Mackenzie went on to become Surveyor-General of India. He
had always planned to put to good use his vast collection of manuscripts, inscriptions, drawings and other material gathered during
his surveys but he died in Bengal in 1821 with his papers uncata-
logued. Dr Horace Wilson, then Secretary of the Asiatic Society of
Bengal, was assigned the task and with the help of Kavali Venkata
Laksmiah produced a catalogue that when published in 1828 filled

two volumes. The bulk of the papers were sent to the Library of the Madras College, where they lay largely untouched for some decades, which meant that Mackenzie's hoard of Jain manuscripts remained unexamined.[5]

In the meantime it was India's other 'lost' religion that became the main focus of antiquarian interest, leading to the sidelining of Jain studies for over half a century, so that it came to be regarded, in the words of a later student of Jain studies, 'as grey and unappealing, as austere as its followers ... its tenets less profound than Buddhism, its mythology less spectacular than that of Hinduism'.[6] This neglect lasted into the 1870s, the turning point being the visit in 1874 of the German Indologists Hermann Jacobi and Georg Bühler to the remote outpost of Jaisalmer in the Rajasthan desert, where they found a cache of neglected Jain manuscripts in the library of the local Rajput rulers. These documents included the teachings of the sect's founder, Mahavira, as well as accounts of the lives of Mahavira and his predecessors recorded in the *Kalpa Sutra*.[7] With the support of their German academic colleagues in Oxford and Berlin, Jacobi and Bühler brought the Jain religion to the attention of the wider world, showing its philosophy and culture to be as rich as that of its rival.[8]

The Jain faith had emerged as a distinctive religion with defined beliefs and practices in the late sixth or early fifth century BCE in the most technologically advanced of the Arya *mahajanapada*s in the Gangetic plains, Magadha. Trading between these *janapada*s had led to the growth of an increasingly wealthy mercantile class, creating an urban elite of Kshatriya landlords and Vaishya traders who now had the wealth, power and opportunity to challenge Brahminical orthodoxy, giving rise to a variety of heterodox but mostly ascetic movements. Of these, Jainism and Buddhism enjoyed the greatest success. Both faiths shared the Brahminical belief in *moksha* – liberation from the endless cycle of birth, death and rebirth – as an ultimate goal. What made them heterodox and heretical was their belief that this could be achieved not through the intervention of divine forces directed by priest-led prayers and sacrifices but by individual action, by following the teachings of those who had already achieved such *moksha*.

The revolutionary nature of the teachings of Gautama Sakya-muni (the Buddha), the founder of Buddhism, was first articulated by the German Indologist Albrecht Weber in the 1880s when he wrote that Buddhism was 'in its origin one of the most magnificent and radical reactions in favour of the universal human rights of the individual against the oppressing tyranny of the pretended privileges of divine origin of birth and of class'.[9] That 'radical reaction' was equally a feature of Jain teaching as originally expounded by a Kshatriya named Vardhaman, who came to be known as Mahavira, 'the great hero', believed to be the last in a line of twenty-four *tirthankara*s or 'ford-crossers' who were said to have preceded him. It was to these departed saints rather than to any deities that Jains directed their prayers as a means to obtaining their own liberation.

Thanks to royal patronage and the extensive trading links of the mercantile classes, Jainism spread throughout the Gangetic plains and beyond, even though theological differences led to its division into two sects: the Digambaras, or 'sky-clad', who spurned clothing and believed that women lacked the spiritual qualities to attain *moksha* and had first to be reborn as men; and the Svetambaras, or 'white-clad', who accepted women as nuns. That schism may well have been the real reason why the leader of the Digambaras decided to migrate south.

At Sravana Belgola, Mackenzie's pandits had been unable to read the mysterious script today known as Brahmi in its local variant: Purvadahalegannad, or Pre-Old Kannada. As a result, they missed the significance of why one of Sravana Belgola's twin hills was named Chandragiri, 'the hill of Chandra'.

That breakthrough was left to Benjamin Lewis Rice, the Bangalore-born son of missionaries who had returned to South India in 1861 to become principal of the Bangalore High School but later joined the Mysore State Civil Service as a school inspector. In 1873 Rice was shown some photographs of rock inscriptions in his area and asked if he could translate them. He had come across apparently similar inscriptions during his tours through Mysore and Coorg and he now became obsessed with finding, copying and deciphering them. The first fruit of his labours was Volume I of *Mysore Inscriptions*, published in 1879, the first systematic survey of South Indian inscriptions. More volumes followed over the years, now collected in the twelve volumes of *Epigraphia Carnatica*, containing facsimiles and translations of some nine thousand inscriptions from the Mysore region.

In 1885, soon after being appointed head of Mysore's Department of Archaeology, Rice and his Kannada-speaking assistants began work on the Sravana Belgola inscriptions. Over the course of four years they located and translated more than eight hundred, the oldest and the most revealing of which were on the walls of a Jain temple known as the Chandragupta Basti, overlooking a cave on the lower slopes of the Chandragiri hill called the Bhadrabahu Gupha. 'Before these inscriptions were deciphered by me,' wrote Rice (not a man to hide his light under a bushel), 'no one had succeeded in reading them, nor was the object with which they were engraved known, so completely had knowledge of the ancient alphabet been lost ... The first I managed to decipher was No. 26, and this gave me the key.'[10]

Rice's Inscription No. 1 proved to be the oldest of the inscriptions and the most valuable, because it gave an account of the Jain migration south more than two thousand years earlier under the direction of their leader Bhadrabahu: 'It states that Bhadrabahu Swami ... having foretold in Ujjayaini [Ujjain] the approach of a dreadful famine which would last twelve years, the whole *sangha* or Jain religious brotherhood forsook the northern regions and under his leadership migrated to the south ... When approaching a wild mountain called Katavapa the *rishi* felt his end drawing nigh. He therefore sent on all his followers and, remaining behind with only one disciple, performed the last rites of a *sunnyasi* and there died.'

FAÇADE OF CHANDRAGUPTA BASTI

(Above) The elaborately decorated façade of the Chandragupta Basti on the Chandragiri hill at Sravana Belgola. (Below) The Bhadrabahu Gupha (cave) on the same hill, where the ex-emperor Chandragupta Maurya is said to have fasted to death early in the third century BCE.

Among those who had accompanied Bhadrabahu's great trek south was his most important follower, none other than the first great emperor of India, Chandragupta Maurya, who had unified most of Northern India under one banner in about 316 BCE – only to become a Jain, renounce violence and abdicate in favour of his son Bindusara in order to join Bhadrabahu's epic migration south. That abdication probably took place just before or about 300 BCE, with Chandragupta's journey ending at Sravana Belgola. Having faithfully served his teacher until his death, the ex-emperor Chandragupta had then followed his example by becoming an ascetic, eventually choosing the moment of his own death by self-starvation.

Along with their religion, the Jain immigrants brought new ideas – hardly surprising, considering that they were led by well-educated monks versed in teaching and in such spheres of knowledge as mathematics. All the available evidence suggests that they had an immediate and dramatic impact on the South.

The worship of the Mother Goddess, along with the linga fertility cult, snake-worship, tree-worship, hero-worship and other forms of folk-worship, had long been practised in Tamil country, but it was the Jains who introduced the first clearly defined creed, with the Buddhists hot on their heels. Both heterodoxies were flexible enough to accommodate elements of existing religious practices by turning local deities into protectors and supporting demi-gods. So the widely worshipped Naga snake deities became protectors of both Jainism and Buddhism, which is why we find Jain images in stone and bronze of the Naga snake-king Dharana sheltering the twenty-third *Tirthankara*, Parshvanatha, with his hood from a storm sent by a demon, Buddhist images of the Naga snake-king Muchalinda sheltering the Buddha-to-be for seven days and nights while he meditates, and, in due course, Hindu images of the thousand-headed cosmic Naga snake-king Ananta offering his coils as a couch for Lord Vishnu.

The Jains and Buddhists also gave roles as guardian attendants to the male and female nature-spirits known as *yakshas* and *yakshis*, the Jains giving particular prominence to a nature-spirit named Ambika Devi, or 'goddess-mother', who became the protector of the twenty-second *Tirthankara*, Neminatha. The two heterodoxies also developed a great partiality for the overtly sexual tree-and-water *yakshi* Vrikshaka, better known as a *salabhanjika*, or 'branch-breaker', who by symbolically breaking a branch of a sal tree – perhaps a rudimentary form of pruning – brought increased fertility. Exquisite carvings of these *salabhanjikas*, naked but for a jewelled girdle and with one arm grasping a tree's branch and one leg wrapped round its trunk, decorated the earliest Buddhist and Jain stupa railings at Bharhut and the Great Stupa at Sanchi. In time, Hinduism followed suit, with some of the finest images ever carved in stone taking the form of *salabhanjikas* that decorate the twelfth-century temples of the Hoysalas in Belur and Halebid in south Karnataka. Pairs of these tree-grasping sprites can also be seen at the entrance gates of many South Indian temples, but now acting as purely decorative guardians.

Many of the Jain immigrants who came south would have been Brahmin by caste but there is no evidence that Vedic Hinduism, whether introduced by Agastya or any other rishi, entered Tamil country before the arrival of Jains at the start of the third century BCE. The earliest surviving literary work that records the presence of Brahmins and the performance of Vedic rites in Tamil country is the poem *Pattinappalai*, written by a Brahmin poet in praise of the Chola king Karikala, dating from the last decades of the second century CE.

The Digambara Jain leader Bhadrabahu and his followers had entered a region dominated by three rival dynasties, whose common ancestor is said to have given birth to three sons known as the Muvendar, or 'Three Crowned Kings', all supposedly born at

(Left) A twelfth-century Hoysala *salabhanjika yakshi*, now transformed into a dancer, from the Vaishnava temple of Chennakeshava at Belur. (Above) A second-century *salabhanjika yakshi* on a gatepost of the east gateway of Stupa 1 at Sanchi.

Korkai, near the mouth of the Thamirabarani River. Each brother was too ambitious to be content with sharing power, so the eldest brother, Pandya, stayed put while the other two, Chera and Chola, established their own kingdoms to the north and west respectively. The Cholas went on to rule the country around Thanjavur and Trichy, the Cheras in Travancore and Coimbatore (Kovai), leaving the Pandyas to rule in Madurai and Tirunelveli.

External historical sources support the legendary antiquity of these three dynasties. The Greek Megasthenes, appointed as ambassador to the Mauryan rulers of Northern India in about 310 BCE by the successor to Alexander the Great in Babylon,

wrote of South India being governed by queens, with the
'Pandae' (Pandyas) and the 'Charmae' (Cheras) as rulers. Half
a century later, the Buddhist emperor Ashoka Maurya declared
in his famous major rock edicts that his Dharma, or Moral Law,
extended 'on its borders among the Chodas [Cholas], the Panidas
[Pandyas], Satiputras, Keralaputras and as far as Tambrapani' –
which could refer to the river of that name but more probably to
the island of Lanka, which the Greeks knew of as Taprobane.

The kings of these three dynasties are among those celebrated
in the earliest literature of the Tamil South, collectively known
as Sangam (also written Cankam), taking its name from three
assemblies of scholars and poets who between them are said to
have created a great corpus of poetic literature, of which very
little survives. The most detailed account of these Sangams was
set down by a literary commentary written in about the eighth
century by a poet of Madurai named Nakkirar. By his reckoning,
the first Sangam took place at Then Madurai, or 'South Madurai',
under the patronage of a Pandya king named Ma Kirti, with the
sage Agastya acting as the convenor. It lasted for 4440 years,
involved 4449 poets, including gods and sages, and it produced
Agastya's lost grammar *Agathiyam*. The second Sangam was held
at a place called Kapatapuram, lasted 3700 years, had Agastya's
disciple Tholkappiyar as convenor and produced his *Tolkappiyam*.

These first two assemblies were held in cities located to the south
of Kanyakumari in the country of Kumarikkantam or Kumarinadu.
Here, it seems, was the cradle of ancient Tamil civilisation, South
India's Atlantis, occupying a continental shelf that was lost to the
sea in one or more catastrophic inundations. The third Sangam was
held in Uttara Madurai, or 'North Madurai', so in the present city of
Madurai. It lasted a mere 1850 years and involved 449 poets, its first
chairman being a survivor of the inundation.

A lot has been said in recent years about this supposed lost

continent of Kumarikkantam, which in some quarters also goes by
the name Ilemuriakkantam, 'the country of Ilimuria'. This last is no
more than a Tamilisation of the word Lemuria, coined by a British
zoologist named Philip Sclater in 1864.[11] Sclater's researches into
fossils had led him to conclude (wrongly) that the engaging long-
tailed, bug-eyed primates known as lemurs found on the island of
Madagascar had once had ancestral cousins in India. This led him
to propose that there must at one time have been a 'great continent'
that had formed a land-bridge linking India to Africa, which he
named Lemuria. Other zoologists as well as geographers picked
up the idea, just as the concept of continental drift was becoming
established, among them the German evolutionary biologist Ernst
Haeckel, who proposed in his *History of Creation* that this Lemuria
was the cradle of mankind, the original paradise from which humans
had emerged to populate the Earth by way of India and Africa.[12]

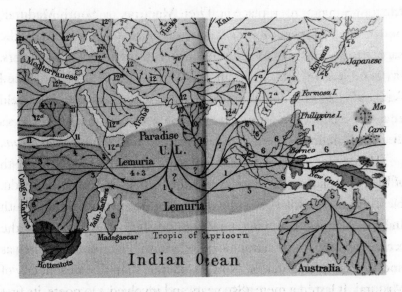

Lemuria or Paradise as the cradle of mankind. Detail from Ernst Haeckel's map
'Hypothetical sketch of the monophyletic origin and of the extension of the 12
races of man from Lemuria over the earth', as it appeared in English in 1876.

Haeckel's theory first became known in India when it was mentioned in the three-volume *Manual of the Administration of the Madras Presidency*, an official government document published in the mid-1880s, which stated that the Dravidians were the original indigenous people of India. According to its author, the Madras civil servant Charles Maclean, there were a number of circumstances which suggested that 'the primeval home of man was a continent now sunk below the surface of the Indian ocean ... given the name Lemuria. By assuming Lemuria to have been man's primeval home, the explanation of the geographical distribution of the human species is much facilitated ... Southern India was once the passage-ground by which the ancient progenitors of northern and Mediterranean races proceeded to the parts of the globe which they now inhabit.'[13]

So the Lemuria theory caught on, gaining further credibility when it was picked up by the founder of the Theosophical Movement, the occultist Madame Blavatsky, and promoted by her in her esoteric teachings, reaching its most bizarre apotheosis in the writings of three of her disciples: Charles Leadbeater, William Scott-Elliott (author of *The Lost Lemuria*, 1904) and Rudolf Steiner (author of *Cosmic Memory: Prehistory of Earth and Man*, 1959). Ridiculous as many of the ideas promoted under the aegis of the Theosophical Society now appear, the relocating of its headquarters from New York to Madras in 1895, coupled with the wholehearted support given to the Indian home rule movement by the Theosophist, political activist and social reformer Annie Besant, ensured that Theosophy and those same ideas about the lost continent of Lemuria found a place in the hearts of many South Indians.

Kumarikkantam and Ilemuriakkantam fitted very neatly into the new Tamil self-image as promoted by the Tamil revivalists in the early decades of the twentieth century, because it accorded with their own perceptions of the Sangam golden age. These revivalists spearheaded what became known as the Thanittamil Iyakkam, or 'Pure Tamil Movement', largely drawn from a newly emergent urban elite created in large part by the colonial and missionary educational system and largely made up of higher-caste, non-Brahmin Shaivas determined to reject what they saw as the polytheistic religious practices introduced by the Arya Brahmins through the medium of Sanskrit in favour of *Tamilar matam*, the true Tamil religion, which they saw as the worship of Lord Shiva alone through the liturgical medium of Tamil.

Some notable Tamil Brahmins also joined their ranks, including the historian T. R. Sesha Iyengar, whose book *Dravidian India*, first published in 1925, is still widely read today.[14] 'Geological research has shown that the Indian Ocean was once a continent,' wrote Iyengar, 'and that this submerged continent, sometimes called Lemuria, originally extended from Madagascar to Malay Archipelago, connecting South India with Africa and Australia ... There are unmistakable indications in the Tamil traditions that the land affected by the deluge was contiguous with *Tamilakam*, and that, after the subsidence, the Tamils naturally betook themselves to their northern provinces.'

This still appears to be a widely accepted Tamil view of its history today, a reading promoted in schools, colleges and temples and in Tamil Nadu government publications. The rest of the world may have moved on in accepting the validity of a dating that puts the Indian Plate's final break with Gondwanaland towards the close of the later Mesozoic – approximately seventy million years too early for the human race – but in Tamil country the lost continent of Kumarikkantam comes close to being accepted as an established fact of history as *Kumarinatu*, the fountain-head of Tamil identity.

There is no reason why a belief in a lost or drowned land

should not be taken seriously. As mentioned earlier, the last major glaciation caused sea levels to fall, resulting in the extension of coastlines, the exposure of continental shelves and the formation of connecting land-bridges. Subsequent deglaciation involved at least three significant meltwater pulses, when huge quantities of trapped water were suddenly released. The last of these is reckoned to have taken place between 8200 and 7600 years ago, with a central peak during which sea levels are believed to have risen by some seven metres within a space of 150 years.[15] So it is entirely possible that in about 6000 BCE human settlements located off Kanyakumari, the Malabar coast and in what is now the Gulf of Cambay could have been engulfed by some form of tsunami.

Memories of such traumatic events would certainly have been passed down through the generations. But it does not follow that an advanced civilisation was lost to the sea. It is quite feasible that one or more rudimentary settlements were established on the exposed shelf off the present Kanyakumari eight thousand years ago. What is entirely unrealistic is to credit them with a degree of sophistication capable of supporting literary assemblies of the kind ascribed to the first two Sangams.

The best evidence of the state of Tamil society at the time of the late Iron Age that I am aware of comes from an extensive urn-burial cemetery at Adichallanur, on the south bank of the Thamirabarani River some 25 miles (40 kilometres) inland. This was first excavated by Dr Alexander Rea, Superintending Archaeologist of the Archaeological Survey of India (ASI), between 1889 and 1903. His digs uncovered numerous urn burials, each containing complete human skeletons in squatting positions, together with many grave goods, including swords, spears and metal utensils. 'The objects yielded by these burial sites,' Rea wrote, 'are finely made pottery of various kinds in great number; many iron implements and weapons; vessels and personal ornaments in bronze; a few gold ornaments; a few stone beads; and some household stone implements used for grinding curry or sandalwood.'[16] The gold items were of particular interest because they were in the form of diadems with a hole at each end for tying them round the forehead, suggesting that these were symbols of kingship. Among the bronze objects were lids with finely executed finials in animal shapes depicting elephants, tigers, buffalo, goats and chickens.

Continuing excavations at Adichallanur by the ASI have uncovered many more burials as well as evidence of extensive opencast mining for copper, iron and gold, although no identifiable township has yet been located.[17] A few early Tamil-Brahmi letters have also been found scratched on potsherds, possibly dating as early as the second century BCE, as well as a six-character inscription scratched inside an urn which the discoverer has rather optimistically dated to the fifth century BCE.

But that is not to dismiss the Sangam tradition as nothing more than a Tamil nationalist fantasy.

It has been noted that the years of the three supposed Sangams all involve multiples of thirty-seven, suggesting a Jain involvement, since the Jains considered *Sankhyana*, the science of numbers, to be one of the highest accomplishments of their monks. That very word 'Sangam' is itself derived from the Sanskrit word *Sangha*, first used by Jains to describe their assembly of monks and nuns – and afterwards adopted by the Buddhists. The bulk of the early Tamil literature that has survived is credited to Jain authors, including three of five surviving Tamil epics – *Cilappatikaram*, *Civaka Cintamani* and *Valayapathi* – as well as a sixth epic that did not survive. Other writings such as the *Kural* and *Nalatiyar*, as well as a number of important grammars and lexicons, are also credited to Jain authors. Some scholars have even suggested that the oldest surviving Tamil text,

Tholkappiyar's *Tolkappiyam*, may have been the work of a Jain, on account of its promotion of vegetarianism and its abhorrence of animal sacrifice. It has even been argued that Thiruvalluvar, author of *Thirukkural*, could have been a Jain.[18]

Given this Jain dominance in early Tamil literature it is entirely reasonable to suppose that it was the Jain monks whose presence kick-started the early Tamil civilisation known as the Sangam Age by presiding over regular literary assemblies held in Madurai, even if the first of these is unlikely to have taken place before the start of the second century BCE. To my mind, these Sangams must have been very like the bardic festivals of poetry, music, singing and dance known as eisteddfods ('sessions') that have been a feature of Welsh culture for many centuries – and which themselves have also been subject to a great deal of fanciful nationalistic embellishment.

A quite remarkable characteristic of this early Tamil literary creativity is the absence of all-powerful deities. Instead of the gods it is the local rulers who are showered with praise as patrons of the arts of peace and war. What survives from the very earliest phase divides into two groups: the Pathupattu ('Ten Idylls') and the Ettuthogai ('Eight Anthologies'). One of those sets of anthologies – and the most revealing from a historian's point of view – is the *Purananuru*, or 'Four hundred poems about the exterior', the word *puram* ('exterior') referring to public as opposed to domestic life. Its four hundred poems are addressed to more than fifty named Chola, Chera and Pandya kings, as well as eighty-three lesser kings. The chief concern of their authors is to enumerate a particular ruler's virtues: his greatness, his generosity as a patron and his prowess as a warrior. So patently, the king was the fulcrum around which much of ancient Tamil society revolved, imposing order out of chaos, keeping enemies at bay and even bringing the rains to water the fields and keep them fertile. But what I find so fascinating about these poems is their coverage of wider aspects of life and death and, in particular, observations of the natural world.

There is a delightful freshness and a muscular vigour to the *Purananuru* that makes them instantly accessible, nowhere more so than in the recent translations into English by the combined team of George L. Hart, Professor of Tamil Language at UC Berkeley, and Hank Heifetz, also a scholar of Tamil and an outstanding poet in his own right. One of the shortest poems, Poem 128, for example, is composed in honour of a king of the Ay dynasty, which was one of the major powers in the South before the rise of the Cheras, and whose descendants continued to rule parts of South India as vassal kings into the tenth century:

> *On Poti mountain, the realm of Ay who wears sliding*
> *bracelets,*
> *in the giant branches of the jack tree growing in his*
> *courtyard,*
> *a monkey, thinking it a fruit, beats on the clear*
> *sweet-singing*
> *eye of a drum left hanging there by some who travelled to*
> *him*
> *in their need and a wild goose calls out as if keeping time!*
> *Unless a woman will approach it dancing,*
> *Mighty kings have no hope of ever coming near that hill!*[19]

What is so striking about these works – indeed, quite remarkable in the Indian context – is their essentially secular nature. 'The *Purananuru*,' writes Professor Hart, 'is one of the few works of classical India that confronts life without the insulation of a philosophical façade; it makes no basic assumptions about *karma* and the other world; it faces existence as a great and unsolved mystery.'

This early classical Tamil literature is a boon to historians because of what its tells us about Tamil society before Arya or Brahminical influence had penetrated the South. Even before the *Purananuru* had been tracked down, transcribed and published by U. V. Swaminatha Iyer in the 1890s, Robert Caldwell was able to able to enthuse about how much information they revealed:

> They had 'kings', who dwelt in 'strong houses' and ruled over small 'districts of country' ... They were well acquainted with 'agriculture' and delighted in 'war'. All the ordinary or necessary arts of life, including 'spinning', 'weaving', and 'dyeing' existed among them. They excelled in 'pottery' ... They had 'minstrels' who recited 'songs' at 'festivals' and they seem to have had alphabetic 'characters' written with a style [stylus] on Palmyra leaves. They were without hereditary priests and idols, and appear to have had no idea of heaven or hell, of the soul or sin, but they acknowledged the existence of God, whom they styled *ko*, or 'king' – a realistic title little known to Hinduism. They erected to his honour a temple, which they called *ko-il* [usually written *kovil*], 'God's house'; but I cannot find any trace of orthodoxy in the nature of the worship which they offered to him.[20]

As Caldwell also noted, this poetry was written as well as spoken, which brings us to another crucial innovation that can be credited to one or other or even both of the heterodoxies.

From the *Rig-Veda* onwards, the entire canon of Vedic and Brahminical 'literature' was preserved by memory alone. These were spoken texts, handed down by direct transmission from one initiate to the next, from *guru* (teacher) to *chela* (pupil). By this means what was contained within these spoken texts remained hermetically sealed, too sacred to be accessible to the uninitiated.

This same tradition was followed by the early Jains and the early Buddhists. But everything changed with the establishment of what fully deserves to be called the first Indian empire by Chandragupta, founder of the Maurya dynasty.

Prior to his abdication, Chandragupta's long-time teacher and counsellor had been a Brahmin named Chanakya, also known as Kautilya, who has been called 'the Indian Machiavelli', although it really ought to be the other way round, with Chanakya by far the more astute of the two, and, of course, earlier by some fifteen hundred years. This is because Chanakya was the author of a famous treatise on political economy and statesmanship entitled *Arthashastra*. It was known about but thought to be lost to history until 1891 when the Maharaja of Mysore set up the Mysore Oriental Library as a repository for the growing collection of ancient manuscripts gathered by Benjamin Rice and his colleagues. Shortly after its opening a Brahmin from Tanjore appeared with a tattered manuscript which the librarian, Shama Shastry, recognised as a medieval copy of Chanakya's legendary lost masterpiece and subsequently (in 1909) published in English to widespread acclaim.

Chanakya drew on his own first-hand experience of politics and statesmanship as a chief minister at the very heart of Chandragupta's growing empire. He also appears to have served Chandragupta's son and successor Bindusara, who was a more orthodox supporter of Brahminism than his father and extended his empire with further conquests in the west and east. How far south this conquest extended is unknown, although the *Arthashastra* describes the Dakshina as abounding in 'conch-shells, diamonds, precious stones of other kinds, pearls and articles of gold', and the Dakshinapatha or 'road into the Deccan' as being 'frequented by many and easy to travel by'. So clearly there was some interaction at that time between the Mauryan

empire north of the Narmada and the country beyond. This new
stability in the North may well have provided a spur for the export
of settlers and new ideas in the persons of Brahmin and Buddhist
missionaries eager to challenge the superiority of the Jains who
had gone before.

It was at this juncture that writing, and thus literacy, was first
introduced, not just to the South but to most of India.

The Greeks who accompanied Alexander the Great on his epic
rampage talked of the Indians as having no writing. However, the
Achaemenid empire had been in political control of the Indus
region since about 500 BCE onwards, and had introduced a written
language based on a Persian Aramaic script known as Kharosthi.
The wily counsellor Chanakya and his star pupil Chandragupta
would surely have cut their teeth on this Kharosthi script in
Persian-controlled Taxila. Chandragupta subsequently graduated
to become one of many Indian mercenaries who initially fought
for the Persians against Alexander, only to change sides and then
change sides again to lead a revolt against Alexander's Greek successors in India. He went on to form an alliance with other Greeks
and Indians which ended with his becoming sole ruler of much of
Northern India.

But no empire can function without good communications.
Chandragupta's extensive contacts, first with the Persians and
then with Alexander and his exceptionally literate Macedonian
officers, can only have impressed upon him the need for a local
equivalent of the Kharosthi script. So, with Kharosthi and Greek
as models, the Brahmi alphabet came into being, if not in the last
years of Chandragupta's reign then very soon thereafter. When
you compare the Kharosthi alphabet with Brahmi you can see
obvious similarities, but Brahmi was a step up, thanks to the
introduction of diacriticals to express more complex vowel sounds.
So well thought out was this new alphabetical system that it went

on to become the mother of all the Brahmic scripts of South and South-East Asia, including written Dravidian and its local variants.

In 1882 the Madras civil servant Robert Sewell, Collector and Judge in Chingleput, Malabar and Tirunelveli, came to the little village of Mankulam, just north of Madurai. This was well outside his area but Sewell's enthusiasm for antiquarian pursuits had led to his being given the additional role of recorder of sites of archaeological and historical importance in the Madras Presidency. This was what had brought him to Mankulam village, which nestles in the shadow of the Kalugumalai ('vulture hill') rock, rising like a great beached whale out of the dark greenery of the plains.

(Above, left) The Kalugumalai rock seen from the Murugan temple and tank at its foot. (Above, right) Images of Jain *tirthankaras* cut into the rock on the summit of Kalugumalai hill, Mankulam, near Madurai.

The Kalugumalai rock is probably best known for its striking ninth-century Pandyan temple in the form of a monolith, cut out of the rock from the top downwards, but it was also known locally as Samanamalai, 'the hill of the *sramana*s (ascetics)'. This is because on its summit, approached by a perilously exposed walkway made up of narrow steps cut into the rock, are three caves and a water tank. Every cave is adorned with carved bas-reliefs of Jain saints along with inscriptions written in characters that to Sewell's eye closely resembled the ancient Brahmi script of the Ashokan edicts. Unable to make any sense of the writing, Sewell simply noted the discovery in his report, which duly became part of the first volume of *Inscriptions of the Madras Presidency*. Years passed before there was any follow-up.

The same thing happened in 1897 when six more inscriptions were spotted cut into the side of a cliff beside a mountain pass known as Sultan's Battery, which took its name from an incident in the Mysore Wars when Tipu Sultan turned a Jain temple into an armoury. In this case, the finder was the Superintendent of Police for Malabar District Fred Fawcett, an enthusiastic amateur antiquarian. Fawcett got in touch with his old friend Bruce Foote, who was far more interested in the petroglyphs and stone tools that Fawcett had also found at the site. However, he sent Fawcett's rubbings of the inscriptions to the Government Epigraphist in Madras, Dr Eugen Hultzsch, who declared four of them to be written in what appeared to be defective Brahmi and the remaining two 'decidedly archaic' but unreadable. More than seventy years passed before these copies were re-examined, by which time the originals had been obliterated under modern graffiti.

Such cave inscriptions only began to be taken seriously in 1906, after the Deputy Collector of Tirunelveli reported the existence of an inscription in a rock-shelter on a hill above the village of Marukaltalai, 15 kilometres west of Tirunelveli. Two more rock-shelters with inscriptions were then discovered in quick succession near Madurai, leading to a scramble that resulted in the discovery of no fewer than thirty-nine new inscriptions from twelve sites all within easy reach of Madurai – in fact, wherever there were rocky outcrops with caves or rock-shelters.

Several trained archaeologists and epigraphists now became directly involved, including Valaiyattur Venkayya, head of the Epigraphical Department of the Government of Madras, and his

assistant, K. V. Subrahmanya Aiyer (also written Iyer).[21] The outcome was the publication in 1924 of Subrahmanya Aiyer's justly
celebrated paper 'The earliest monuments of the Pandya country
and their inscriptions', in which he proposed for the first time
that these inscriptions were not only written in a Tamil version
of Ashokan Brahmi script but also employed the Tamil language
itself rather than Prakrit.

But if U. V. Swaminatha Iyer and K. V. Subrahmanya Aiyer laid
the foundations of Tamil philology and Tamil-Brahmi epigraphy
respectively, it was left to an outstanding scholar of our own times
to complete what they had started: that exceptional epigraphist
Iravatham Mahadevan, who as I write is still very much with us at
the ripe old age of eighty-seven.

Born of a Tamil Brahmin family in Thanjavur in 1930, Dr
Mahadevan began his professional life as a member of the Indian
Administrative Service, successors of the colonial Indian Civil
Service. After five years in Coimbatore he was posted to a desk job
in Delhi where he met the veteran historian K. A. N. Sastri, who
suggested he might be the right man to take another look at what
Subrahmanya Aiyer had claimed to be early Tamil inscriptions in
caves. That opportunity came in 1962 when Mahadevan secured a
posting to the Government of Tamil Nadu's Industrial Department
in Madras (soon to become Chennai) as Director of Handlooms and
Textiles. This allowed him to spend his weekends and leaves going
over both old ground and new – although it was not until 1965 that
he began the first of a series of dramatic discoveries that made his
name as an outstanding interpreter of ancient inscriptions.

In February of that year Mahadevan made his first visit to
Pugalur, on the south bank of the upper course of the Cauvery
River some 15 kilometres from Karur, the ancient Chera capital.
On the southern slopes of a hill overlooking the river were two
caves, both known to have inscriptions. The brow of the first

cave bore two, both said to be damaged and unreadable. 'I had come prepared to see a damaged or fragmentary inscription,' wrote Mahadevan. 'What I saw was a weather-worn inscription which was otherwise not damaged at all ... As I read the words *ko*, *atan* and *irumporai*, I realised with astonishment that the inscription was indeed the record of a Cera [Chera] king of the Irumporai line which ruled from Karur in the Cankan [Sangam] Age.'[22] Owing to imperfect copying their significance had been missed. Mahadevan's new reading now suggested a very early dating, with the royal patron in question most likely being Yanaikatcei Mandaran Irumporai, an ally of the Cheras captured in battle by the Pandyas and taken as a prisoner to Madurai.

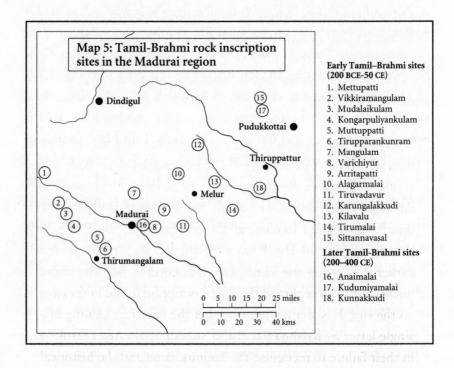

Map 5: Tamil-Brahmi rock inscription sites in the Madurai region

Early Tamil–Brahmi sites (200 BCE-50 CE)
1. Mettupatti
2. Vikkiramangulam
3. Mudalaikulam
4. Kongarpuliyankulam
5. Muttuppatti
6. Tirupparankunram
7. Mangulam
8. Varichiyur
9. Arritapatti
10. Alagarmalai
11. Tiruvadavur
12. Karungalakkudi
13. Kilavalu
14. Tirumalai
15. Sittannavasal

Later Tamil-Brahmi sites (200–400 CE)
16. Anaimalai
17. Kudumiyamalai
18. Kunnakkudi

Early Tamil-Brahmi inscription sites in the Madurai region, all associated with Jain retreats in caves or rock-shelters.

In that same year of 1965 Mahadevan began to re-examine all the known cave inscriptions in the Madurai area, beginning at Alagarmalai, another imposing rock just east of Madurai (see Map 5). Here there were no fewer than thirteen of what were now recognised as Tamil-Brahmi inscriptions, carved on the brow of one large cave at the foot of the hill. The script was more evolved than at Pugalur, pointing to a later date, but all the inscriptions recorded the patronage of a variety of Jain donors from Madurai, mostly merchants with specific trades ranging from goldsmiths to salt-traders, including a nun and a local prince. Here was striking evidence of wide-ranging support for the Jain religion in the South in the first centuries of the Common Era.

From Alagarmalai, Mahadevan and his team moved north to the Mankulam caves, where Robert Sewell had first reported the existence of inscriptions back in 1882. 'The bright winter sun had lit up the façade of the upper southern cave and the long one-line inscription on the brow of the boulder caught my eye,' he was afterwards to write:

It was weather-worn and looked more like bruising on the rock than engraving, but was otherwise undamaged. The bold and legible letters were clearly visible to the naked eye. As I spelled out *ne-tu-n-ca-li-ya-n* and *va-lu-ti-y* I realised with astonishment that I was indeed looking at an inscription of the Pantiyan [Pandyan] king of the Cankan [Sangam] Age not reported earlier ... During the same visit, I discovered that the name *netincaliyan* also occurs in the long inscription in the lower cave on the site. It is strange but true that the incorrect reading of a single letter by Krishna Sastri and Subrahmanya Aiyer resulted in their failure to recognise the famous name and the historical significance of the record.

(Above, left) The Tamil epigraphist Iravatham Mahadevan chalking in a Tamil-Brahmi inscription on the walls of a cave at Alagarmalai in 1992. (Above, right) The longest inscription from the Mankulam caves, shown by Mahadevan to be the earliest Tamil-Brahmi inscription yet found. It reads: 'Charity to Nanta-siri Kuvan, the kani [senior Jain monk]. Behold! The hermitage was caused to be carved by Katalan Valuti, the servant of Netuncaliyan.'

Both inscriptions stated that a Pandyan king named Netun-caliyan had ordered the rectangular beds to be cut into the floor of the cave as a donation for Nanta-siri Kuvan, head of the Jain monks. 'The two inscriptions,' wrote Mahadevan, 'are the oldest historical records in Tamil discovered so far. Their archaic linguistic and palaeographic features indicate a date around the second century BC.' This matched the finding of Mahadevan's colleague K. A. N. Sastri, who placed Raja Netuncaliyan in about 160 BCE as a contemporary of the Chera king Senguttuvan. The Sangam literary work *Mathuraikkanci*, written to extol his virtues, had credited him with winning a battle against an Arya army from the North.

Thanks to Mahadevan and his colleagues, many more Tamil-Brahmi inscriptions were either discovered or reinterpreted over the next four decades, ranging in date from the second century BCE to the fourth century BCE. Mahadevan's direct involvement ended in 2000 but he continues to keep in touch with developments, and in a recent newspaper interview he lamented the damage being inflicted on these precious early inscriptions by ignorant tourists and quarriers: 'Already in my lifetime many Tamil-Brahmi inscriptions have been lost or damaged severely. The destruction is now proceeding much faster. It is sad that the public are indifferent and the State and Central Governments helpless to stop this wanton destruction of our cultural heritage. I can only shed tears at what has been lost and, frankly, I am not hopeful that what remains will be saved.'[23]

More than ninety Tamil-Brahmi inscriptions from over thirty cave-sites have so far been identified in Tamil Nadu and Kerala, of which all but five are directly associated with Jain retreats. They show that over a period of some five hundred years Chera and Pandya rulers, as well as local mercantile communities, supported the Jain monks and nuns in their austere hill retreats. These inscriptions also confirm the major impact of Jain learning on Tamil culture, strengthening the case for the Jains being the real initiators of the first Sangam, held in Madurai probably no earlier than towards the end of the second century BCE, but which gave rise to more such assemblies and so helped to create the legend of a Sangam golden age.

Their emphasis on education and social equality makes the Jain monks and nuns prime suspects in the introduction of the Brahmi script to Tamil country in the form of Ashokan Brahmi, out of which emerged Southern Brahmi and Tamil-Brahmi in the second century BCE, after which came the Vatteluttu, or 'rounded script', and then the Pallava script in the sixth century CE, resulting in the distinctive Tamil script we have today.

A *chakravartin* or 'universal ruler', representing the perfect monarch, together with the seven symbols of his reign, including his queen, heir, counsellor, the wheel of the moral law, precious jewel, horse and elephant. In this delicately incised slab from the much-damaged Buddhist stupa of Jaggayyapetta in the Krishna River valley the *chakravartin* raises his hand to cause gold to rain down from heaven. (From a drawing by James Burgess following his excavation of the site in 1882.)

5

BUDDHISTS
AND ROCK-CUT CAVES

A large bas-relief with a short inscription identifying the male figure
as *rayo asoko*, or King Ashoka, with his queen and female attendants.
Detail of a photograph taken (by force of circumstances, without permission) during the period between 2001 and 2014 when all on-site
photography at the Kanakanahalli stupa site was prohibited.

The earliest known examples of the Brahmi script are the words
set down in stone by Chandragupta's grandson Ashoka Maurya
from about 260 BCE onwards. This does not mean that Brahmi
was not employed before then, only that there is no solid proof

that it was.[1] That is the established view, although it is being challenged by recent claims that Brahmi lettering originated not in India's north-west but either in Lanka or in Tamil country, and as early as the fourth or even the fifth century BCE. These claims are based partly on ongoing excavations at the ancient Lankan capital of Anuradhapura but also on the discovery of hundreds of very short inscriptions on pots and sherds at an excavation site at Kodumanal, a small village on the north bank of an upper tributary of the Cauvery River in Tamil Nadu. This was once an important trading centre known as Kodumanan, sited on the ancient highway through the Palakkad Gap that linked the Cauvery delta and the Chera capital of Variti (modern Karur) with the great sea-port of Muciri, known to the Romans as Muziris.

This site had been either abandoned or destroyed by conquest in about the fifth century CE and subsequently forgotten, only to be rediscovered in 1983 by a young student named K. Rajan, now the respected Professor of History at Pondicherry University. In the course of research for his PhD on megalithic culture Rajan came across a site east of the village of Kodumanal dotted with cairn circles and menhirs (standing stones) which he recognised as a cist burial site, where the dead are placed within stone compartments. Seven seasons of excavations have since shown Kodumanan to have been a major centre for the early production of high-quality steel. But it also had a huge burial complex, only part of which has so far been uncovered. Many of the compartmented chambers contain grave goods in the form of pots, the earliest of which are inscribed with rudimentary symbols such as suns, swastikas, wheels and fishes. However, in the later burials the pots carry the names of the dead, inscribed in local characters clearly derived from the Brahmi alphabet but adapted to allow for elements in spoken Tamil, hence 'Tamil-Brahmi'. So far, more than a hundred shards of pottery have been uncovered bearing characters in Tamil-Brahmi script, which Rajan and his colleagues initially dated from well-stratified layers to the third century BCE but subsequently revised to the fourth century BCE.

Subsequently, a second cist burial site was excavated at Porunthal, also in Tamil Nadu but some 90 kilometres due south of Kodumanal. This was also sited on an ancient trade route, running through the Western Ghats from Madurai. Here grave goods from four graves excavated in 2009 and 2010 included pots containing grains of rice, two samples of which were subjected to radiometric measurement by Accelerator Mass Spectometry (AMS) to give datings of 490 BCE and 450 BCE. This was clear evidence of paddy being cultivated in that area at that date. However, this early AMS dating was further said to prove the existence of Tamil-Brahmi writing at that same period. 'For the first time,' wrote Professor Rajan and his colleague, Dr V. P. Yatheeskumar, in 2013, 'an AMS date is obtained for a grave that is associated with Brahmi script ... Thus the AMS date obtained for the paddy grains from the Porunthal site has the following implications: the Brahmi writing system in India can be pushed back to fifth century BCE.'[2]

Such a dating would turn the history of writing in South Asia on its head. However, its critics argue that its authors have not satisfactorily established the link between the inscribed potsherd found in the Porunthal excavation and the dated rice grains. My own view is that more and better evidence will have to be produced before the text-books are rewritten on the issue of the first appearance of Brahmi in India.

In the meantime, the earliest writings that can be dated with absolute confidence remain Ashoka's proclamations, inscribed initially on rock faces and large boulders and later on sandstone pillars.

Ashoka Maurya's thirty-seven-year rule over more territory than any other ruler before or since is one of the most remarkable episodes in India's long history. I have written elsewhere about Ashoka's achievements[3] so allow me to restrict myself here to his impact south of the Narmada.

Ashoka had to fight for several years before wresting his father's throne from his elder half-brothers, but by about 269 BCE he was fully in control of his empire in the North, whereupon he embarked on the violent subjugation of the as yet unconquered kingdom of Kalinga, modern Odisha. This was achieved at such cost that it may well have been the catalyst that converted Ashoka from a nominal supporter of Buddhism into a genuine and remorseful convert. Some two and a half years later Ashoka began an extended tour of his empire. We can plot at least part of the ground he covered from the earliest of his four main sets of written proclamations, which have come to be known as his Minor Rock Edicts (MREs), inscribed in what is known as Ashokan Brahmi script.

These MREs mark the first public appearance of a written language, initially inscribed on boulders, and later on pillars, plaques and copper plates. Ashoka's rule also sees the first sculptures carved out of rock, and the first excavating into rock to make cells for ascetics – new techniques made possible by advances in ironworking that produced harder steel.[4] Of these three innovations the one that had the most far-reaching impact was Ashoka's use of the new Brahmi script to make his pronouncements known in the furthest corners of his empire. What is also striking is that the language Ashoka chose for these pronouncements was not priestly Sanskrit but the less ornate vernacular language of North India known as Prakrit, which carries the meaning of 'ordinary' or 'artless'. Ashoka seems to have been determined that all his subjects should know what he thought and felt, using the new medium of writing.

Nearly all these first MREs are found carved on the smoothed-out walls or floors of existing rock-shelters, and all are dated, as Ashoka himself informs us, from two and a half years after he had become what he himself called an *upasake* or 'follower of Sakya' – in other words, a Buddhist lay-follower of Buddha Sakyamuni. He goes on to tell his readers (of whom there must have been very few at that time) that he is engaged on a 256-day tour of his dominions. He ends by calling on parents, elders and teachers to be respected, for kindness to be shown to all living things, for truth always to be spoken and for the Dharma to be promoted.[5]

Autocratic ruler though he was, Ashoka believed passionately that his interpretation of dharma was the means by which all people could live in harmony with each other, nature and the gods. It called for all religions to be respected and it remains to this day an astonishing message to come from a ruler, quite without parallel in history. It is under Ashoka's aegis that Indian civilisation, in the sense of a shared culture embracing everything from administration to art and architecture, makes a great leap forward, with tolerance as its watchword. One of his edicts is entirely devoted to this subject, with the great emperor under his regnal name of Piyadasi calling on his subjects to respect all religions. It ends with these words:

Whoever praises his own religion, due to excessive devotion, and condemns others with the thought 'Let me glorify my own religion', only harms his own religion. Therefore contact (between religions) is good. One should listen to and respect the doctrines professed by others. Beloved-of-the-Gods, King Piyadasi, desires that all should be well-learned in the good doctrines of other religions.[6]

Ashoka was also the first Indian ruler known to have concerned himself with animal rights. In his second tranche of rock edicts (known simply as REs and not to be confused with the earlier MREs), he orders that 'not a single creature should be slaughtered or sacrificed', only to qualify this a few sentences later by making an exception for himself: 'Formerly, in the kitchen of Beloved-of-the-Gods, King Piyadasi, hundreds of thousands of animals were killed every day to make curry. But now with the writing of this Dharma edict only three creatures, two peacocks and a deer, are killed, and the deer not always. And in time, not even these three creatures will be killed.'

Some twelve years later, when Ashoka came to set up the last set of his edicts on enormous polished sandstone pillars, he was even more specific about what creatures could and could not be slaughtered, even to the extent of setting down a most bizarre list of animals, birds, fishes and reptiles that were to be spared, ranging from rhinoceroses, porcupines, lizards, tortoises and certain species of deer to cranes, geese, ducks, doves, mynah birds and parrots, to say nothing of nanny goats, sheep and pigs suckling their young, as well as all quadrupeds which had no economic use or which were not habitually eaten. Cows are not mentioned.

It was initially thought that Ashoka's proclamations were confined to north and central India, the most southerly being the RE discovered in the 1850s on a hilltop overlooking the rectangular walls of the buried city of Jaugada, on the southern borders of what is now Odisha. Here its royal author reassures his neighbours to the south that he has turned his back on conquest by force and will henceforth conquer by moral force alone. So it was assumed that this was as far as Ashoka's empire extended. However, in 1892 Benjamin Rice made what he always considered to be his most important contribution to Indian history when he came across three Ashokan MREs while exploring in the Chitaldurga District of what is now Karnataka but was then part of Mysore State. Two were inscribed on boulders near the village of Siddapura, some 50 kilometres south of Bellary (Ballari), and the third on a hilltop a short distance to the north.

(Above, left) The Ashokan Minor Rock Edict at Siddapura, discovered by Benjamin Rice in 1892, here showing the eminent epigraphist Professor Harry Falk chalking in the letters. (Above, right) Professor Georg Bühler's rubbing of the nearby Brahmagiri MRE, also discovered by Rice. (Below) The Govimath MRE discovered in 1931 at Koppal, then in Mysore State.

In 1928, shortly after Benjamin Rice's death in England at the age of ninety, a fourth Ashokan MRE was discovered to the east of Bellary. Another two were found in 1931, this time west of Bellary. In 1946 the Tamil historian and numismatist T. G. Aravamuthan came across an eye-copy of a Brahmi inscription while going through the papers of Colin Mackenzie. Attached to it was a note explaining where the inscription had been found: 'Opposite the west Gopuram of Pedda Rama Devalayam in the southern part of a village called Rajula-Mandagiri in the Panchapalayam Taluk'.[7] Thanks to these directions the seventh Ashokan MRE was duly located, north-west of Bellary. Finally, in 1978 and 1979, two more MREs were found north of Bellary, making it nine in all.

These nine Ashokan MREs in the Bellary area of Karnataka make up half of the eighteen known MRE sites so far rediscovered. The eminent epigraphist Professor Harry Falk has determined that at least five of the nine are the work of the same scribe, who signs himself Capada, calls himself a *lipikara*, or 'engraver of words', and writes that word not in Brahmi lettering but in Kharosthi.[8] So he was a Gandharan from north-west India, or Gandhara-trained, which is just as one would expect, because this surely is where that Brahmi alphabet was first dreamed up.[9] What Ashoka also tells us in these Bellary MREs is that he is currently based at a provincial capital called Suvarnagiri, or 'golden hill', which to judge from the spread of these nine MRE locations must have been somewhere at or close to the modern town of Bellary and the imposing hilltop fort at its centre (see Map 6).

It seems that only after his conquest of Kalinga did Emperor Ashoka become fully aware of the consequences of his actions and begin to take his new faith seriously. In what must surely be one of the most remarkable confessions ever made by an all-powerful ruler, Ashoka tells us in his REs that in conquering

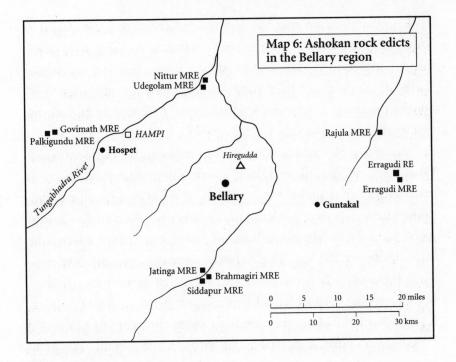

Map 6: Ashokan rock edicts in the Bellary region

The nine Ashokan minor rock edicts found in the Bellary area of Karnataka, together with one major rock edict found at Erragudi. These are the most southerly Ashokan edicts yet discovered. The Hiregudda ridge north of Bellary, site of the Neolithic stone factory and petroglyphs, is also shown, along with the main river systems in the area.

Kalinga he caused a hundred thousand to be killed and a hundred and fifty thousand to be deported, with many others dying from other causes. He declares himself full of sorrow for the suffering caused and goes on to state that he has changed his ways and he now 'desires non-injury, restraint and impartiality to all beings, even where wrong has been done. Now it is conquest by Dharma that Beloved-of-the-Gods considers to be the best conquest.' He then lists all the places within and beyond his borders where the message of his Dharma is now being heard, ending with an explanation as to why he has had this edict written: 'So that my sons and great-grandsons may not consider making new conquests, or that if military conquests are made, that they be done with forbearance and light punishment, or better still, that they consider making conquests by Dharma only, for that bears fruit in this world and the next.'

One of the eleven known Ashokan major rock edict sites is at Dhauligiri, or 'the hill of Dhauli', little more than a modest rise overlooking an equally modest river, the Daya, just above the point where that river joins the much larger Kuakhai to flow north past the town of Bhubaneshwar in Odisha and then eastwards into the Bay of Bengal. The Sanskrit word *daya* means 'compassion'. Precisely when this little river was first given that name is not known but it must have been soon after the terrible battle of Kalinga, which was fought here in or about the year 263 BCE.

Ashoka's words have been cut into the smoothed side of a large rock that is topped by the figure of a standing tusked elephant, of which only the head and front legs have been carved (see illustration). That the battlefield massacre took place here at Dhauli seems indisputable. The late conservationist and founder of the Elephant Family charity Mark Shand told me how in the course of his journey with the elephant Tara that became the subject of his best-seller *Travels with my Elephant* he rode Tara into this area completely unaware of its past history. As they approached Dhauli the elephant refused to go forward; nothing that Mark or the mahout did could persuade her to cross the open ground in front of them. Only then did Mark learn that they had come to the Kalinga battlefield, on which hundreds of war elephants are said to have died. Mark ascribed Tara's behaviour to ancestral memory, passed on from one elephant to another over two thousand years and more. 'Elephants never forget,' he reminded me.

(Left) The half-carved Dhauli elephant, cut into the top of the rock on which a set of Ashoka's major rock edicts are incised. It was carved in about 259 BCE, making it one of the earliest stone sculptures of India's historical age. Detail of a photograph taken in 1895 by Alexander Caddy of the ASI, whose pitched canvas tent can be seen in the background. (Above, right) Mark Shand, champion of the Indian elephant, here seen with the elephant Tara and mahout at the Jain rock-cut caves at Udayagiri, Bhubaneshwar, in 1990.

The Buddhists and Jains saw the elephant as a symbol of unmanageable brute power brought under control by the dharma of their respective faiths. Emperor Ashoka obviously thought likewise, using the elephant as a symbol of his vision of dharma. The half-carved elephant that guards the Dhauli edicts is echoed in another elephant carved above another set of Ashokan REs several thousand miles away at Kalsi in the Himalayan foothills. Here and at virtually every other surviving RE site these edicts have been cut into the sides of huge rounded boulders deliberately chosen for their elephantine appearance.

Although Buddhism was already taking a more outgoing course than Jainism as a proselytising religion, the Buddha's teachings had made little impact outside Maghada – until Ashoka began to propagate the Buddhist dharma alongside his own ethics-based Dharma as set down on his rock edicts. His first action was to redistribute the original cremated remains of the Buddha, which had been buried under eight simple mounds, or stupas. These remains were now divided into fragments and placed in new stupas built throughout his empire – supposedly eighty-four thousand of them but more likely something closer to eighty-four. These early stupas were no more than simple brick domes enclosed within wooden railings. Under the direction of Ashoka's religious commissars, known as *mahamatyas*, the veneration of the stupa as the embodiment of the Buddha became a quintessentially Buddhist phenomenon, briefly copied by the Jains with their own saints.

This stupa-building programme in conjunction with Ashoka's edicts impacted so dramatically on the landscape as to make Ashoka's name known in almost every corner of the land. A further boost came in the wake of a great Buddhist gathering convened by Ashoka in his capital in Pataliputra (modern Patna in Bihar) in about the year 250 BCE which led to the setting up of an ambitious missionary programme which saw the most qualified Buddhist monks being despatched to preach the Buddha's gospel beyond the borders of Ashoka's empire. The many inscribed reliquaries recovered by General Alexander Cunningham in 1851 from his excavation of the stupas on Sanchi hill and the surrounding hills, each identifying the names of the elders and missionaries whose ashes they contained, testify that Sanchi came to be regarded by Buddhists as a central necropolis of Buddhism, to which the relics of its saints and its missionaries were brought to be interred.

The Great Stupa at Sanchi, just a few miles east of Bhopal in the central Indian state of Madhya Pradesh, is something of a miracle, being the only one of many from the early years of Buddhism to have survived more or less intact. However, it has no place here, other than in its significance as the jumping-off point from which many of the Buddhist missionaries embarked, most notably Ashoka's son Mahendra by his first known wife, the Buddhist Devi, also known as Vidisha Devi, who had her home in nearby Vidisha town and her own nunnery on Sanchi hill.

All this is set out in the *Mahavamsa*, the 'Great Chronicle' of the island of Lanka, which presents Emperor Ashoka as a hero for his role in bringing Buddhism to the island through his own actions and those of his two children by his wife Devi, Mahendra and Sanghamitta. It tells us that Mahendra and four of his fellow missionaries flew from Vidisha hill (Sanchi) and landed in Lanka on the hill of Mihintale, although it seems more reasonable to assume that they took ship and made their way south along the east coast, halting at various places that were subsequently settled by Buddhist communities and marked by memorials, one of these sites being Amaravati, where the original stupa built there (probably on Ashoka's order) was greatly enlarged over the course of five centuries to become the largest and most impressive stupa complex in South India.

The *Mahavamsa* further relates how a Buddhist missionary named Mahadhammarakkhita was sent to Maharattha (modern Maharashtra) where he converted eighty-four thousand persons; another elder, Mahadeva, was sent to Mahishamandala – probably the Mysore region; 'Dammarakkitha the Greek' was sent to Aparantanka ('the western ends') where he converted thirty-seven thousand; and Rakkhita was sent to Vanavasa ('forest country') where he converted sixty thousand and founded six hundred *viharas*, or monasteries – this Vanavasa most probably being Banavasi in western Karnataka, which later became the capital of the Kadambas in the fourth century. The Buddhist traveller Xuanzang passed through this same Vanavasa region in about the year 642 and reported the existence of more than a hundred monasteries with over ten thousand monks. He also noted the presence of several hundred non-Buddhist temples where 'heretics of different faiths live together'. Modern Banavasi is now an important centre of Shaivism, dominated by the honey-coloured stones of the ninth-century Madhukeshvara temple, one of many Shaiva temples suspected of having originated as Buddhist shrines.

A later chapter of the 'Great Chronicle' describes how the Chola prince Elara (Ellalan) of Thiruvarur invaded and captured the throne of Lanka in about 205 BCE but was later killed in battle by the Sinhala prince Dutugamunu in about 161 BCE. The peace that followed allowed King Dutugamunu to complete the building of the giant stupa of Ruwanweliseya at Anuradhapura to house the Buddha's begging bowl, after which many thousands of Buddhist monks came from all over India to attend the ceremony, including 'the great *thera* [elder] Candagutta from the Vanavasa country together with eighty thousand ascetics'. Even if we knock off the usual two or three noughts, this list shows that Buddhism was well established in several regions of South India by the second century BCE.

That same Chola prince Elara (or Ellalan) mentioned above is also celebrated in Tamil folklore as Manu needi Cholan, 'The Chola who followed Manu (the Lawgiver)'. The story goes that as ruler of Lanka he installed a bell outside his courtroom which anyone seeking justice could ring. One day the bell was rung by a cow, and on enquiry it was discovered that the king's son had accidentally driven over the cow's calf in his chariot. In the interests of justice the king then killed his son under the wheels of his own chariot. But how should one interpret such a horrifying tale – as an example of extreme piety or of religious fanaticism? To me it suggests the beginnings of Brahminical influence at the court of a Chola ruler early in the second century BCE, since the Jains and the Buddhists were as much against cow-slaughter as the Hindus, but as pacifists were also opposed to all forms of violence.

*

The identification of Emperor Ashoka and his edicts was the result of what must surely rate as Indian historiography's single most important breakthrough: the deciphering of the Brahmi alphabet by the Calcutta-based director of the Bengal mint James Prinsep in 1837, which not only opened the door for every early text to be read but also restored Emperor Ashoka to Indian history. Scarcely less important, to my mind, was the formation of the Archaeological Survey of India (ASI) and the appointment in 1861 of General Sir Alexander Cunningham as its first director. However, Cunningham's brief never extended to South India. Here the first official archaeologist was a Scots educationalist named James Burgess, who in 1871 was appointed head of the new Archaeological Survey, Western India. After Cunningham's retirement in 1886 Burgess stepped into his shoes, so that for the first time the whole of British India came under the authority of one archaeological body.

At the risk of boring the reader with more names of pioneering Orientalists I must add another, also a Scot: James Fergusson, who having made enough money from indigo to be able to retire while still in his mid-twenties chose to reinvent himself as an architectural historian.

Fergusson had become fascinated by one particular form of architecture that he had first explored in and around the great natural harbour of Bombay, visiting the cave on Elephanta Island with its huge Shaiva carvings and the Buddhist caves at Kanheri, now located within the Sanjay National Park on the northern outskirts of the Mumbai megalopolis. Fergusson was also aware of two other cave complexes that had recently come to public attention: the great horse-shoe of rock-cut caves at Ajanta, with their mouldering but still exquisite wall paintings, and the Hindu rock-cut temples at Ellora, both in Maratha country.

These elaborately carved-out caves, dug out of solid rock, had struck him as being uniquely Indian. They were being spoken of as 'cave-temples', but Fergusson gave them the more precise name of 'rock-cut caves'. Determined to make them his object of study, Fergusson sailed to England, learned all he could about the principles of architecture, and returned to India in 1838. He then spent the next five years zig-zagging across the country, beginning in the Western Ghats and working his way down the coast as far as Mahabalipuram, south of Madras.

What Fergusson was unaware of when he embarked on his study was that this was another of the innovations begun in Emperor Ashoka's time, after which rock-cutting spread very rapidly to virtually every corner of India wherever the local geology lent itself naturally to this form of excavation. There are well over a thousand such artificial caves scattered across the Indian subcontinent, of which the majority are at least two thousand years old. They extend from Jain caves in the hills around Madurai to the Buddhist caves in the Tora Bora mountains on Afghanistan's side of the border with Pakistan.

In December 1843 Fergusson read his paper, 'On the rock-cut temples of India', at a meeting of the Royal Asiatic Society in London. This was a genuinely ground-breaking work of art history, first printed in the Society's *Journal* and then republished in 1845 with nineteen lithographic plates to illustrate the text (see illustration). Fergusson showed that rock-cut caves were an integral feature of early Buddhism and, to a lesser extent, early Jainism.

The practice had begun with ascetics of every persuasion making use of natural rock-shelters in the hills for their rainy-season retreats. Then in Emperor Ashoka's time his royal patronage had enabled communities of Buddhist, Jain and Ajivika ascetics to employ masons to cut out custom-built caves in Magadha (now Bihar). At first these were no more than square cells, but with each generation the rock-cutting of the Buddhist community had become ever more ambitious. 'All the Buddhist caves we know of belong to one of two classes,' wrote Fergusson.

> They are either *Viharas* or monasteries, or they are *Chaitya* caves or churches ... The oldest *Viharas* consist of one cell only. In the next stage they are extended to a long verandah, with one long cell behind it ... In the third, and by far the most numerous class, the cell expands into a hall, generally with pillars in the centre, and around these the cells of the monks are arranged ... In ancient times, no sculptures or images were introduced into the *Vihara*, but as early, certainly, as the first or second century of our era we find a chapel always facing the principal entrance and in it we find an image of Buddha ... In the *Viharas*, we can trace the progress from the simple cave to the perfect monastery.

As for what Fergusson called '*Chaitya* caves': 'These are the temples, or if I may use the expression, the churches of the series, and one or more of them is attached to every set of caves in the west of India, though none exist in the eastern side.'

One curious feature of this Buddhist rock-cut architecture was the way it imitated in stone features of contemporary wooden structures, so that the vaulted ceilings of the caves incorporated quite unnecessary beams, and the doorways and window frames echoed the decorated horse-shoe shapes of wooden buildings shown on bas-reliefs. Even when the caves were later enlarged to serve as *chaitya-griha*s or prayer-halls these archaic features persisted.

Fergusson's paper also included an account of the Ellora caves, which were unusual in being a mix of ten Buddhist caves, six Jain and four of what Fergusson called Brahminical. However, these last had been cut centuries later than the others and were quite different in conception. Instead of burrowing into the rock from the side the masons had started at the top, working downwards

A fold-out from James Fergusson's *Rock-cut Cave Temples of India*, (1842)
showing a plan and cross-section of one of the oldest rock-cut caves
at Ajanta: Fergusson's Cave 10, an apsidal *chaitya-griha* or prayer-hall
begun in the third century BCE under the patronage of the Satavahanas.

to carve magnificent temples out of the solid rock, no longer as
monastic retreats but as sites of popular worship, with the vast
Kailas temple at Ellora the supreme example, conceived on a
quite stupendous scale: 'Every thing is Brahminical, every thing is
copied from structural buildings; and had it been cut out of a rock
on a plain, no stranger would have suspected that it was a monolith, without at least a most careful examination of its structure ...
Whatever faults may be inherent in the design, we owe to it the
most splendid excavation in India.'

Fergusson was puzzled as to why the Hindus had ignored this
technique of cutting into rock for so long, only starting in the fifth
century CE. Part of the answer was that the Brahmins had no need
to retreat into isolated monastic communities and no wish to copy
what the heretical faiths were doing; but there was also their ancient
Vedic heritage to be taken into account – their ancestral reluctance

to build anything solid in the way of temples. Perhaps the earth itself, Prithvi, was still accounted their mother, not to be cut into or built upon. The innate conservatism of religious orthodoxy has also to be taken into account. As so often, it was heterodoxy and its challenging of orthodoxy that brought about change.

More than a quarter of a century after the publication of his *Rock-cut temples* Fergusson joined forces with James Burgess to produce in 1880 a greatly enlarged version of Fergusson's early work as *The cave temples of Western India*. First editions of this superbly illustrated publication now sell at a thousand dollars and more, but for me the work is marred by the knowledge that both Fergusson and Burgess had little time for the Indian assistants they worked with or who worked for them. When the Bengali social reformer and highly respected Sanskritist Rajendralal Mitra – the first Indian scholar to state publicly in writing that cow-worship and beef-eating had gone hand in hand in the Vedic era[10] – dared to challenge some of Fergusson's datings in his own two-volume work *The Antiquities of Orissa*, published in 1875 and 1880, Fergusson reacted with a vitriolic personal attack on Mitra and his scholarship which he published as *Archaeology in India with especial reference to the works of Babu Rajendrala Mitra*. As for Burgess, he singularly failed to acknowledge publicly the huge debt he owed to the Indian pandit who acted as his chief translator and epigraphist, and who also carried out numerous field trips on Burgess's behalf.[11]

The Indian in question was a remarkable Gujarati named Bhagwan Lal Indraji, who had grown up in Junagad, on the Kathiawar peninsula of Gujarat, and while still a teenager had taught himself to read the Brahmi script, so enabling him to make his own translation of the well-known Ashokan RE carved on a boulder on the nearby Jain sacred hill of Girnar. This led to him being employed as a field researcher by the already well-known Bombay scholar Dr Bhau Daji (after whom the delightful Bhau

Daji Lad Museum in Mumbai's Byculla District, formerly the
Victoria and Albert Museum, has been renamed).

It was in this last capacity that Indraji came to the Udayagiri
hill outside Bhubaneshwar in 1885 to examine its so-called
Hathigumpha inscription. Its existence had first been reported
half a century earlier by the local Assistant Collector, Andrew
Stirling, who had noted that many of the caves were then occupied by Hindu ascetics who had expressed a strong aversion to a
natural rock-shelter known as the Hathigumpha, or 'Elephant's
Cave', which carried an extensive but mutilated seventeen-line
inscription cut across its brow. 'The Brahmins refer to the inscriptions with shuddering and disgust,' wrote Stirling, 'and to the
Budhka amel, or time when the Buddhist doctrines prevailed, and
are reluctant even to speak on the subject.'[12]

Rajendralal Mitra had previously examined the inscription
and had declared it to be all but unreadable, due to its poor state
of preservation. Indraji thought otherwise, and after many hours
of poring over the faint letters came up with a reading that was
a significant advance on earlier readings, even if it was never
given the recognition it merited. What Indraji had recognised
was that the Hathigumpha inscription, along with many of the
lesser inscriptions from the Udayagiri and Khandagiri hills, had
been written in yet another local version of the Brahmi script,
Kalinga-Brahmi.

Indraji was also able to identify the author of the Hathigumpha
inscription as a ruler of Kalinga named Kharavela, who had caused
the inscription to be made in the thirteenth year of his reign. A
reference to a canal dug in the fifth year of his reign and 'in the
165th year of the Mauryan era' led Indraji to calculate that Raja
Kharavela had ruled from 103 BCE to at least 90 BCE. Later epigraphists have read that same phrase differently, arriving at dates
ranging from 18 BCE to 50 CE, but for myself, I'm happy to go

along with Indraji in placing Raja Kharavela's rule early in the first decade of the first century BCE.

The Hathigumpha inscription announces itself as written by order of 'illustrious Kharavela, the *aira*, the great king, the descendant of Mahameghavahana, the increaser (of the glory) of the Chedi dynasty, (endowed) with excellent and auspicious marks and features, possessed of virtues which have reached (the ends of) the four quarters, overlord of Kalinga'.[13] Indraji interpreted that word *aira* as the Sanskrit 'Arya', which, if correct, shows that Kharavela saw himself as such. He goes on to declare himself to be a devoted supporter of the Jain religion, after which he enumerates his own many virtues, achievements and public works. Having consolidated his kingdom he had set out on a series of wars against his neighbours, all described with much bombast, starting with a ruler named Satakamini: 'In the second year, disregarding Satakamini, (he) dispatches to the western regions an army strong in cavalry, elephants, infantry and chariots and by that army having reached the Kanha-bemna [Kanhan and Waingana rivers?], he throws the city of the Musikas [Muziris?] into consternation.'[14] More on this defeated ruler Satakamini (more popularly known as Satakarni) and his long-overlooked dynasty in the next chapter.

Kharavela had next attacked the Graeco-Bactrian ruler Demetrius in the north-west and then the Shungan successors of the Mauryas in Maghada:

In the twelfth year he terrifies the kings of the Uttarapatha [north country] with .... thousands of .... and causing panic amongst the people of Magadha (he) drives (his) elephants into the palace, and makes the King of Magadha, Bahasatimita bow at his feet. And (he) sets up (the image of) 'the Jina of Kalinga' which had been taken away by King Nanda .... and causes to be brought home the riches of Amga and Magadha along with the keepers of the family jewels, horses, elephants, jewels and rubies as well as numerous pearls in hundreds.

Kharavela's proclamation ends very much as it begins, with the king declaring himself to be 'the king of peace, the king of prosperity, the king of monks, the king of dharma, who has been seeing, hearing and realising blessings ... respecter of every sect, the repairer of all temples, one whose chariot and army are irresistible, one whose empire is protected by the chief of the empire, descended from the family of the royal sage Vasu, the great conqueror, the king, the illustrious Kharavela'.

There were two good reasons why Kharavela chose Udayagiri as this site for his proclamation. The first was that the Jain teacher Mahavira was said to have preached his doctrines on the hill, making it an especially propitious site for Raja Kharavela to place on record his devotion to Jainism. The second was that the rock face he chose for his inscription looked directly out across the plain to Ashoka's inscription on Dhauli hill. It was a homage to his great predecessor, whom he himself had set out to emulate, perhaps even overshadow.

Following Ashoka's death in about 232 BCE his empire had fragmented in the classic pattern as local governors staked their own claims as rulers. There is some evidence of a Brahminical backlash, with the last of the Mauryas ruling in Magadha being assassinated in about 185 BCE by the Brahmin commander of his army, Pushyamitra Shunga. A bout of anti-Buddhist violence and iconoclasm by Pushyamitra then seems to have taken place, followed by a friendlier attitude towards Buddhism under the aegis of the Shungas that allowed a number of damaged Buddhist stupas to be restored and enlarged.

Largely thanks to Ashoka's promotion of sculpture, Buddhist monastic communities now began to replace the wooden railings of their stupas with carved stone balustrades, enclosures and gateways. Panels were carved to illustrate in bas-relief some of the key elements of Buddhist worship along with episodes from the Buddhist Jatakas, moral tales built around the past lives of the Buddha. Initially, both the Jains and the Buddhists were reluctant to show their respective teachers in anything other than aniconic form, representing them instead by such symbols as a pair of footprints, an empty throne, a royal umbrella or a wheel representing their respective dharmas. As mentioned earlier, both faiths sought to make their teachings more accessible by incorporating elements of folk-worship as protectors and attendants in the form of statues of *yaksha*s and *yakshi*s (nature-spirits), and such celestial creatures as *apsara*s and *gandharva*s, drawing on existing local traditions of ivory-carving and modelling in clay fired into terracotta.

One particular goddess now began to emerge as the first clearly identifiable female deity to appear in Indian art. She is habitually described as the goddess Lakshmi but it would be more accurate to describe her as the rice-providing deity Shri, who has claims to be a genuinely Vedic divinity, rising out of the first churning of the milk-ocean as radiant light to make her mark in the *Atharva-Veda*. She is always shown being lustrated by two elephants while seated or standing on a lotus, which the Buddhists first sought to claim for themselves as the symbol of Buddhist dharma, so her first appearance in Indian art is as a bringer of good fortune to the followers of Buddhism (see illustrations overleaf).[15]

One known early centre of ivory-carving was the town of Vidisha, close to Sanchi hill, and it may well have been here that the exquisite statuette misleadingly called the 'Pompeii Lakshmi' was carved. This was found in a charred wooden chest disinterred from the volcanic ash of Pompeii in 1939 and took the form of a *yakshi* fertility goddess just under 10 inches in height (25 centimetres). She is clad in nothing more than bangles, beads and garlands, and – as almost invariably in portrayals of Indian women

(Above, left) One of the earliest depictions of the goddess Shri standing or seated on a lotus while being washed by elephants, in the form that came to be known within Hinduism as Gajalakshmi, or 'Lakshmi and elephants' (from a roundel on the Barhut stupa railing, c. 160 BCE). (Above) The so-called 'Pompeii Lakshmi'; more correctly, a carved ivory figure of a *yakshi* fertility goddess, with two attendants at her sides. (Left) The Ashmolean terracotta goddess, a moulded plaque recovered in 1883 from modern Tamluk in West Bengal, site of the ancient port of Tamralipti.

from the very earliest times – has elaborately coiffed hair which she is engaged in adjusting. As with the earliest stone *yakshi*s, this dainty little goddess, most likely fashioned in about the first century BCE, is overtly sexual in the unashamed way she displays herself. A very similar ivory figurine was recently found at Ter in central Maharashtra, known to the Romans as the trade centre of Tagara, which suggests that the Pompeii Lakshmi was exported from India by way of one of the half-dozen or so major entrepots dotted along the Gujarat or Malabar coasts that came into their own in the first century BCE. Alternatively, she could have taken ship from Tamralipti, identified as the modern town of Tamluk, which is sited some 25 miles (40 kilometres) east of Kolkata beside what was formerly one of the many channels of the Ganges. This was the port from which Ashoka's daughter Sanghamitta set sail for Lanka with her father's gift of a cutting from the Bodhi tree of Bodhgaya in about the year 250 BCE.

In 1883 a terracotta plaque of a goddess figure with a wonder-fully elaborate coiffure was recovered from the river bank at Tamluk (see illustration). This is now recognised as a product of what is coming to be known as the Chandraketugarh culture, which came into its own with the rise of the Shunga dynasty in what is now West Bengal and Bihar in the second century BCE. But that is another story, still waiting for another historian to write.

The tenth and last of the Shunga rulers, Raja Devabuti, fol-lowed precedent by being assassinated by his chief minister, Vasudeva Kanva, who then founded his own short-lived Kanva dynasty in about 80 BCE. But soon afterwards the fourth and last of the Kanvas was himself overthrown by a new power in South India, named in the Puranas as the Andhras but better known today by the name they gave themselves: the Satavahanas, who to this day remain perhaps the most undervalued of all the great dynasties of Indian kings.

A slab from the Kanaganahalli stupa before restoration. It shows a victorious Satavahana king named as Raja Pulumavi pouring water over the hand of a defeated ruler in a traditional gift-bestowing ceremony. This could portray Vasishthiputra Sri Pulumavi I, who ruled for twenty-eight years c. 110–138 CE, or Sira Sri Pulumavi II, who followed him some seven years later and ruled for seven years.

6

SATAVAHANAS
AND ROMAN GOLD

(Above, left) The upper section of the Naneghat cleft, the ancient pass through the Western Ghats, looking down from near the summit. (Above, right) The Naneghat Cave, on the walls of which the Satavahana queen Naganika carved a series of family portraits and a detailed account of her late husband's and her own religious sacrifices.

National Highway 222 follows an ancient trade route running inland from the Konkan coast just north of modern Mumbai. If you stay on the road it will take you to Ahmednagar, but a point comes when you see ahead of you what looks like an unbroken line of cliffs topped here and there by jagged peaks. To avoid these cliffs the metalled road veers to the north-west, and it is precisely at this point that it deviates from the old track, which

now has to be followed on foot. The trail winds through paddy
fields and across little rivulets for a couple of hours' walking before
you arrive at the foot of the cliff-wall, which at this point sticks
out to form a crescent-shaped bastion with a distinct cleft in the
middle. You now have to climb, an ascent that grows increasingly
precipitous until the path gives way to uneven steps cut directly
into the rock. Above and to your right you can see two tiers of
caves crudely cut into the cliff-face, the nearest of which has been
shored up with some modern walling and a protective railing to
stop you falling into the abyss.

Above the caves the path widens out on to an open, grassy
plateau soaked in mist. If this mist was not so thick the view
across the great void behind you would, I suspect, be pretty
spectacular, because this is the ancient Naneghat Pass, which
sits like a cleft on the watershed of the Western Ghats. Whatever
rain falls east of this barrier drains away across the Deccan to
join either the Godavari or the Bhima, the upper course of the
Krishna.

The Naneghat Pass takes its name from what at first glance
looks like a small Buddhist stupa set beside the path. This turns
out to be a large stone container made out of two sections of
carved stone. It was used to collect tolls from travellers who used
the pass. *Nane* means 'coins' in Marathi and *ghat* in this context
means 'pass', hence 'toll-pass'.

The cave at the top of the Naneghat Pass first came to the
notice of the scholarly world in the form of a letter dated 1
August 1828 written by Colonel William Sykes, subsequently
read to the members of the Bombay Literary Society under the
title of 'Inscriptions of the Boodh [Buddhist] caves near Joonur'.[1]
For the previous four years Sykes had been employed collecting
statistical information from the Bombay Presidency, very much as
Buchanan and Mackenzie had done earlier in Madras and Bengal.

This included reporting on the many rock-cut caves that now came to light in the mountains around Poona (now Pune), and making eye-copies of their inscriptions.

Sykes's letter included two drawings of the inscriptions which lined the two side walls of the Naneghat Cave. Owing to the monsoon rains entering the west-facing chamber these had suffered 'great obliterations', although in Sykes's view they had also been crudely incised, which he attributed to carelessness. 'They bear marks of having been quickly done, as a person writes when careless or in haste,' he wrote. 'The chamber was probably intended as a resting place for persons passing the Ghat, as there is a stone seat all round the bottom of the walls.'

But it was Sykes who was guilty of carelessness, because he failed to notice that the back wall of the cave had originally carried a line of eight life-sized figures in semi-relief which had been so thoroughly hacked away that only bits of their feet remained, although each was identified by a short inscription.

Like other antiquarians of his time, Sykes could make no sense of what he termed the 'Boodh letters' of the inscriptions. But he did note 'the very singular fact that, in comparing Boodh inscriptions with very ancient Sanskrit inscriptions, Boodh letters are discovered in the latter, and the prevalence of the Boodh letters is in the ratio of the antiquity of the Sanskrit letters ... Can it be that these Boodh letters are a very ancient form of the Sanskrit alphabet, and that the inscriptions themselves are in the Sanskrit language?' This was spot on. The Brahmi script of his 'Boodh letters' is indeed the prototype of modern Devanagari.

Another nine years passed before James Prinsep proved with his deciphering of Brahmi that Sykes's conjecture was correct, and decades before parts of the Naneghat inscription were satisfactorily read by the Bombay-based German epigraphist Georg

Bühler – enough to show that this was the work of a power-ful widowed queen named Naganika who had married a king named Satakarni, son of the illustrious king Simuka. Her hus-band was now dead, but they had had four sons, one dead and one who was now the ruler. It was their portraits in stone that had originally lined the back wall of the cave. Queen Naganika's husband Satakarni had evidently enjoyed a long and prosper-ous reign because most of the inscription was taken up with a detailed account of the many vows, ceremonies and Vedic sacri-fices they had together performed, all of which had entailed the donation of vast amounts of silver coins and mountains of grain, but, above all, huge numbers of cows – in one instance twenty thousand, but more usually the auspicious number of 1001.

Of the gods acknowledged at the start of the Naneghat inscrip-tion nearly all were Vedic – Dharma (lord of all creatures), Indra, Surya, Chandra, Yama, Varuna, Kubera and the four guardians of the quarters – but also mentioned were two manifestations of the same Hindu god now on the rise: Sankarshana (Vishnu as Balarama, older brother of Krishna) and Vasudeva (Vishnu as Krishna). Patently the author of the inscription saw her royal line as part of the Arya family, even though it was probably Dravidian in origin. The inscription named them as the Satavahanas.

None of the Hindu Puranas lists a royal dynasty named Satavahana, but five give details of the Andhras, a dynasty founded by a Raja Simuka, with many of his ruling descendants bearing the regnal name Satakarni. Emperor Ashoka in his major rock edicts had referred to just such a people called Andhra living within the southern borders of his empire. The Greek ambassador Megasthenes, who had attended the courts of Ashoka's grandfa-ther and father, had also written in his *Indika* of a people he called 'Andarae', describing them as a 'powerful race, which possesses numerous villages, and thirty towns defended by walls and towers, and which supplies its king with an army of 100,000 infantry, 2000 cavalry, and 1000 elephants'. The Naneghat inscription names Simuka as the Satavahanas' founding father and Satakarni as his son, so patently the Satavahanas and the Andhras are one and the same, most probably originating in the region between the Krishna and Godavari rivers that still carries that name of Andhra to this day.

The *Matsya Purana* lists the name of thirty Satavahana kings who together ruled for a total of 460 years. Of these, ten carried the name Satakarni or a close approximation. Although the *Matsya Purana* places the first Satakarni sixth in the line of Satavahana kings, the other Puranas all put him third and name him as successor to Kanha, brother of Simuka. A Jain text translated by Professor Bühler states that Simuka, founder of the Satavahana dynasty, was a great builder of Buddhist and Jain temples but became so tyrannical that he was killed by his younger brother Kanha. This led Bühler to conclude that this Raja Simuka was the ruler named and portrayed in the Naneghat Cave, as well as being the Satavahana king named in the Hathigumpha inscription against whom the Jain ruler of Kalinga, Raja Kharavela, went to war in about 166 BCE.

Most modern historians consider Bühler's dating to be a century too early, although the case is by no means proven. This majority view holds that the early Satavahana rulers suffered a setback but bounced back in the first half of the first century BCE, with the first Raja Satakarni playing a leading role in restoring and extending Satavahana rule. The *Matsya Purana* credits him with ruling for a remarkable fifty-six years, which is so unusual as to suggest that it has a solid basis in fact. He or some other early Satavahana ruler with the same name certainly suffered a defeat at the hands of Raja Kharavela of Kalinga, after which came a series of victories, first over the Shungas or their successors, the

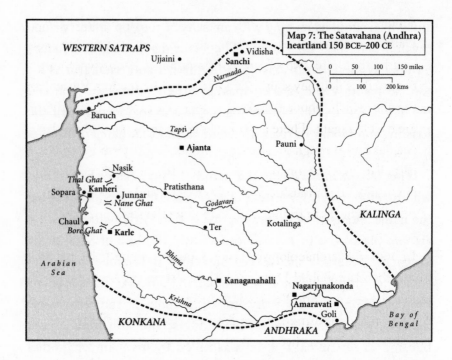

The Satavahana empire at its height, showing major trade centres (marked ●), main passes (marked ⪥), major Buddhist rock-cut caves and main Buddhist stupa sites (marked ■).

Kanvas, to the north, and then the Indo-Greeks (the so-called Western Satraps) in the north-west. This opened the way up and over the Naneghat Pass and on to Pratisthana, situated on the upper reaches of the Godavari River in the Aurangabad District of Maharashtra. Pratisthana then became the Satavahanas' northern capital – today Paithan, south of Aurangabad, best known for its hand-woven Paithani saris (see Map 7).

Two thousand years ago Pratisthana was important enough for the early Graeco-Roman shipping guide known as the *Periplus Maris Erythraei*, or 'Voyage round the Erythraean [i.e. Arabian] Sea', to declare it, as 'Paethana', to be one of the two most important trading centres of the Deccan, the other being 'Tagara':

Among the market towns of Dachinabades, for *dachanos* [i.e. Dakshina, Deccan] in the languages of the natives means 'south', there are two of special importance: Paethana, about twenty days' journey south from Barygaza [the modern Broach], beyond which, about ten days' journey east, there is another great city, Tagara. There are brought down from these places by wagons and through great tracts without roads, from Paethana carnelian in great quantity, and from Tagara much common cloth, all kinds of muslins and mallow cloth, and other merchandise brought there from the regions along the sea coast.[2]

In 1901 the archaeologist Henry Cousens visited the town of Ter in the Osmanabad District of Maharashtra to check if it might indeed be the ancient Tagara. His findings led him to believe that it was – since confirmed by modern excavations and some exceptional finds such as the Ter 'Lakshmi' ivory figurine mentioned earlier. However, Cousens' outstanding discovery lay in recognising that a tiny Vaishnava shrine outside the town was actually a rare surviving example of an early Buddhist *chaitya-griha* from perhaps as early as the fourth century, built of brick but itself modelled on an earlier wooden temple (see illustration). These same little apsidal temples almost certainly provided the models for the group of Hindu temples carved out of the rocks at Mahabalipuram in the seventh century. Although misleadingly known as *ratha*s, after the chariots that carried deities in procession during temple festivities, these structures in turn served as templates for the classical Pallavan style of temple building in South India.

Also mentioned in the *Periplus* are two important ports on the west coast named 'Calliena' and 'Suppara', which had apparently become so silted up that shipping had had to be diverted elsewhere. Calliena was identified without difficulty as the modern town of Kalyan, now part of Greater Bombay. Suppara proved

(Above, left) The Vaishnava temple of Trivikram at Ter, originally a Buddhist *chaitya-griha* or prayer-hall, photographed by Henry Cousens, who identified Ter as the ancient Tagara of the Romans. The flat-roofed structure is a later addition. (Above, right) The Drapaudi Ratha, with a curved roof that mimics thatch, one of five rock-cut monoliths known as the Pancha Rathas, or 'Five Chariots', at Mahabalipuram (Mamallapuram). From an album of photographs taken by an unnamed photographer in the 1860s.

more elusive, until Bhagwan Lal Indraji was asked in 1882 to examine some inscribed stone fragments at modern Sopara, north of Bombay. He instantly recognised them as the remains of one of Emperor Ashoka's major rock edicts. He stayed on to excavate a mound outside Sopara town known locally as *buruda rajacha qila* or 'the fort of the king basket-maker'. This proved to be the remains of a Buddhist stupa containing relics and a silver coin of the Satavahana king Raja Yajna Satakarni.

The *Periplus* also refers to two local rulers, 'the elder Saraganus' and 'Sandares'. The first name probably refers to Satakarni I and the second to Sundara Satakarni, the twentieth ruler on the *Matsya Purana*'s list of Satavahana kings, who ruled very briefly in about 50 CE – a link that helps to date the Indian information in the *Periplus* as gathered very soon after that year.

The *Periplus* reinforces the archaeological and numismatic evidence, which shows that the Satavahanas took over control of both the interior and coastal trades of the Deccan just at the time when the Romans discovered the secret of the shifting monsoon trade winds. With the Roman takeover of the Ptolemaic kingdom of Egypt in 30 BCE the Eritrean Sea became accessible to Roman shipping, opening the way for maritime trade with India on a grand scale.

In 1507 a well-known antiquarian in the European city of Augsburg named Konrad Peutinger was shown eleven sheets of a parchment scroll which when joined together extended to 22 feet (6.74 metres). The learned Dr Peutinger recognised it for what it was: a medieval copy of a much earlier map of the world as it was known to the Romans. The town of Pompeii, destroyed in 79 CE, is shown on the map but so too is Constantinople, the former Byzantium, which had only acquired that name change in 330 CE, so the map is a compilation of information built up over several centuries. What became known as the *Tabula Peutingeriana* is essentially an overland route map, not intended to be geographically accurate but with lines drawn between cities, not to scale but in zig-zags, and the distances between them marked in Roman miles. The further it moves away from Rome the less accurate the map becomes (see illustration).

The last of *Tabula Peutingeriana*'s eleven sheets shows far Asia, with a great mountain range, 'Mons Imaeus' (the Himalayas), dividing China from India, and the rivers 'Ganges' and 'Indus' clearly but confusingly marked. A lesser mountain range in the bottom right-hand corner named as 'Mons Lymodus' has written under it in smaller letters *In hic locis elephanti nasciunter* ('In this place elephants are born'), which suggests that it represents the Western Ghats, which was famous elephant country. At the very bottom of the map is the misplaced island of Lanka, 'Insula Taprobane'. Only one major land route is shown extending into South India. It runs south from the head of the Persian Gulf and crosses the Western

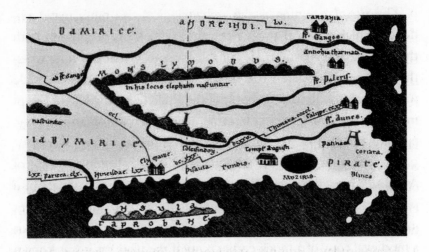

The bottom right corner of the last section of the *Tabula Peutingeriana*, showing the South Indian peninsula and Sri Lanka ('Insula Taprobane', or 'Island of Taprobane') at a time when the Satavahana rajas were the dominant powers in central and South India. The major trade port of Muziris is given prominence, with the temple of Augustus nearby and a lake representing what are now the Kerala backwaters.

Ghats to emerge on the east coast between two rivers named as the 'Paleris' and 'Aunes', probably representing the Krishna and Cauvery. South of the latter are two regions named 'Patinae' and 'Comara' which we can link to Nagapattinam and Comorin. Below Comara the word PIRATE is written in bold letters in red.

But as the eye proceeds up the other coast it meets the most striking features of this corner of the map: a large lake coloured dark blue, 'Lacus Musiris', and under it in capitals MUZIRIS. On the left (north) side of the lake is a drawing of a classic Roman temple with columns and pediment and above it the inscription 'templum Augusti', or 'temple of Augustus'. We can interpret the lake as the famous backwater lagoons of Kerala, while Muziris can be matched to the port of Muciri, situated at the mouth of the

Periyar River on the Malabar coast. The presence of an Augustan temple on Indian soil shows that in the first half of the first century CE there were enough Roman traders settled in Muciri for them to put up their own temple in the name of their ruling or recently deceased emperor.

One of these Roman citizens could well have been the Christian missionary Judas Thomas, because, according to South Indian Syrian Christian tradition, Muciri was where the founding father of their church stepped ashore in 52 CE, going on to found seven churches along the coast and convert eleven prominent Brahmin families before being martyred, with his remains buried at Mylapore, today a Brahmin stronghold in modern Chennai. Jewish refugees are also said to have entered India by way of Muciri, in the wake of the Roman destruction of Solomon's temple in Jerusalem and the dispersal of the Jews in 70 CE.

A poem in the early Tamil bardic anthology *Akananuru* describes Muciri as 'the city where the beautiful vessels, the masterpieces of the *Yavanas* [Westerners], stir white foam on the Culli [Periyar], river of Chera [Kerala], arriving with gold and departing with pepper, when that Muciri, brimming with prosperity, was besieged by the din of war'.[3] Another poem, from the *Purananuru*, speaks of Muciri as 'the city that bestows wealth on its visitors', and as a treasure-house where sacks of pepper were piled up alongside heaps of gold.

The Romans thought equally highly of Muciri, to the extent of describing it as 'primum emporium Indiae' and 'the most important trade-centre in India'. However, Pliny the Elder in his *Natural History* notes that it was inconveniently sited up-river and much troubled by pirates – presumably those same pirates the *Tabula Peutingeriana* warns about in capital letters. 'If the wind, called *Hippalus* [the South-west Monsoon], happens to be blowing,' Pliny writes, it is possible to arrive in forty days at the nearest market in India, *Muziris* by name. This, however, is not a very desirable place for disembarkation, on account of the pirates which frequent its vicinity ... Besides, the roadstead for shipping is a considerable distance from the shore, and the cargoes have to be conveyed in boats, either for loading or discharging. At the moment that I am writing these pages, the name of the king of this place is Caelobothras [Keralaputra]. Another port, and a much more convenient one, is that which lies in the territory of the people called Neacyndi, *Barace* by name. Here king Pandion [Pandya] used to reign, dwelling at a considerable distance from the market in the interior, at a city known as *Modiera* [Madurai].

So extensive was the India trade at this time that it had begun to threaten Rome's gold and silver reserves, with Pliny complaining that India, Arabia and China were together taking a hundred million sesterces from Rome every year, the bulk of it ending in South India. This is confirmed by the remarkable number of hoards of Roman coins reported in Kerala from the nineteenth century onwards. One such hoard of gold and silver coins, said to amount to 'five coolie loads', was reported near Cannanore (Kannur) in 1847. Most of the coins quickly disappeared but fifty-one were saved for the Madras Museum: ten from the reign of Emperor Augustus, four from Tiberius, four from Caligula, fifteen from Claudius, thirteen from Nero and five from Antonius Pius. In 1945 another major Roman hoard was found in an earthen pot near one of St Thomas's seven churches at Palayoor, including twelve gold and seventy-one silver coins and covering a period from the first century BCE up to Trajan in 117 CE. A third major hoard of reportedly two thousand coins came to light in 1983 in Parur, the site of another of St Thomas's churches, near Cranganore (Kodungallur), sited beside the mouth of the present course of the Periyar River, just a few miles north of Cochin. This, too, was rapidly dispersed but some two hundred and fifty coins were saved for the local museum.

It was this last discovery that renewed interest in establishing the exact location of ancient Muziris/Muciri and its attendant Augustan temple. From 1945 onwards efforts had been made to locate the famous port, initially with little success, largely because a major cyclone strike back in the fourteenth century had radically altered the coastline, diverting the mouth of the Periyar a mile or two north, silting up the old port and in the process creating what later became the harbour of Cochin. Today the focus has shifted to the hamlet of Pattanam on the south bank of the present estuary, where a series of ongoing excavations by the Kerala Council for Historical Research led by Professor P. J. Cherian have so far uncovered a brick-lined wharf studded with teak bollards and some early Roman amphorae and glassware, as well as medieval Arabian glazed pottery and Chinese porcelain. But, as yet, no signs of an Augustan temple.

The number of Roman coins found throughout what was then Satavahana territory shows that this was something of a golden age, more funded by trade than conquest. It was Rome's precious metals that paid for the Vedic sacrifices listed by that pious couple of son and mother Raja Satakarni I and Rani Naganika on the walls of the Naneghat rock-cut cave, besides giving them and their successors the security to accommodate and even patronise other faiths within their empire.

The reader will not be surprised to learn that the first serious collector of Satavahana coinage was that remarkable self-made scholar Bhagwan Lal Indraji. When a certain Surgeon-Major Codrington read his paper 'Coins of Andhrabhritya kings of South India' to members of the Bombay branch of the Royal Asiatic Society in Bombay in September 1877, he had the grace to acknowledge that it had been prepared 'from information given by

(Above, left) A copper coin from the Bhagwan Lal Indraji bequest
to the British Museum showing Gautamiputra Satakarni, stern-
faced, shaven-headed and with pendulous earring, c. 110 CE.
(Above, right) Drawing of another Satavahana coin from the Indraji
bequest, showing a two-masted Roman ship. It carries the name of
Sri Vasishthiputra Sri Pulumavi, ruler of Paithan c. 110–138 CE and
known to the historian Ptolemy the Elder as Siriptolemaios.

Pandit Bhagvanlal Indraji, honorary member of the Society'. Much
of Indraji's collection is now in the British Museum, which received
no fewer than 1809 early coins from him in the form of a bequest.

From an Indian perspective this Roman coinage was valued
only for its worth as bullion, to be melted down and reworked
into bangles and other ornaments, hence the hoards. Even so, this
flood of coins carrying the names and portraits of Roman emper-
ors seems to have encouraged the Satavahana kings to follow suit,
the first to do so being Gautamiputra Satakarni (see illustration),
following his defeat of the so-called Western Kshatrapas (Satraps)
in the north-west in about 100 CE – a victory that marked the start
of a third revival of the dynasty's fortunes.

An inscription on the wall of a rock-cut cave in Nasik placed
there by Gautamiputra Satakarni's mother describes him as

the conqueror who 'crushed down the pride and conceit of the Kshatriyas [the Arya Rajputs], who destroyed the Sakas [Western Kshatrapas], Yavanas [Indo-Greeks] and Pahlavas [Indo-Parthians], who rooted out the Khakharata family [of Nahapana, the Kshatrapa ruler who had earlier defeated the Satavahanas], who restored the glory of the Satavahana race'.[4] It goes on to declare Gautamiputra lord of the Vindhya, Malaya, Mahendra, Krishnagiri and other mountain ranges, whose horses drank from the waters of three oceans, which suggests that he also briefly conquered the Cholas and the Pandyas in the far south.

This inscription declares Gautamiputra Satakarni to be an *ekabrahmana*, or 'one Brahmin',[5] yet he also appears to have been a major patron of Buddhism, because under his aegis the Krishna River region became not only the central hub of the Satavahana empire but also a major centre of Buddhist activity in India. A similar policy of religious tolerance appears to have been followed by other Satavahana kings. A donor's inscription on the first of the four magnificent gateways of the Great Stupa at Sanchi links it to Raja Siri Satakarni, who authorised the work and lent his artisans. This was probably Siri Satakarni who ruled for twenty-nine years from about 150 CE. But Siri Satakarni was the last powerful ruler of his dynasty. Although six more named Satavahana rulers followed him, their empire was now being worn away at the edges as one feudatory after another broke away: first the so-called Western Satraps in the west, then the Kadambas and the Ikshvakus in the central regions, and finally the Pallavas, who became the new powers in the deep south.

That these Satavahanas were highly cultured rulers is exemplified by Raja Hala, listed in the *Matsya Purana* as the seventeenth ruler of their dynasty. Hala compiled an anthology of poetry originally written in early Maharashtrian Prakrit entitled *Gaha Sattasai*, or 'Seven hundred songs' (in Sanskrit, *Gathasaptasati*), which included some forty of Hala's own poems, which have something of the Japanese haiku form about them in their compressed delicacy. These were first edited by the German Sanskritist Albrecht Weber in 1881 and some have since been translated into English by the distinguished American poet and translator Andrew Schelling. One of Raja Hala's poems in Schelling's translation reads as follows:

Mother
with the blink of an eye
his love vanished
A trinket gets
dangled
into your world
you reach out and it's gone.[6]

The Satavahanas are, to my mind, the most undervalued of all the great dynasties of kings who ruled India, not least because of the early Buddhist revival that began under their protection. Their very name had been all but lost to history when two rival Orientalists – the Madras civil servant Robert Sewell and Alexander Rea of the ASI – began their surveys in the late 1880s. In 1886 Sewell got to hear of curious remains said to have been built by the ancient Pandavas on a ridge midway between the lower reaches of the Godavari and Krishna rivers above a village called Guntupalle. He was delighted to find a line of rock-cut caves with decorated horse-shoe entrances very similar to those that Fergusson and Burgess had written about in the Maharashtrian country of the Western Ghats. Guntupalle proved to be the most southerly of the hundreds of Buddhist rock-cut caves mined to serve as *chaitya-griha*s (prayer-halls) for monks. Subsequent surveys by the ASI have shown that the first caves here were probably cut by Jain monks in the second century BCE under the patronage of Raja Siri Sada or Srisata, a successor to Raja Kharavela of Kalinga. The site had then been taken over by Buddhists at the time of the Satavahanas. They had enlarged the caves, reshaping one into a circular *chaitya-griha*, turned the rest into cells with platforms for beds, and cut a flight of steps up to the top of the ridge, where they built a pillared assembly hall and a cluster of small stupas – all now neatly restored by the ASI.

Sewell criticised his rival Rea for not doing more at Guntupalle and in the Krishna Valley region generally. But Rea was being expected to cover an area that was enormous both in geographical and historical terms and had concentrated his resources on clearing and restoring the 'lost' city of Vijayanagara, spread over many acres of the south bank of the Tungabhadra River – better known today as the magnificently restored World Heritage Site at Hampi – which had been abandoned after its sacking by the armies of the sultans of Bijapur and Golconda in 1565. Mackenzie and his pandits had briefly visited the ruins back in 1799 but it was Rea and his small team who did the donkey work that made it possible for Sewell to write the ground-breaking study that restored the Vijayanagara empire of the little-known Sangama dynasty of Karnataka to history.[7]

Rea also deserves more than a pat on the back for his surveying of what has since come to be recognised as the 'Krishna River Civilisation': a predominantly Buddhist culture that appeared quite suddenly in that area in the second century BCE, and ended almost as suddenly in the third century CE – dates that more or less match the rise and fall of the Satavahana empire and its hugely profitable trade with the Western world.

What was left of the Amaravati stupa had already been explored by Mackenzie and others but Sewell carried out a more thorough excavation, resulting in further finds that now grace the Chennai Museum. He then worked his way along the banks of the Krishna River examining other potential sites, one of which was a large mound near the little village of Bhattiprolu, 80 kilometres downstream from Amaravati. This also had been plundered for its building material, although in this case the culprit was the officer in charge of the local Public Works Department, who had used its slabs to make a sluice gate for a nearby canal. However, the foundations were untouched, leading to the recovery of three untouched stone receptacles, each containing small reliquary caskets of copper, silver, gold and crystal as well as tiny bone fragments. The reliquaries carried a total of ten short inscriptions written in early Brahmi, all but one lacking the usual diacriticals used to distinguish between vowel sounds, as well as employing other previously unknown characters. Rea speculated that this was a local variant of Brahmi, which it was afterwards shown to be – an embryonic version of the Telangana script, written in the second century BCE.

However, Rea missed one prime site: Nagarjunakonda. This only came to light in 1926 when A. R. Saraswati, the Telugu language expert in the Madras Department of Epigraphy, explored the Krishna upstream of Amaravati and came across mounds and standing marble pillars dotted across 'a wild and desolate spot shut in by a ring of rocky mountains' and overlooked by 'a large lozenge-shaped hill of rock about a mile in length with a plateau of sheet rock on top, the edges of which form rugged cliffs all around the summit, converting the latter into a natural fortress, strengthened by brick and stone fortifications now in ruins but showing that at one time the plateau was used as a citadel'. What the scrub in the plains below this citadel concealed were the remains of a city dotted with monastic complexes and small Buddhist *chaitya-griha*s, all in the form of a semi-circular apse at one end and a barrel-vaulted brick roof.[8] This was the once famous Buddhist monastic city of Nagarjunakonda, or 'the hill of Nagarjuna', named after one of the great movers and shakers of early Buddhism.

That city is now under water and Nagarjuna's hilltop monastery is an island. Following the building of the Nagarjuna Sagar dam and reservoir in the 1960s, whatever could be saved in the way of statuary and worked stones from the many Buddhist sites in the valley was taken to pieces and reassembled on the new island above the rising waters. To get there you have to take a boat, and if you are exceptionally lucky, as I was, you might see a pair of amorous leopards frolicking by the water's edge.

Nagarjunakonda had been named after the Buddhist teacher Nagarjuna, arguably the most important figure in Buddhism after the Buddha himself – although Theravadins, who follow the older and more austere traditions of Buddhism, would disagree. Most of what we know about him comes from Chinese and Tibetan accounts written centuries after his death, much of it fantastical. He is said to have been a Brahmin from Vidarbha, in what is now Maharashtra. As a child he learned all the Vedas by heart, then travelled widely, gaining in knowledge wherever he went. But when he believed he had nothing more to learn, Nagaraja, king of the snake-spirits, took him to his palace at the bottom of the ocean to show him hitherto unknown sutras, including the *Prajnaparamita Sutras*, or 'Wisdom Discourses'. After studying them Nagarjuna returned to South India, where the ruling king was a follower of heretical teachings who refused to grant Nagarjuna an audience. Believing that the king had to be converted in order for the dharma to spread, Nagarjuna joined the king's bodyguard and duly became their commander. His name finally reached the ear of the king, who summoned Nagarjuna and asked him who he was, to which the sage replied that he was a man of perfect wisdom. The king then put him to the test, which ended with the king accepting his teaching, along with all the Brahmins in his court, who 'shaved off their tufts of hair and received full ordination'.[9]

The kernel of this tall tale is that Nagarjuna became an adviser to a king of the Satavahana dynasty. Inscriptional evidence from the Amaravati stupa railing points to that king being Yajna Sri Satakarni, believed to have ruled between about 167 and 196 CE, which fits Nagarjuna's presumed dating. There is nothing to show that Yajna Sri Satakarni converted to Buddhism, but he and his successors undoubtedly created a tolerant and peaceful environment in which new ideas could be freely explored and exchanged without fear of giving offence.

It is no exaggeration to state that under these later Satavahanas Buddhism in the South underwent a transformation quite as dramatic as that experienced under Ashoka in Northern India. From the first century CE onwards radical schools of philosophy in Buddhist monastic institutions were established throughout the Krishna River valley and along the coast of what is now Andhra Pradesh, giving rise to a new teaching of Buddhism that came to be known as Madyamaka or the 'Middle Way', which in turn laid the foundations for what we know of today as Mahayana, the 'Great Vehicle or Path'. It placed new emphasis on compassion and the intervention of a class of enlightened beings known as Bodhisattvas, whose transcendent wisdom had allowed them to achieve Buddhahood but who out of compassion for their fellow beings postponed their own entry into nirvana in order to end human suffering. This reinterpretation would eventually lead to a final schism that had long been coming between these new thinkers and those who continued to follow the more austere teachings of Theravada, the Path of the Elders.

Nagarjuna was perhaps the foremost but only one of the new

thinkers who now emerged out of this hothouse of philosophical debate. Many of the central texts of the Madyamaka teaching are attributed to Nagarjuna but are more likely to have been written by his chief disciple Aryadeva or later adherents. The one text that all scholars seem happy to accept as his is the shastra known as the *Mulamadhyamakakarika, or* 'Fundamental Verses from the Middle Way', which covers the essentials of his thinking in 448 verses. The higher metaphysics behind the teaching that so profoundly reshaped the course of Buddhism are quite beyond me, so I refer the interested reader to someone who knows what they are talking about.[10]

This Satavahana-sponsored Buddhist culture extended as far north across the Narmada as Sanchi and the Ajanta caves. Within the Krishna Valley itself it was long thought that the only important stupa sites were at Amaravati, Bhattiprolu, Jaggayyapeta and Nagarjunakonda. However, thanks to the work of the Andhra circle of the ASI two more important stupa sites have in recent years been added to the list: Phanigiri and Kanaganahalli. These names still mean very little in India, which is a pity, because Kanaganahalli in particular will in time become as world famous as Sanchi or Ajanta as one of India's very few well-preserved early Buddhist sites.

In 1989 four of Emperor Ashoka's major edicts were found carved on a stone slab on the floor of a collapsed Kali temple in a little village called Sannati on a bend of the Bhima River, which is an upper tributary of the Krishna. Five years later, as plans were being drawn up to build a dam upstream of Sannati, archaeologists carried out a wider survey of the immediate area and uncovered the remains of a massive stupa and attendant monastery near the village of Kanaganahalli. What makes this discovery so important is that even though the stupa itself had collapsed at some point in the distant past, shattering many of the large sculpted limestone slabs lining the body of the stupa, the site had never been plundered for building material. These slabs are little short of sensational as art works, and a magnificent addition to India's limited portfolio of early sculpture. Many illustrate the Jataka tales and the life of the Buddha – shown in aniconic form as appropriate to this early stage of Buddhist art – very much as found at Bharhut, Amaravati and Sanchi.

The added bonus is that Kanaganahalli comes with a portrait gallery of eminent rulers from the Satavahana dynasty, all identified and presented in idealised form (see below and at the start of the chapter). They include Rajas Simuka Satakarni, Sri Pulumavi (either Pulumavi I, but more probably Shiva Sri Pulumavi) and Yajna Sri Satakarni (c. 152–181 CE), as well as a number of Buddhist heroes of whom the most striking is Emperor Ashoka, shown in the company of his queen and female attendants, and named in Prakrit and Brahmi in a brief inscription in the top left corner of the panel as *rayo asoko*, Raja Ashoka.

Two fragments of bas-reliefs from the Kanaganahalli stupa. (Above, left) Gods and human kings worship the Buddha in aniconic form, represented by an empty throne and a pair of footprints. (Above, right) The Buddha's shorn hair, with turban, is brought before the gods to worship.

Regrettably, it seemed to both local and foreign scholars that for some years after the initial excavation some elements within the ASI appeared to be doing little to conserve the site and its incomparable statuary. Thankfully, that is certainly no longer the case and a full report entitled *Excavations at Kanaganahalli* has been published (if still very hard to obtain).

The smaller archaeological site of Phanigiri, or 'serpent-hill', is on a hilltop some 50 miles due east of Hyderabad in what is now Telangana State. Here there is a happier story to tell. It was first seriously excavated in 2001 by an ASI team led by the distinguished archaeologist Dr B. Subrahmanyam, the leading authority on the Buddhist archaeology in Andhra Pradesh, and excavations continue to this day, revealing an extensive site that had been plundered in the past but still retained a number of its carved bas-reliefs, statuary, pillars and gateway architraves, all much damaged but of exceptional quality.[11] As yet no portraits of rulers have emerged but several inscriptions bear the names of Satavahana rulers as well as those of the dynasty that succeeded them, the little-known Andhra Ikshvakus.

In the middle of the second century CE the fortunes of the Satavahanas began to decline. The eastern Deccan fell to the Ikshvakus, who took over the Krishna and Godavari valleys and made Nagarjunakonda their capital. Their origins are uncertain. One theory is that their founder Siri Camtamula was an invader from the North, but two of the epithets given to them in the Puranas – Sriparvateya, meaning 'of the forest', and Andhrabhrtyas, or 'servants of the Satavahanas' – suggest that they are more likely to have been local tribal people who rose up against their masters. Unlike the Satavahanas, the Ikshvakus were overtly Buddhist and for a hundred years they presided over the continuing spread of Madyamaka Buddhism, supporting new monastic centres such as Phanigiri and enlarging existing ones such as Amaravati and Kanaganahalli. It was at this time that the first iconic – that is to say human rather than symbolic images – portrayals of the Buddha began to make their first appearance in south and central India.

Little is known about these Andhra Ikshvakus, but we know even less about the mysterious Kalabhras who may – or may not – have followed them, and who are said to have been responsible for a supposed 'dark age' that engulfed the Tamil South over this same period. Until recently historians used to speak of a two-and-a-half-century 'Kalabhra interregnum' that disrupted the ancient lines of the Chola, Pandya and Chera kings between the end of the third century and the sixth century, their most prominent king ruling in the last quarter of the fifth century under the name Vikranthaha or 'idol destroyer'. References to these Kalabhras are invariably hostile, describing them as 'enemies of civilisation' and as 'evil kings who brought chaos and took away the rights of the Brahmins', because from their point of view the Kalabhras were heretics who destroyed Brahminical culture. They appear to have entered the Tamil country from the North, most probably from the Karnataka region, spoke Prakrit rather than Tamil and were apparently strong enough to overthrow the incumbent Tamil rulers and disrupt the existing social order, confiscating land given to the Brahmins.[12] However, there now appears to be a growing body of opinion that argues that there was no Kalabhra dark age, though there may have been a period of turmoil, *kalavaram* meaning 'turmoil' in Tamil. I remain unconvinced.

What is indisputable is that during this supposed Kalabhra ascendancy there was a dramatic expansion of Buddhist centres of learning at Conjeeveram (Kanchipuram) and Nagapattinam, creating what could almost be called a second Buddhist renaissance in the South, now centred on the Cauvery River delta. Students came to study here from as far afield as Gandhara and China and took the new teachings of Madyamaka away with them. And as it spread north and east so these Madyamaka teachings solidified into Mahayana, the Great Vehicle, today followed by the majority of Buddhists worldwide.

Other schools of Buddhism also flourished side by side with Madyamaka. The seventeenth-century Lankan text known as the *Gandhavamsa*, or 'History of Literature', speaks of Kanchipuram as one of three major centres of early Theravada learning in South India and of ten great teachers of Kanchipuram, beginning with the fifth-century theologian Buddhadatta, who in his own writings speaks of a king named Achchuta Vikranta of the Kalabhra clan ruling over the country from his capital at Kaveripattinam. Today the site of the former port of Kaveripattinam is better known as Poompuhar or Poompatinam ('estuary town') and is little more than a collection of fishermen's huts strung along a sandy beach. Little evidence of a glorious past has survived and little has emerged from surveys. However, the submerged wharves and piers of an ancient harbour have been located offshore, which seem to confirm old stories of the city being overwhelmed by some natural disaster, possibly a tsunami such as the one that wreaked such havoc along this same coast in 2004.

Being sited on the coast beside the estuary of the Cauvery River meant that Kaveripattinam was well placed to take advantage of the increased traffic between Lanka and the mainland that began in Ashoka's time in the third century BCE, so much so that it expanded into an important trade emporium known to Pliny the Elder as 'Khaberis'. One of the poems in the Tamil *Purananuru* describes how even the greatest ships could enter its port without having to lower their sails, how they poured precious cargo from overseas on to the beach, and how the merchants' mansions in the city were so tall that the upper floors could only be reached by ladders. The city was further said to be divided into two districts, with a docks and warehouse area beside the sea inhabited by ship-builders, fisherfolk and foreign traders, and a city proper further inland where the nobility, the wealthy and the intellectuals lived.

The natural disaster that overwhelmed Kaveripattinam probably occurred in the third century CE, after which the sea-trade switched to the port of Nagapattinam further down the coast, marked as 'Patinae' on the *Tabula Peutingeriana* map. Nagapattinam has a starring role in the Buddhist epic *Manimekalai*, composed by a Buddhist poet named Seethalai Saathanar towards the end of the fifth century CE and set in what was then a busy and prosperous sea-port, thronging with foreign merchants from afar speaking different languages, and ships unloading cargoes of fine horses from Arabia, gold from the northern sea and coral from the western sea. This is where the poem's beautiful heroine Manimekalai, after much personal suffering, comes looking for answers from the competing philosophies of Hinduism, Jainism, Ajivikism and Carvakism before becoming a Buddhist nun. The first modern translation of *Manimekalai* was the last of the translations of the three surviving Tamil epics undertaken by that great scholar Swaminatha Iyer.

Manimekalai shows Nagapattinam to have been as much a mixing-bowl of competing ideas as it was an international market-place, largely because of its strong trade links with China and Lanka. Innumerable Buddhist teachers and students passed through the city as they came and went between Lanka and the mainland, among them four outstanding Pali scholars of the fifth century each of whom made significant contributions to Buddhist learning: Buddhadatta, Buddhaghosa, Dinnaga and Dhammapala, all of them Tamils writing in Pali rather than Sanskrit, and all promoters of Theravada Buddhism.

However, even these great teachers have to give pride of place to the South Indian guru who became known as Bodhidharma, famous for his trademark unblinking stare, hairy eyebrows and even hairier chest – the monk credited as the founder of Zen Buddhism and kung fu. Chinese Buddhists came to regard Bodhidharma as one of the most important of the early propagators of Mahayana Buddhism, and most of what we know about him comes from those sources, among them a Chinese monk who provided a brief biography of his master in a book on the core teachings of Zen Buddhism. 'The Dharma Master was a South Indian of the Western Region,' he wrote. 'He was the third son of a great Indian king. His ambition lay in the Mahayana path, and so he put aside his white layman's robe for the black robe of a monk ... He subsequently crossed distant mountains and seas, travelling about propagating the teaching in Han and Wei.'[13] Another Chinese account makes Bodhidharma the third son of a great king of South India who was a Brahmin. This suggests Pallavan ancestry, since the Pallavas were unusual in claiming Brahmin status, in which case Bodhidharma was probably born and raised in Kanchipuram.

By one account Bodhidharma went to China to establish Prajnatara's *Sarvastivada*, or 'theory of all existence', teaching there. By another it was because Buddhism was now under threat within India, so he migrated to ensure its continuance elsewhere. He is believed to have had an audience with the Chinese Emperor Wu of Liang in 527 CE, after which he settled in the Song mountains near Luoyang and the Shaolin monastery, where he meditated without speaking and with his face to the wall for nine years, and where he died no later than 554.

What Bodhidharma achieved in China is the stuff of legend, quite literally. That he followed the teachings of Nagarjuna is exemplified by his famous two-word answer of 'Vast emptiness' when asked by Emperor Wu to explain Buddhism. His and his chief disciples' rigorous promotion of the regulation of the mind

The South Indian monk Bodhidharma, who exported Mahayana Buddhism to China in the second quarter of the sixth century CE and whose meditation practices laid the foundation of Chinese Chan, which evolved into Zen in Japan. He is always depicted with bulging eyeballs, having cut off his eyelids after falling asleep while meditating. The eyelids are said to have turned into the first tea-leaves. Detail from a painting by a twentieth-century Japanese Zen master.

through *dhyana*, which loosely translates as 'meditation', undoubtedly helped lay the foundations of Chan Buddhism, which evolved into Zen in Japan, where Bodhidharma is known as Daruma and is most often represented as a round, hollow wooden doll with blank staring eyes.

The legendary element lies in the claim that Bodhidharma brought Tamil martial arts – and, by some accounts, yoga – to China and taught them to the monks at Shaolin as kung fu. Its proponents argue that Bodhidharma introduced a form of Tamil martial arts known as *Kalaripayattu*, closely associated with the Nadars of Travancore. They cite what seem to me to be the very tenuous similarities between Shaolin kung fu and the form of *Kalaripayattu* known as *Varma kali* once widely practised among the Nadars, with its emphasis on sparring with a variety of weapons ranging from swords-and-shields to unarmed grappling with blows aimed at pressure points. The facts are that Shaolin monastery had been established in 495 CE by order of the Chinese emperor for the Indian monk Buddhabada, who taught a form of Theravada Buddhism. He became its first abbot and among his first disciples were several exponents of the Chinese martial art of *Shuai Jiao*, which had already been in existence for several centuries. So when Bodhidharma came to Shaolin in or about 527 a martial arts tradition was already well established, with his first disciple, Huike, being a known exponent. The first known manual of *wushu*, better known as kung fu, was written by a visitor to Shaolin in about 1610 and makes no mention of Bodhidharma as the originator of the art.[14]

Much of the success of Mahayana Buddhism came from its promotion of Bodhisattvas as interceders on behalf of mankind. Of these Bodhisattvas by far and away the most popular was Avalokiteshvara, 'the lord who looks down on the caller', who helped to make Buddhism accessible to the masses, in part by taking on some of the traits of the Vedic demi-god Purusha along with elements of Shiva, Vishnu, Indra and Surya. The earliest written text in which Avalokiteshvara appears is the famous *Lotus Sutra*, versions of which had reached China by the third century CE. There is a strong case for locating Avalokiteshvara's origins in second-century Nagarjunakonda as a product of Madyamaka teaching. From there he went on to occupy a place within Mahayana Buddhism second only to the Buddha himself. In Tibet he became Chenresig, the protector of Tibet, with the Dalai Lamas as his manifestation; in China he changed sex to become Guanyin, 'goddess of mercy', and Guazon or Cannon in Japan; and in Lanka he came to be worshipped at Natha, with Taradevi as his *shakti*.[15]

The accounts of the travels of the Chinese monk Xuanzang, who visited practically every major Buddhist community in India between 630 and 645 CE, show that in most of these places Mahayana and Theravada schools co-existed side by side with other lesser schools of Buddhism. Thanks to the translations into French and English of Xuanzang's *Great Tang Records on the Western Regions*, Alexander Cunningham and his successors were able to track down virtually every one of the Buddhist centres he visited in India. But what Xuanzang's account also shows is that by his time Buddhism was on the wane and Hinduism very much in the ascendant.

Xuanzang had arrived in Tamil country not long after the Pallavas under the leadership of the warrior-king Mahendravarma had recaptured their former capital at Kanchipuram. Then in 642 CE, at just about the same time as Xuanzang's visit, Mahendra-varma's son Narasimhavarman defeated the so-called 'Early Chalukyas' to the north with the aid of an exiled Lankan prince. In return Narasimhavarman lent the prince an army, which he used to invade Lanka and win the throne for himself. Xuanzang was about to set sail for Lanka from Nagapattinam when a party of refugee monks came ashore with news that the Buddhist king of Lanka was dead and the island in turmoil.

Xuanzang was forced to change his plans and move up the west coast, but not before he had taken note of a sacred mountain on the eastern flank of the Malaya mountains known to him as 'Po-ta-lo-ka'. On its summit was a stone palace frequented – not by Agastya but by the Buddhist Bodhisattva Avalokiteshvara! By his account, pilgrims hoping to see Avalokiteshvara in his palace on this Potala peak had to risk their lives by climbing the mountain. Those who succeeded were granted an apparition of Avalokiteshvara – not as himself but, in Xuanzang's words, 'as a *Pashupatha Tirthaka* or as *Mahesvara*'. Maheshvara, or 'great

A damaged but rare example of early South Indian Chola 'bronze casting' in the form of a seventh-century copper alloy statuette of Avalokiteshvara from the Krishna River region, obtained by Robert Sewell from an unknown source and later sold by him to the Victoria and Albert Museum for £3 in 1914.

lord', is an epithet for Lord Shiva, and a Pashupatha Tirthaka is an ascetic devotee of Shiva, so by Xuanzang's time Shaivas were firmly in control of this holy mountain, whether as Potala, Pothigai or Agastya Malai. This also helps to explain why in Tamil Buddhist accounts it is Avalokiteshvara and not Shiva who is credited with teaching Agastya the Tamil language.[16]

The Pallava alliance with Lanka gave Narasimhavarman and his successor Parameswaravarman the security to concentrate their efforts on utterly crushing their remaining enemy, the Chalukyas, so that by the time Narasimhavarman's great-grandson and namesake Narasimhavarman II had ascended the throne in 700 CE the Pallavas were once again the unchallenged power in the South.

Known popularly as Rajasimha, the 'Lion King', Narasimha-varman II was as ardent a follower of Lord Shiva as his forefathers – and he now had the peace and the prosperity to direct his devotion into temple-building, beginning with Kanchipuram's modest little Kailasanatha temple, undoubtedly one of the earliest stone-built (as opposed to carved out of stone) Hindu temples in Tamil country, although some would argue that the famous breaker-lapped 'Shore temple' on the coast south of Chennai at Mahabalipuram (Mamallapuram) is older and that it, along with the little cluster of rock-cut *rathas* nearby, was actually begun by Rajasimha's great-grandfather Mahendravarma I.

The latter was popularly known as Mamallaballa, 'the great wrestler', on account of his martial prowess, and this is said to have given that area its local name of Mamallapuram. The British knew of the sculpted *rathas* as the 'Seven Pagodas'. They were the very first temples I explored on my first visit to South India in the late 1960s, and their very simplicity and scale left a lasting impression, so much so that for many years I found myself quite unable to appreciate the majesty of the vast temple cities of the South that evolved from here by way of Rajasimha's temples at Kanchipuram. I now better understand why it was that Kanchipuram came to be listed as one of India's seven sacred cities and why it came to be known as 'the Varanasi of the south'.

Yet even as Hinduism came into its own, Buddhism clung on – but only in isolated patches, and with only limited royal patronage. Centuries later, in 1820, a British missionary named Elijah Hoole visited Nagapattinam and was surprised to see in one of its streets what he described as 'a well-executed sculpture of Buddhu, full size and seated as though in meditation'. He also saw on the

town's outskirts a ruined tower known to the British as the Silver
Pagoda and a well-known landmark for sailors. It was said to have
been a Buddhist temple built by a local ruler for the Chinese, and
it remained standing until 1854, when it was knocked down to
make way for a Jesuit seminary. But in the course of clearing the
ground workmen uncovered a brick chamber under the roots of
a fallen tree, which was found to contain five Buddhist bronzes.
They had been buried with great care, as if for their protection,
and were judged to be at least eight hundred years old. Since then
more than 350 bronze statues have come to light, either from
under the streets of Nagapattinam or from its immediate environs,
all of them Buddhist.

Nor are these relics of the region's Buddhist heritage confined
to Nagapattinam. In the summer of 2004 a local landowner
set some labourers to dig the foundations for a new house in
the little village of Sellur, beside a side-channel of the Kaveri
known as the Vettaru River, about 30 kilometres upstream of
Thiruvarur. At a depth of six feet they came across a hoard of no
fewer than forty-five Buddhist statuettes, lying face down and
protected by a brick surround. All but three were metal figurines
cast in copper alloy (usually but incorrectly described as bronze)
using the so-called lost-wax process. Ranging in height from
7 to 52 centimetres, these 'bronzes' represent just about every
aspect of Mahayana and Theravada Buddhism, from popular
Bodhisattva figures such as Avalokiteshvara and Lokesvara to
the rarer image of Maitreya, the Buddha to come.

Remarkable as the Sellur hoard is, it represents only part
of the Buddhist statuary that has come to light in recent years
in just this one district of Tamil Nadu alone, largely thanks to
the efforts of a handful of local enthusiasts, none more ener-
getic than Dr B. Jambulingam, Superintendent of the Tamil
University in Thanjavur. Since 1993 Dr Jambulingam has been

(Above, left) The Buddha in meditation under the Bodhi tree guarded by two Naga snake-kings, one of the many Chola 'bronzes' found under the streets of Nagapattinam, now in the Chennai Museum. (Above, right) Dr Jambulingam kneels by a damaged torso of the Buddha found in January 2015 in a field of sugarcane in the village of Manalur, near Thanjavur.

tracking down long-neglected Buddhist statues or following up reports of new discoveries in the countryside around Thanjavur. In his doctoral thesis delivered in 2000 Jambulingam listed sixty granite Buddha images found in five of Tamil Nadu's thirty districts.[17] And Buddhist statues continue to come to light. In July 2012 a life-size stone statue of the Buddha was unearthed during construction work in the village of Kandramanikkam, in the same district as Sellur. Three months later the discovery of a slightly smaller decapitated statue was reported from the hamlet of Kiranthi, just south-west of Nagapattinam – making it the sixty-seventh stone statue to be recovered in this prime Chola country since Independence.

Most of these stone and bronze Buddhas can be dated to between the ninth and twelfth centuries, when the Imperial

Cholas were at the height of their power. This is long after Buddhism in Tamil country is supposed to have become extinct. They show not only that pockets of Buddhism survived but that it was tolerated by the Cholas, the most ardent devotees of Lord Shiva.

Jagannat'h.

The three murtis worshipped in the temple of Jagannath at Puri, with Krishna in the role of Jagannath, 'lord of the universe', his brother Balabhadra and his sister Subhadra. An early nineteenth-century watercolour, probably from Benares.

7
JUGGERNAUT

The seafront at Puri, with the temple of Jagannath in the distance, as drawn in a watercolour by an unknown European artist in September 1820.

JUGGERNAUT A corruption of the Skt. *Jagannatha*, 'Lord of the Universe', a name of Krishna worshipped as Vishnu at the famous port of Puri in Orissa. The image is called an amorphous idol ... and it has been plausibly suggested (we believe first by General Cunningham) that it was in reality a Buddhist symbol, which has been adopted as an object of Brahmanical worship, and made to serve as an image of a god. It was, and is, annually dragged forth in procession in a monstrous car, and as masses of excited pilgrims crowded round to drag or accompany it, accidents occurred ... The popular impression in regard to the continued frequency of immolations on these occasions – a belief that has made *Juggernaut* a standing metaphor – was greatly exaggerated.

Col. Henry Yule and A. C. Burnell, *HOBSON-JOBSON, A glossary of colloquial Anglo-Indian words and phrases*, 1886

Today the seafront at Puri looks very much like any other seaside resort, with a long sandy shore, the Golden Beach, lined by an esplanade, the Marine Drive, and backed by large hotel blocks catering for families on their annual holidays. Two centuries ago this seafront was almost entirely empty. A watercolour from 1820 (see page 205) shows a cluster of thatched bungalows on the beach put up for European visitors. Everything changed with the opening in 1888 of the Bengal Nagpur Railway's line linking Calcutta with Madras. For the first time Puri became accessible from virtually every corner of India.

Yet even before the railways Puri drew vast crowds, as a watercolour drawn in July 1818 by one of Colin Mackenzie's draughtsmen illustrates (see illustration). It shows the ceremony for which Puri was famous throughout India – and, to some degree, also notorious: the procession known as the *ratha yatra, or* 'chariot journey', in which three pyramidal carts with vast wooden wheels are drawn by hand in a procession that circles the central temple and its immediate environs. Each *ratha* contains one of a trinity of *murti*s, or 'images of deities', who normally reside on a platform in the innermost sanctum of the city's Jagannath temple: Krishna as Jagannath, 'lord of the universe', his brother Balabhadra and his sister Subhadra.

The anglicisation of the word 'Jagannath' into 'Juggernaut' and its corruption in the English dictionary into a pejorative meaning an unstoppable and merciless destructive force serves as a classic example of the colonial demonisation of the 'other' of the sort that made it possible for an otherwise decent man like the Christian evangelist and slavery abolitionist William Wilberforce to speak of Hinduism as 'one grand abomination, a dark and bloody superstition' and to describe the Hindu deities as 'absolute monsters of lust, injustice, wickedness and cruelty'. Indeed, this Western vilification of the Jagannath cult began long before the colonial era, as that marvellous portmanteau of Anglo-Indianised words *Hobson-Jobson* demonstrates. *Hobson-Jobson* provides a dozen lurid accounts of devotees hurling themselves under the wheels of the Jagannath chariots, beginning with that of the Italian friar Odorico of Pordenone, who stopped at Puri in 1319 on his way to Sumatra and China and who noted that 'many pilgrims who have come to this feast cast themselves under the chariot, so that its wheels may go over them, saying that they desire to die for the god'.[1] Over the next five centuries other European travellers would give similar accounts.

In 1803 the East India Company (EICo) drove out the occupying Marathas and installed a British Commissioner in Puri, Andrew Stirling, who soon afterwards declared that as far as he

A watercolour of the Jagannath procession in Puri in 1820, showing the 'lord of the universe' being drawn through the street in his sixteen-wheeled *ratha* attended by the British Commissioner Andrew Stirling, shown seated with his wife on an elephant (far left).

could ascertain these ritual suicides had ended some time ago: 'That excess of fanaticism which formerly prompted the pilgrims to court death by throwing themselves in crowds under the wheels of the car of Jagannath has happily long ceased to actuate the worshippers of the present day.'[2] Over the course of four years' service he took part in several *ratha yatra* processions but witnessed only three fatalities, one of which was accidental.

Today such acts of self-harm are even less infrequent but the cult of Jagannath continues to fascinate scholars, and with good reason, because the Jagannath temple at Puri and its contents do have a quite extraordinary history.

Recent excavations at Udayagiri and Ratnagiri in the hills north-west of Cuttack have revealed a number of monastic sites where Buddhism continued to be practised as late as the twelfth century. As for the temple city of Bhubaneshwar, visitors who tour these restored temples today can hardly imagine how utterly different the scene was when the EICo took over the region. The entire temple area had been largely abandoned following the desecrations inflicted by the raider Baki Khan in the 1640s, and all but the central Lingaraja temple – described by James Fergusson as 'the finest example of a purely Hindu temple in India' – lay derelict and overgrown by thick jungle. Photographs taken by the ASI in the 1860s and 1870s and those published by Rajendralal Mitra in his *Antiquities of Orissa* in 1875 show how extensive this dilapidation was. In the circumstances it is easy to see why Colin Mackenzie and General Charles 'Hindu' Stuart – whose Hindu statues now make up a large portion of the British Museum's outstanding collection[3] – felt free to help themselves to a number of stone images, in particular those from the niches of the Raja Rani temple.

When Stirling toured the temples in the early 1820s he noted that one, known as the Bhaskareshwara shrine, had been

(Above, left) The archaeologist and Sanskritist Rajendralala Mitra, author of *Antiquities of Orissa*. (Above, right) Part of the Lingaraja temple complex in Bhubaneshwar.

built around a large 40-foot stone column. However, when the Bhaskareshwara temple was next reported on, by Rajendralal Mitra in the 1880s, the column had shrunk to a mere 9 feet. Even so, Mitra had no hesitation in declaring it to be Ashokan in origin, which appeared to be confirmed when in 1929 the head and shoulders of an Ashokan-type lion capital were found in a pit beside the temple, followed by the discovery of an Ashokan bell (base of a capital) and fragments of a pillar in an old tank known locally as the 'Asoka jhara' or 'Asoka kund'. What had apparently begun as an Ashokan-style pillar, probably standing beside a Buddhist stupa, had been converted into a Shaiva linga and a temple built around it.

One of the many puzzles of the Ashokan era is why that great emperor, having introduced a pan-Indian script, should have stuck with India's remarkably crude system of punch-marked coinage when his Greek neighbours next door were producing high-quality coins bearing the ruler's portrait and name on the obverse and images of their deities on the reverse. Such coins only began to appear in India in the first half of the second century CE during the rule of the Kushan king Kanishka, whose kingdom of Gandhara extended deep into Northern India and who came to be regarded by Chinese Buddhists as a second Ashoka even though his coinage shows him to have patronised a range of Vedic, Zoroastrian and Graeco-Bactrian deities besides Buddhism.

One of these gods was Oesho, a deity largely derived from the proto-Vedic wind god Vayu, who came into his own during the extended rule of King Kanishka's father Vima Kadphises (c. 95–127 CE). Coins from this time show Oesho in several different forms: in aniconic form as a trident to which is attached the blade of a battle-axe, an erect phallus and a *vajra* (thunderbolt); as a naked ithyphallic human figure, holding a trident-cum-battle-axe in one hand and a stylised animal skin in the other; and as a crowned figure clad in a dhoti and accompanied by his vehicle, the bull Nandi – at which point he can definitely be said to be more Shiva than Oesho (see page 211). By the time Kanishka comes to the throne in about 127 CE Shiva has started to be depicted with three faces and four arms, even though still named as Oesho – and still arguably ithyphallic.

Just as Lord Shiva set the pace among the Hindu gods north of the Narmada, so a very similar process took place in the Deccan and worked its way southwards with Lord Shiva made manifest as Shiva linga, the unmistakable human phallus. Nowhere is this more magnificently and puzzlingly displayed than in a tiny Parasurameswara temple at Gudimallam, an otherwise insignificant hamlet lying about 30 kilometres to the south-east of Tirupati

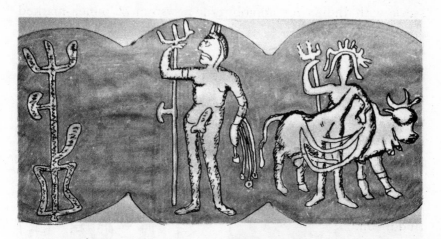

Oesho/Shiva as he appears on three coins of the Kushan ruler Vima
Kadphises, first in aniconic form as a phallic trident, then in human
form with trident, and finally with his bull Nandi.

in southern Andhra Pradesh. This is now a scheduled monument
maintained by the Archaeological Survey of India (ASI) – and
with good cause, because at its heart is the truly remarkable
Gudimallam Shivalinga, rising out of the floor to a height of about
5 feet (1.5 metres), an unmistakably rampant phallus carved in
hard dark stone with the figure of Lord Shiva in warrior pose on
the front (see below).

This quite extraordinary carving, breathtaking in its vigour
and sharpness of detail, may well be the earliest known sculpture
in stone that can be linked indisputably with Shaivism, and on
that score alone it is hugely important. Just about every historian
of Indian art has had his or her say on its dating, beginning with
its discoverer in 1903, the archaeologist and epigraphist T. A.
Gopinatha Rao, who headed Travancore State's Archaeological
Department until his early death in 1919. Rao believed it to date
from the third or second century BCE but was promptly challenged
by many of his contemporaries, with Ananda Coomaraswamy

(Above) The Gudimallam linga, showing in deep relief the figure of Lord
Shiva as a forest-god, photographed
by I. K. Sharma when the base of the
statue was excavated in the 1990s.
(Right) A drawing of the Gudimallam
linga, showing the deity's battle-axe
front and side.

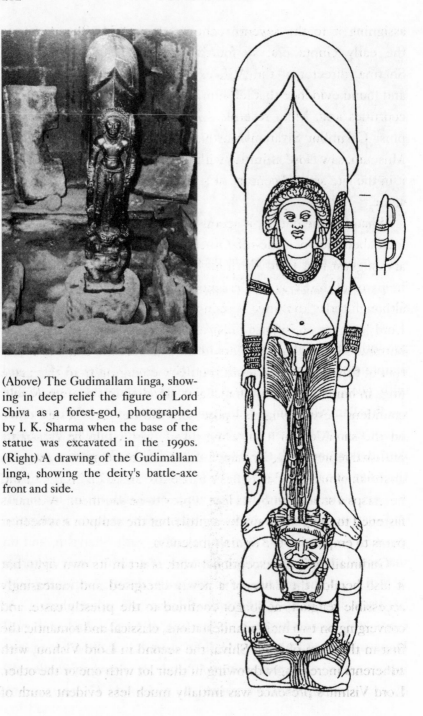

assigning it to the seventh century CE and Dr Bhandarkar to the early Gupta era, so fourth century. In 1994 Karthikeya Sharma, director of the ASI, excavated the base of the statue and found evidence that led him to ascribe it to the third–second centuries BCE. More recently still, the art historian and epigraphist Calambur Sivaramamurthi, long associated with Chennai Museum, saw close affinities with the Bharhut *yaksha*s and placed it in the late second century BCE – a verdict with which I tend to agree.

Whatever the dating, it seems that Gudimallam was not some local aberration or a one-off. Other early examples of priapic statuary[4] suggest that Lord Shiva may initially have been worshipped in parts of India as the essence of male virility and fertility, although today the linga is seen as an aniconic representation of Lord Shiva as an infinite pillar of fire and energy without top or bottom.[5] Gudimallam appears to show the second stage of evolution of this early phallic cult: the deity emerging from that same linga in human shape as a forest god, standing in a supremely self-confident – even arrogant – pose, legs astride, feet pressed down on the shoulders of a kneeling dwarf, who could be Apasmara purusha, representing ignorance and death, but equally a *yaksha* or guardian of nature. He cradles a battle-axe and with his right hand he grasps a small ram by its feet, a prey to be sacrificed. A dhoti is fastened to the god's waist by a girdle but the sculptor has been at pains to emphasise the figure's maleness.

Gudimallam is an exceptional work of art in its own right, but it also heralds the dawn of a newly energised and increasingly accessible religion, no longer confined to the priestly caste, and converging on two main manifestations, classical and romantic: the first in the form of Lord Shiva, the second in Lord Vishnu, with adherents increasingly throwing in their lot with one or the other. Lord Vishnu's presence was initially much less evident south of the Narmada divide but he too begins to assume physical human form at this same time, dramatically coming into his own in a great surge of popular belief that had its beginnings in the Tamil South in the seventh century and spread northwards, replacing Brahminical Vedism with the popular Hinduism that so many millions follow today.

At its heart was the new concept of bhakti ('devotion or piety'), which turned its back on priest-led ritual to embrace personal devotion to a particular deity as the path to salvation. This enabled ordinary men and women to engage in their own ecstatic and even mystical relationship with their chosen deity without priestly intercession – the key word here being *bhagavata*, or 'devotee of the Lord (Bhagavan)', describing that close connection between deity and worshipper. As an aid to bhakti, the so-called agamic texts were introduced, derived from the Sanskrit *agama*, 'what has been handed down'. These were essentially devotional manuals of service that purported to be ancient but were newly written, their core texts being the eighteen *Mahapurana*s – 'the great ancient (writings)' – which prophesied events to come that had already taken place.[6] These played a key role in the propaganda battles for popular support waged between the two rival religious parties that is still being waged today.

This was nothing less than a Hindu revolution, which sidelined the old abstract Vedic deities in favour of younger and more interactive and accessible gods. The two clear winners were Vishnu, along with his ten avatars – extending from the axe-wielding warrior Parashurama to Krishna and Rama and even sometimes the Buddha as the ninth avatar – and Shiva in all his forms. The triumph of these two super-deities was made complete with the absorption of Shakti, the female element, so that the two opposite forces of male and female were joined in union – in the case of

Lord Shiva *devis* ranging from Parvati to Durga by way of Sati, Chamunda and Kali, and in the case of Vishnu his *shakti* Lakshmi, and the much-loved consorts of Rama and Krishna, Sita and Radha. To this we should add Shiva's sons and daughters, beginning with Ganesha and Kartikeya (the god of war, and known to the Tamils as Murugan), but accumulating over time, with the important addition in the South of Ayyappan, to say nothing of all those local folk *devas* and *devis* absorbed into one or other of these two great streams of Hinduism.

This new pantheon had also to take account of the myriad sub-sects and local sects within Shaivism and Vaishnavism, such as the yogis known as Naths or Nathas whose founder, Matsyendranath, was swallowed in the manner of the Biblical Jonah and so overheard the esoteric teachings given by Shiva to his wife Parvati. This rich diversity is what gives Hinduism its extraordinary resilience, its flexible capacity to be all things to all men and women.

Spearheading this great transformation in the Tamil South were two rival movements of missionary saints of Vaishnavism and Shaivism, each championing their deity with the aid of their own agamic texts and supported by an ever-growing pool of writers, poets and musicians using their art to express their devotion and to inspire others. Among the Vaishnavas, bhakti found its most vocal expression in the twelve Alvars ('those immersed in god'), poet-saints drawn from every level of society from Brahmins to Shudras and even including in their number one woman saint, whose devotional hymns helped to create a native Tamil religious literature largely but not wholly free of Sanskrit.

Among the Shaivas the lead came from the sixty-three Nayanars, or 'masters', also known among Tamils as the Arupathu Moovars. These in turn were followed by a second bhakti movement promoted by mostly young celibate monks, many of whom took their lead from the Shaiva reformer Adi Shankara, born in Kaladi in present-day Kerala and said to have been disabled by dwarfism but a man of immense intellect and vigour, of uncertain date but most probably active in the first quarter of the ninth century, and as much vilified within the Buddhist world as 'the enemy of Buddhism' as he is admired by Shaivas for his militant proselytising and for taking on the Buddhists on their own terms and showing them to be wanting.

Despite his physical handicap, Shankara is said to have personally led a *digvijaya* or 'tour of conquest' that took him as far north as Kashmir and Nepal, in the course of which he challenged through debate every opposing philosophy, most obviously Buddhism and Jainism. Having defeated all his opponents, he founded seminaries to promote his *advaita vedanta* teachings, built around the three elements of *shastra* (the scriptures), *yukti* (reason) and *anubhava* (experience). Of these seminaries, the most famous today are the four *matha*s (Hindu colleges or monasteries) established at the four corners of India, each headed by the best and brightest of his army of highly disciplined disciples, each of whom then established their own line of leaders, called Shankaracharyas. The first of the four *matha*s was set up at Sringeri,[7] in the hill-country of Karnataka, the other three being in Puri on the east coast, Dwaraka on the west coast and Badrinath in the Himalayas. Two of the four, Badrinath and Puri, are believed to have been places of Buddhist worship before they were Hindu.[8]

Shankara died at thirty-two years of age, but his movement spread the cult of the Shivalinga allied with *advaita* to every corner of the subcontinent and with such vigour that it has come to be seen by many today as the supreme expression of Hindu spirituality. That this fervour was accompanied by the active persecution of Buddhists, as claimed by the Dalit reformer

Dr Ambedkar and others, is denied by Shankara's present-day followers, who claim that Shankara achieved the expulsion of both Jains and Buddhists from the mainstream simply by defeating them in public debates – albeit debates in which the winner took all, with the loser required to accept either Shankara as guru, banishment, or even, as a third option, suicide by self-immolation.

All the same, there are texts which record the persecution and expulsion of all Buddhists from Kerala by an eighth-century Malayali king named Sudhavana, supposedly at the instigation of an anti-Buddhist Brahman named Kumarila Bhat. The earliest biography of Shankara, *Sankara Digvijaya*, tells the same story, and has King Sudhavana ordering his servants to 'kill all Buddhists from Himalaya to Rameshwaram, even children and the elderly. Whosoever will not kill them, will be killed at my hands.' There are also twelfth-century inscriptions on the walls of a number of Shaiva temples in the districts of Bijapur and Dharwad in Karnataka lauding the anti-Jain activities of three feudatory chiefs of the Western Chalukyas named Ekantada Ramayya, Viruprasa and Vira-Goggideva, the last described as 'a fire to the Jain scriptures' and 'a hunter of the wild beasts in the form of the followers of the Jina'. The temple of Somesvara in Ablur village, for example, contains several sculptured panels with graphic descriptions attached. One shows Ekantada Ramayya smashing a Jain statue and replacing it with a linga, the accompanying inscription reading (in P. B. Desai's reading): 'At this place Ekantada Ramayya breaking the Jaina and setting up the Sivalinga.' A second inscription above another panel is longer: 'This is the place representing how at the temple of the illustrious Brahmeshvara, Ekantada Ramayya laid a wager, at the cost of the Jina of the shrine, of cutting off his head and receiving it back on again. When Sanka-gavunda would not let him destroy the shrine of the Jina, arraying his men and horses against him, Ekantada Ramayya fought and vanquished him and installed the linga.'[9]

And what are we to make of the supposed instance of the massacre of eight thousand Jains in Madurai? According to the Shaiva chronicles, this was perpetrated by a Pandyan king known as Koon Pandiyan, 'the hunchback Pandyan', who had abandoned Shaivism to embrace Jainism but was then restored to his original faith by one of the sixty-three Nayanars, a Shaiva boy saint named Sambandar, acting at the behest of his faithful queen. The Jains first set fire to Sambandar's house, whereupon the saint deflected the fire at the king. The Jains were unable to alleviate the king's suffering, whereas Sambandar not only removed the pain but also cured the king's hunched back. Sambandar and the Jains then engaged in a series of wizardly challenges, from which the Shaiva saint emerged triumphant, whereupon the eight thousand Jains willingly allowed themselves to be impaled on stakes.

This supposed impaling of the Jains was until very recently depicted in frescoes on the walls surrounding the Golden Lily Tank of the Meenakshi Amman temple in Madurai. Yet not a hint of this catastrophic event can be found in any Jain chronicle, and they surely would have had most cause for complaint. The earliest known account of the Jain massacre comes from a twelfth-century Shaiva source, while the (now effaced) Lily Tank fresco dated from the seventeenth century. To me, this seems to be more a case of Shaiva triumphalism than anything else, a way of celebrating the success of Sambandar and his fellow Nayanars over the Jains in Madurai by making out that the Jains killed themselves in their humiliation.

As for Shankara's alleged persecution of Buddhists, the plain facts are that Buddhism was losing popular support long before the advent of Shankara, while he himself was wise enough to learn from Buddhism even as he rejected its central philosophy, so much so that Shankara's more orthodox opponents accused him of spreading Buddhism in the guise of Hinduism, even giving him the epithet *pracchanna bauddha*, or 'Buddhist in disguise'.

Royal patronage was everything, and here the Brahmins held two trump cards. They alone could ensure caste respectability and status, and they alone could provide the seal of sanctification by carrying out their complex rituals and sacrifices, as in the instance of all those royal sacrifices listed on the walls of the Naneghat Cave. Furthermore, the Brahmins had no truck with celibacy and so could hand down their calling from father to son, ensuring continuity and stability. So it was the celibate Jains and the Buddhists who lost out. The increasing withdrawal of royal patronage and public support left the Jains with no option but to rely on their own resources, while many Buddhist monks and nuns retreated to Lanka. Many others, no doubt, did what many of their lay followers must have done, which was to take the easier course of returning to Hinduism.

That many Jain and Buddhist places of worship or retreat became Hindu temples is beyond doubt, but this is more likely to have taken place through simple abandonment rather than forced expulsion. There are scores of places in Kerala that include *palli* as a suffix, which was the original term for a Buddhist *vihara*, which suggests that these were originally Buddhist sites. But then when the first Christians built their churches on the Malabar coast they too used the word *palli*, as did the Muslims in later years. It is simply that *palli* had become the local word for a temple.

That said, the continuing rediscovery of scores of mostly eleventh- and twelfth-century pieces of Buddhist statuary

scattered up and down the Tamil heartland, as recounted earlier, does suggest that in some instances these had been taken
out and dumped, often with the heads decapitated or defaced.
Dr John Samuel, director of the Institute of Asian Studies in
Chennai, has reported on more than 150 Buddhist statues or
parts of such statues found in close proximity to ancient Hindu
temples.[10] In a number of instances Buddha statues too large to
be removed have been converted into Hindu deities or simply
concealed from sight by the building of a wall. According to the
well-known Bengali scholar and archaeologist Dr Nagendranath
Vasu,[11] the great temple of Jagannath at Puri is said to have one
such hidden statue of the Buddha concealed behind a wall of
the shrine to Surya, the existence of which is denied by the
temple authorities, so it is impossible to know if Dr Vasu's
claim was based on anything more than rumour. Enquiries are
not made easier by the fact that this is one of those temples
to which non-Hindus are forbidden entry, although Jains and
Buddhists are now allowed in – provided they can prove Indian
ancestry.

This brings us back to Puri and Jagannath, and those three
curious images of Krishna and his brother and sister that are
annually paraded before the vast crowds of the *ratha yatra*. The
Jagannath temple is the very heart and soul of Puri and Odisha
and its people's beliefs, and the first point to be made about it
is that the temple itself has been attacked and violated perhaps
more often than any other temple in India.[12] By one account it
has been plundered nineteen times, the first by the Rashtrakutas
in about 800 and the last in 1881, when the members of a local
religious cult known as the Alekha or Mahima Dharma raided
the temple and burned its three images in the street.[13] Sixteen
of these raids were led by Muslim generals, for the most part
motivated by politics rather than religious fanaticism. Despite

all these depredations the Jagannath has come through. It is a
survivor.

But what was there in Puri before that first attack in 800?

The Jagannath temple's legendary origins were first set out in
the *Purusottama Mahatmya*, one of many books that make up the
Skanda Purana, the longest of the eighteen Puranas and believed
to have first been assembled in the sixth century CE with later
interpolations. It tells how a king of Kalinga named Indradyumna
got to hear of a deity being worshipped in secret in the forests
by a tribal king named Viswavasu. A Brahmin named Vidyapati
was sent to find this deity but had no success until he won
Viswavasu's confidence by marrying his daughter. The tribal king
then agreed to take the Brahmin to see the deity but insisted that
he wear a blindfold. However, Vidyapati outwitted Viswavasu by
dropping mustard seeds on the way, and when these had grown
into shoots he was able to retrace his footsteps to a cave, where he
found the deity in the form of Neela Madhava, or 'Blue Vishnu'.
On hearing the news, King Indradyumna hurried to the cave to
worship the deity, only to find it gone and the entire area covered
in sand. Deeply disappointed, he began a death fast, as well as
performing the ancient horse sacrifice and building a temple
to Lord Vishnu at Puri. He then had a dream in which Lord
Jagannath appeared and told him to seek out a fragrant-scented
tree on the sea-shore. This he found on the beach at Puri in the
form of the trunk of a *neem* tree, from which he fashioned three
wooden images – Krishna as Jagannath, 'lord of the universe',
his brother Balabhadra and his sister Subhadra – which he duly
installed in his temple.

This myth highlights the possibly tribal and non-Vedic origins
of the deity, its formlessness and the three *murtis* cut from wood
to give that formlessness shape. An engraving of the dressing
of Sri Jagannath published in 1869 (see page 223) shows that

the deity's face is a painted mask dominated by two huge eyes and that the humanoid hands and feet are stuck on to projections from a wooden core, known as *daru*. The Jagannath *daru* is the largest of the three *murti*s, being nearly 6 feet in height, with his arms spanning 12 feet, and so heavy that it takes more than fifty men to lift him. Balabhadra is slightly smaller but still 12 feet from finger-tip to finger-tip, and Subadhra smaller still at 5 feet.

Every twelfth year these three *daru*s are replaced by fresh wood cut from the forest in a complex secret ceremony. As soon as the new mask has been painted on, the three images are treated as living deities. They have their own dedicated staff who wake them, wash them and dress them in a series of outfits and jewellery that are changed as often as eight times a day, with different clothes for every day of the week and special outfits for public dressings, known as *suna besha*, that take place five times a year. Before they are put to bed the images are smeared in sandalwood paste to keep them cool. They are then lodged on a platform in the *garbha griha*, or innermost sanctum of the main temple, from which they are carried out to participate in all the annual festivals. Of these the most important is the annual *ratha yatra* which takes place in June, when they are brought out through the temple's lion gate and placed in their respective chariots, each drawn by long lines of men, to be pulled in procession round the temple and home again.

Similar if less elaborate rituals take place in temples all over India, but what is so strikingly unusual here at Puri is that the three *daru*s have remained deliberately symbolic rather than anthropomorphic. One has to ask why.

One explanation is that the Puri Jagannath was originally a local tribal deity, that these wooden objects echo the original aboriginal worship of wooden totem poles in the forest, and that

An engraving from 1869 showing the wooden core of the Jagannath
daru being dressed by temple attendants.

the myth records a non-tribal ruler winning over the local tribal
peoples by accepting their gods. In support of this theory is the
fact that the *daru*s have to be cut from particular trees display-
ing specific auspicious signs in specific wooded areas, with an
anthill and water nearby and a snake-hole at the foot of the tree,
but no birds nesting or even perching on the tree. Furthermore,
the leading role in the finding and shaping of the *daru*s is
undertaken by the male members of a tribal community called
the Dayitapatis, who are said to be descended from Viswavasu,
the first worshipper of Lord Jagannath. Only these Dayitapatis
are involved in the replacement of the old *daru*s with the new
within the inner temple, the last phase being performed by the
three most senior members of the tribe, who are blindfolded and

their hands bound in cloth. At dead of night the old *daru*s are
then carried out by the Dayitapatis to be buried in their own
cemetery in a ceremony that must not be witnessed by any but
those involved, a prohibition taken so seriously that a black-out is
imposed on the town of Puri for the duration of that night.

But there may also be a very intriguing Buddhist element in
all this. In 1837 James Prinsep, the genius who first translated
the Brahmi script, began a correspondence with George Turnour,
a Ceylon civil servant who was then engaged in translating the
Mahavamsa, or 'Great Chronicle' of Lanka. But Turnour was
also working on a second text, the *Daladawansa* or *Datavamsa*,
'Chronicle of the Tooth', which related how that island's famous
Buddha's tooth had arrived there.[14] It told how after the crema-
tion of the Buddha's remains his right canine tooth was retrieved
from the ashes by a disciple who gave it to Brahmadatta, the
king of Kalinga, who then built a great *chaitya* or prayer-hall in
his capital of Dantapuri, the 'City of the Tooth', and enshrined
the tooth there. This tooth relic was regularly carried in procession around the city, a practice that continued through the
subsequent reigns of Brahmadatta's son and grandson.

Years later a ruler named Guhasiva became king of Kalinga
and expelled his Brahmin ministers. These Brahmins then
went to an all-powerful ruler named Pandu to complain that his
vassal Guhasiva worshipped 'a piece of human bone', whereupon Pandu sent an army to subdue Guhasiva. The tooth was
brought to Pandu, who first threw it into a fire and then, when
it failed to burn, hammered it on an anvil. When that also failed
to destroy the tooth it was thrown into a sewer – whereupon all
sorts of miraculous events occurred which led Pandu to convert
to Buddhism. The tooth was then carried in procession round
Pandu's capital and placed in a great temple built for it. But
the tooth relic's supernatural powers had now become widely

known, leading Pandu's neighbours to make war on him in order to secure it for themselves. He therefore returned the tooth to its rightful owner, King Guhasiva of Kalinga. But now Guhasiva's neighbour, King Kshiradara, desired the tooth, and when he died in battle his sons raised a new army to renew the attack. Fearing for the tooth's safety, Guhasiva arranged for it to be smuggled out of the country by his daughter Hemamala and son-in-law Danta, with Hemamala concealing it in her hair. Having evaded their pursuers, they sailed from the port of Tamralipti to Lanka, where they presented the tooth to King Kittisiri Megha, who built a great temple at his capital Anuradhapura in which the tooth was installed in the year 311 CE.

This was by no means the end of the vicissitudes suffered by Sri Lanka's famous Buddha Tooth,[15] but what concerns us here is that this sacred tooth evidently remained in Dantapuri in Kalinga for several centuries before its removal to Lanka – which raises the question: where was Dantapuri?

One claimant is a small village called Danthavarapuri not far from the coast in the Srikakulam District of northern Odisha. It does indeed have some mud fortifications where excavations by the ASI revealed traces of several ancient wells, possible stupas and various types of early pottery, but not enough to convince that this was the site of the fabled capital of ancient Kalinga.

It was General Cunningham of the ASI who first proposed that Puri was the original site of Dantapuri, and who first suggested that the Jagannath deity may have had its origins in the Buddha's tooth. In examining the Buddhist symbols displayed at Sanchi he noticed that one of the most widespread was the *triratna*, representing the 'three jewels' of Buddhism: the Buddha, his Dharma and the *Sangha*, or Buddhist church (see sketch on page 226). This *triratna*, he observed, was identical in form to the three *daru*s representing Jagannath, Balabhadra

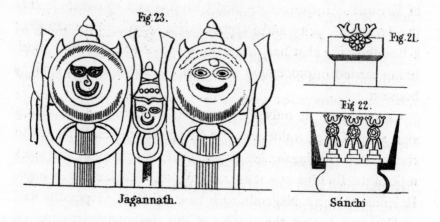

Fig. 23.   Fig. 21.   Fig. 22.

Jagannath.   Sánchi

The three *darus* worshipped at the Jagannath temple at Puri (left)
compared to the Buddhist *triratna* ('three jewels') symbols carved on
the pillars of the Great Stupa at Sanchi (right).

and Subhadra at Puri.[16] Furthermore, wrote Cunningham, 'these
same rude [i.e. crude] Jagannath figures are used in all the native
almanacs of Mathura Benaras as the representative of Buddha
in the Budha Avatar of Vishnu.' All this, Cunningham went on,
'shows in the clearest and most unequivocal manner the absolute identity of the holy Brahmanical Jagannath with the ancient
Buddhist triad'.

So far, so much wishful thinking, but Cunningham was on
firmer ground when he drew attention to the *ratha yatra* procession at Puri, which he regarded has having its origins in the
Buddhist custom of annually parading Buddha relics in a *ratha*.
There was also the fact that all the caste prohibitions which
were then in force in Cunningham's time were lifted during the
festival, which he saw as a sop to the previously Buddhist lower
castes. Finally, there was what Cunningham called 'the belief
that the image [the Jagannath *daru*] contains the relics or bones

of Krishna'. All these facts, led Cunningham to conclude that the Jagannath deity and its *ratha yatra* were a continuation of a Buddhist rite that had originally involved the Buddha's tooth being carried in procession round the Buddhist temple built to house it.

Cunningham, it must be said, had something of an obsession about Greek influences and Buddhist origins. Even so, his theory that the Jagannath temple had its origins in the tooth relic of the Buddha was supported by other scholars, for example Rajendralal Mitra, Nagendranath Vasu and T. A. Gopinatha Rao.

The fact is that the origins of the Jagannath trimurti are wreathed in unfathomable mystery, so perhaps the safest conclusion to draw is that the Jagannath temple with its triple *darus* provides a classic example of how Hinduism came to an accommodation with Buddhism, Jainism and the primal Dravidian gods.

Detail of an eighteenth-century map of India drawn in 1715 to show the empire of the Great Mogul, referring to the Mughal Empire. Shown on the Coromandel coast are the Dutch trading ports of Negapatan (Nagapattinam) and Pellicate (Pulicat), and the EICo's increasingly important 'factories' at Fort St George (afterwards Madras and now Chennai), and Fort St David at Cuddalore (wrongly marked as 'Fort St Davies'), which became the headquarters of the EICo in South India in 1723, only to be twice captured by the French, with their base at Pondicherry, marked 'Pondicheri'.

8

CHOLAMANDALAM INTO COROMANDEL

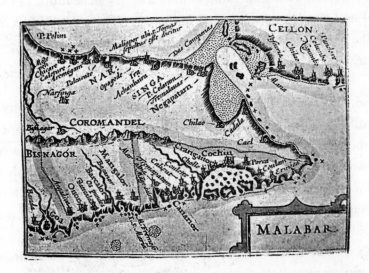

A miniature map of the Malabar and Coromandel coasts drawn by the Flemish cartographer Petrus Bestius of Amsterdam, from *Tabularum geographicarum contractarum* (1606). This was based on an earlier map made in 1580 when the coastal trade was still under the control of the Portuguese.

The word Coromandel makes its first appearance on Portuguese maps at the start of the sixteenth century. It was then picked up in quick succession by the Dutch, the French, the Danes and the English. Like so many Indian words that crept into the English language from late-Elizabethan times onwards, it is a corruption.

That quintessential portmanteau of Anglo-Indian words and their derivations *Hobson-Jobson* has this to say about it:

> **COROMANDEL**, n.p. A name which has been long applied by Europeans to the Northern Tamil Country, or (more comprehensively) to the eastern coast of the Peninsula of India from Point Calimere to the mouth of the Kistna, sometimes to Orissa ... The name is in fact *Choramandala*, the Realm of Chora; this being the Tamil form of the very ancient title of the Tamil Kings who reigned at Tanjore ... The name occurs in the forms *Cholamandalam* or *Solamandalam* on the great temple inscription of Tanjore.

So Coromandel takes its name from the ancient dynasty of Tamil rulers known as the Cholas. That word 'Chola' first appears on rock inscriptions that can be accurately dated to within a year or two either side of 260 BCE, carved by order of Emperor Ashoka, and it continues to reappear century after century on the walls and monuments of the great temple cities of Tamil country, right up to a final appearance in the year 1279 CE.

As to who first coined the word Coromandel, a young Italian adventurer from Bologna named Ludovico di Varthema has a good claim. If Ludovico is remembered at all today it is because he was the first non-Muslim European to visit Mecca, and to live to tell the tale. However, what makes Ludovico and his *Itinerario* – first published in Rome in 1510 and subsequently in English in 1577 – special and so unusual for the time is that the author's main concern was not to enrich himself through trading in spices or slaves, or to boast about slaying idolators or saving their souls for Christ. He travelled for travel's sake, filled, in his own words, with 'a desire to behold the various kingdoms of the world ... with my own eyes'. He goes on: 'Longing for novelty as a thirsty man longs for fresh water, I departed from these places as being well known to all ... Wherefore spreading our sails on a favourable wind, and having implored the Divine aid, we committed ourselves to the sea.'[1]

In December 1502 Ludovico took ship from Venice bound for Egypt and beyond. In Damascus he enrolled as a supposed Mamluk slave soldier under the name of Yunas, or Jonah, and in this disguise served as an escort on a Hajj pilgrimage caravan to Medina and Mecca. In Aden he was imprisoned as a Christian spy and only secured his release by feigning madness. After months wandering around the Persian Gulf he met an Iranian merchant named Cazazioner (probably Khwaja Junair) who also wanted to see the world. So in the autumn of 1504 Ludovico and Cazazioner together sailed across the Arabian Sea to the Malabar coast – only to find themselves in a hornets' nest.

The Arabs had already been trading up and down the Malabar coast for centuries, and had benefited mightily from both their mastery of the sea lanes between India and the Mediterranean world and their monopoly of the spectacularly profitable spice trade. Both these prizes were now in the process of being wrested from Arab hands by a younger and far more truculent power, the Portuguese, under the command of the self-proclaimed Viceroy of Goa. This transfer of power was taking place with bewildering speed, all stemming from that fatal moment on 22 April 1498 when an elderly Omani named Shaykh Ahmed ibn Majid climbed aboard Vasco da Gama's *San Gabriel*, flagship of the First India Armada, in the East African port of Melinde. This was an exceptional stroke of luck for da Gama because ibn Majid happened to be the greatest navigator of the age. He came from a long line of master mariners originally from eastern Oman who had made names for themselves as pilots 'of the two coasts' (meaning the east coast of Africa and the west coast of India) and he was already famous as the author of two books on seamanship that were to remain in use for centuries, so much so that when in 1854 the Victorian explorer Richard Burton embarked in a dhow in the Gulf of Aden he noted that the seaman 'repeated the Fatiha-prayer in honour of Shaykh Majid, inventor of the mariner's compass'.[2]

Arab chroniclers claimed that Vasco da Gama had got ibn Majid to pilot his little fleet of three caravels eastwards to India by getting him drunk. The more likely truth is that within minutes of meeting him and seeing his map the Portuguese admiral had offered ibn Majid a fee he could not refuse. Within days the Omani was piloting da Gama's fleet on the course that brought them to a safe anchorage off 'the most noble and rich city of Calicut [Kozhikode]'. This was now the busiest entrepot in Asia and the most important staging post in the sea route between China, Africa and the Mediterranean world.

Having learned how to make the sea crossing, da Gama then set about driving a wedge between the Arabs and the local Indian ruler, known by the hereditary title of *Samoothri*, or 'one who has the sea as his border', which the Portuguese translated as Zamorin. Da Gama and his fellow Portuguese had been led to believe that the Zamorin, along with his subjects, was a Christian, and for some weeks they managed to persuade themselves that this was so, a fantasy helped along by their loathing of those they called 'Moors' – a hatred born of long memories of the Iberian peninsula under Muslim rule. The Zamorin was in fact a Hindu of the powerful Eradi Nair community, with an army of robust Nair warriors at his back, but having no wish to risk his good relations with the Arabs he played safe, leaving da Gama with no option but to leave India virtually empty-handed.

But the Portuguese now had the key to the India passage. They returned with more ships, greater firepower and better gifts, so that when the so-called Second India Armada reached Calicut in September 1500 its admiral was able to offer the Zamorin the support of his fighting ships in his ongoing wars with his rivals up and down the coast: Cambay to the north and Cochin to the south. This secured the Portuguese a commercial treaty that allowed them to set up in Calicut a *feitoria*, or trading post – a word soon anglicised into 'factory'. As so often in Indian history, rivalries between one kingdom and another allowed a third power to move in to its advantage – a feature of military expansion since time immemorial which for some reason has come to be seen in India as a peculiarly British vice, under the phrase 'divide and rule'.

Such military alliances nearly always end in tears for the weaker party, and so it was here. The Portuguese seized an Arab ship being loaded with spices bound for Jeddah and the Arabs retaliated by attacking the Portuguese factory. Blaming the Zamorin for allowing the massacre that followed, the Portuguese brought all the firepower of their ships to bear on his town, killing hundreds and setting the pattern for what followed.

On 3 October 1502 Vasco da Gama, now admiral of what would become known as the notorious Fourth India Armada, came across the merchant ship *Mirim*, with several hundred Muslim pilgrims aboard. His hatred of Moors appears to us now as bordering on the psychopathic, yet it seems to have been shared by many of his Portuguese compatriots. How else to explain the gratuitous cruelty they displayed at every opportunity hereafter, beginning with that first encounter at sea when the *Mirim* was looted, primed with gunpowder and set ablaze? Twenty children were spared for conversion to Christianity.

Vasco da Gama next anchored his fleet before the harbour of Calicut and ordered the Zamorin to expel the Moors. When he refused, da Gama bombarded the city with his cannons for two days. To reinforce his message, several hundred captured Muslim seamen were hanged from the yardarms of da Gama's nineteen vessels – although not before their hands, ears and noses had been cut off. A boatload of these off-cuts were then sent to the Zamorin with the instruction that he should make a *karil* out of them.

That word *karil*, incidentally, marks the first appearance in Western lexicography of the Tamil *kari*, meaning a 'sauce', out of which the ubiquitous word 'curry' evolved – part of a scarcely perceived but dramatic cultural change for which we must thank, or curse, the Portuguese, for it was they who within a century and a half had transformed the South Indian diet into 'Madras Curry' and variations thereof by introducing from the New World potatoes, tomatoes, maize, peanuts, capsicum peppers and, above all, the fiery chilli, while at the same time challenging the Brahminical ban on onions, garlic and all root vegetables pulled from the earth!

Da Gama continued as he had begun, with further acts of what can only be described as terrorism, designed to send shock waves up and down the coast. Indian rulers and traders alike learned to deal with the Moors at their peril, and when shipping resumed along the coast it was by authority of the Portuguese and the Portuguese only.

The Portuguese acted in the conviction that theirs was the only true religion and that they had a duty to extend its blessings to all, convictions held with equal passion by the people they saw as their chief enemy, the Arabs or Moors. What made the difference in South India was that the Portuguese brought with them leadership and unity of purpose, encapsulated in their mission statement: 'Christians and spices'. Their actual numbers in India throughout the sixteenth century were tiny, but that unity, combined with European advances in ship-building, armaments and military training, was enough to destroy the Arab sea-trade and win them the secure enclave of Goa, where they remained in authority even after Britain had withdrawn from India.

The era of European colonialism that the Portuguese initiated in India with such violence was not in itself exceptional. What set the Europeans apart was not that their behaviour was any worse than what had gone before but that their imperialism – in essence, the exploitation of one people by another – was applied with an efficiency not seen since the days of the Romans, plus superior firepower, as noted by Hilaire Belloc in a famous couplet:

> *Whatever happens, we have got*
> *The Maxim gun, and they have not.*

So by the time Ludovico di Varthema and his friend Cazazioner arrived at Calicut in January 1505 Portuguese carracks and caravels were busy leapfrogging down the Malabar coast in their quest for the 'five glorious spices' of the Indies: pepper, cinnamon, cloves, nutmeg and mace. But on rounding the tip of the peninsula they found their progress up and along India's eastern coast blocked – by an 18-mile chain of rocks and sandbanks linking the island of Lanka to the Indian mainland.

This was the Iramar Palam, or 'Bridge of Rama', the geomorphic umbilical cord that binds island and subcontinent together whether their respective inhabitants like it or not. To this day the Bridge of Rama offers great scope for one set of believers who claim that satellite images prove it to have been built by Lord Rama ten thousand years ago, and another who call the isthmus Al-jeseer Aadham, or 'Adam's Bridge', and are convinced it was built by the giant Adam after his exile from the Garden of Eden.

Until 1480 the Bridge of Rama was indeed a fairly solid land-bridge, but in that year a particularly ferocious cyclone struck the coast and gouged a trough across the isthmus's central section, so creating a channel deep enough for shallow-draught coastal craft to slip through in calm weather, though it remained too risky for bulkier sea-going vessels. This meant that when the Portuguese navigators first came that way they had little option but to turn about and head south, which led them to the natural shelter that became the harbour of Colombo. So it came about that Lanka fell to the Portuguese, who then turned their attentions to the East Indies. It also meant that India's eastern seaboard, the Coromandel coast, was left almost unscathed for later European maritime powers to exploit.

Thanks to the havoc wrought by the Portuguese, Ludovico and his Persian friend were forbidden to sell the merchandise they had brought with them to Calicut. They had no option but to move on. 'And so we departed,' writes Ludovico, 'and made our road by a river, which is the most beautiful I ever saw, and arrived at a city which is called Cacalon [modern Kumarakom]' – a description that will resonate with anyone who has ever travelled by boat along the palm-fringed backwaters of Kerala. They returned to the coast at Colon – modern Quilon (Kollam) – only to find the local raja besieged by his enemies. So they kept on moving, rounding the southern cape by boat to reach the port of Chail, modern Tuticorin (Thuthukodi), which now houses a major container port but was then the centre of a thriving pearl fishing industry very much under the thumb of a wealthy Arab trader.

In order to continue their journey up the coast they hired a vessel known locally as a *ciampana*, which from Ludovico's description – 'they are flat-bottomed, and require little water and carry much goods' – must have been something akin to a Chinese sampan. It was seaworthy enough to get the travellers safely through the Bridge of Rama, despite 'great peril because there are many shoals and rocks there'. They then sailed on up the east coast until they came to 'a city which is called Cioromandel', misapplied by Ludovico to the ancient sea-port of Nagapattinam, on the delta of the Cauvery (Kaveri) River, rather than the region. 'The city is very large,' he writes in his *Itinerario*. 'They gather a great quantity of rice, and it is the route to very large countries. There are many Moorish merchants here who go and come for their merchandise. No spices of any description grow here, but plenty of fruits.'

From Nagapattinam the two travellers sailed first to Ceylon (now Sri Lanka), and then back up the Indian coast to Bengal before continuing on to Burma and beyond. They spent the early summer of 1505 moving from one spice island to another before turning back with a rich cargo of spices and silks. At Malacca they chartered a large vessel which Ludovico terms a *giuncu* – in other words, a junk, showing the continuing influence of the China trade – and in June they sailed back across the Bay of Bengal to 'the said city of Cioromandel'.

Ludovico was now worried that his Muslim disguise had been penetrated. He looked for an opportunity to escape, and when he and Cazazioner returned by sea to Calicut, Ludovico seized the chance to desert his friend and join the Portuguese.

In March 1506 Ludovico fought alongside his new allies in a sea-battle off Cannanore (Kannur) in which eleven Portuguese ships dispersed 209 enemy vessels of the Zamorin of Calicut. He was then caught up in the four-month siege of Cannanore, in which the firepower of the Portuguese again made the difference, enabling them to repulse the assaults of thousands of Nair warriors. It is recorded that what saved the garrison from starvation at a critical point of the siege was a mass of lobsters washed ashore, taken as a sign that God was on their side. Ludovico's courage in battle won him a knighthood, after which he worked for the

Portuguese as a 'factor', or trader, in Cochin for three years before returning to Europe.

When Ludovico di Varthema's *Itinerario* was published in Rome in 1510 every copy was snapped up. Up to that point the Portuguese had successfully guarded the trade secrets of their navigation in the Indies. Thanks in part to Ludovico's descriptions of India's eastern seaboard, the coast of Coromandel now became a target for Portugal's maritime rivals: the Dutch, Danes, French and English. It was the Dutch, through the Vereenigde Oost-Indische Compagnie (VOC), or the Dutch East Indies Company, who went on to show the Portuguese how to trade without scruples. In 1609 they captured the Portuguese fort at Pulicat, which stands at the mouth of the Pulicat lagoon, today a placid bird sanctuary.

'*Negapatnam opde kust van Choromandel*'. Dutch ships off their new enclave of Nagapattinam, having just ousted the Portuguese. Engraving from Wouter Schouten's *Oost-Indische Voyagie*, first published in 1676.

Pulicat subsequently became the headquarters of the VOC for its trading operations up and down the Coromandel coast, with slaving as a sideline. Between 1621 and 1665, VOC ships transported 38,441 slaves from the Coromandel coast, chiefly through Pulicat, for sale to Dutch plantations in Batavia, an activity done with the connivance of local rulers and helped along by several local famines.[3] By such means the VOC became the wealthiest private company the world had ever seen, paying 40 per cent dividends to its shareholders in Amsterdam – which may help to explain why the Dutch named their fort at Pulicat Guelderland.

In 1690 the VOC shifted its Coromandel headquarters from Pulicat to Nagapattinam, which remained under the control of the VOC until 1781, when it fell to the East India Company (EICo) following two sea-battles fought directly offshore between two evenly matched fleets, the British and the French.

When Ludovico di Varthema stepped ashore at Nagapattinam in 1505 he had unknowingly arrived in what had been the Chola heartland for fifteen hundred years and more. Nagapattinam stands at the mouth of the Kollidam, the southern channel of the Cauvery River, and it was here within this fecund triangle of silt threaded with waterways that the Chola kings established their temple capitals: initially, inland at Uraiyur; then on the coast at Kaveripattinam (today Poompuhar); later still in Thanjavur; and then, as their territories continued to expand, at a new site further north which the ruler of the day named Gangaikondacholapuram – 'the city of the Chola who took the Ganges' – which became their fourth and last capital.

No new visitor to these parts should even think of travelling between Thanjavur and Gangaikondacholapuram without stopping halfway to admire the Nageshwaram temple, one of six major Shiva temples in the town of Kumbakonam. For the first-time visitor it is all too easy to get what my wife and I used to call 'templed out' – that is to say, exhausted by these temple cities. The immensity of their ambition and the sheer abundance of artistic endeavour and detail that has gone into each one over the course of centuries tend to overwhelm; all of them being dominated by one or more gigantic entrance gates in the form of pyramidal *gopuram*s built not just to represent a multiplicity of gods and attendants climbing up to the heavens but also, and very deliberately, to overawe. One can easily come away defeated, so newcomers would do well to be selective, whatever the guide or guidebooks might say – or risk suffering the tourist's version of post-traumatic stress.

But Nageshwaram matters, because this is where Chola patronage on the grand scale kicked off, in the last decade of the ninth century or the early years of the tenth century, with much of that patronage coming from the Chola queens.

This is made clear in the majestic array of stone statuary that line the Nageshwaram temple walls, and its long, dark corridors, each figure set in niches and just short of life-size. The local guides may tell you that these represent various gods and goddesses. Some of them do, but some are also portraits in stone of various members of the royal house, along with their spiritual teachers and the occasional minister or two, all donors to the temple.

There is something quite magical about these figures, with their languorous, impossibly elongated limbs, wasp waists and hourglass figures, and their serene gaze, that sets them apart from everything that has gone before. They can only have been the work of one or more master-carvers in stone, perhaps a school of sculptors led by some local unsung Michelangelo or Praxiteles. One of the most beguiling of these statues is said to represent Lord Rama's wife Sita, but without any supporting evidence. A less orthodox view is that she is a portrait in stone of a remarkable Chola queen: Sembiyan Mahadevi.

Each of the Chola kings gave themselves grandiose and identifiable names and titles, but their royal wives had to be content with the single generic title of Sembiyan Mahadevi, 'Great Queen of the Cholas' – or, if they were very lucky and bore a son who went on to rule, the further title of 'The queen who had the good fortune to bear King So-and-so'. As a result it is very hard today to distinguish one queen from another whenever their names are set down on dedicatory or donative inscriptions. However, there was one particular Chola queen whose piety, strength of character and, above all, longevity ensured that she would not be forgotten: the Sembiyan Mahadevi who was also known as 'The queen who had the fortune to bear Uttama Chola Deva [Raja Paratanka II]', and who further distinguished herself from her peers by describing herself as 'The daughter of Mala-Peruanadigal'.

By triangulating these three titles, we can identify this exceptional lady as the queen of the Chola ruler who conquered Lanka in 925 CE and the grandmother of the formidable and formidably named Rajaraja ('king of kings'), which places her as living from about 900 to 980. For more than six decades this Sembiyan Mahadevi was a dominant figure in tenth-century South India, not least as a royal patron of temple-building and donor of bronze images and jewellery. Not only was she extremely pious and extremely wealthy, she was also sufficiently strong to be able to impose her will on her husband, their son and possibly her grandson too, to say nothing of all those Brahmins at court who acted as the ruler's advisers.

The Imperial Cholas have been credited with reviving the ancient South Indian craft of casting in bronze – more properly, in copper alloy – using the so-called 'lost-wax process', which in earlier times seems to have been the preserve of the Buddhists. Our particular queen Sembiyan Mahadevi appears to have been

closely involved in this revival, which her descendants further
refined and took to even greater heights of artistry.

One of the finest surviving examples of tenth-century Chola
copper alloy casting in its first phase is now in the Freer Gallery
of Art in Washington (see page 243). This metre-high statuette
of the goddess Parvati was installed during the queen's lifetime
and under her aegis in the Shiva temple of Kailasanatha Svamin,
a relatively modest temple that she herself built in a new village
named after her near Nagapattinam – perhaps no coincidence,
since Nagapattinam was already the centre of a copper alloy
casting industry dedicated to producing Buddhist images. This
particular statuette would originally have stood alongside her
partner Lord Shiva as well as other images of the temple's *Sapta
Maadhaka* – the seven goddesses Brahmi, Maheshwari, Cowmaari,
Vaishnavi, Varahi, Indrani and Chamundi – all of them subsequently buried for their protection and then lost for centuries in a
pattern repeated many times over at other Chola temples.

One of the recovered images was the Parvati bronze. Some
inspired detective work by the distinguished art historian Vidya
Dehejia has all but proved that this exquisite work of art, acquired
by an American collector back in the 1920s in somewhat shadowy
circumstances, is nothing less than a representation of the great
queen Sembiyan Mahadevi herself, albeit in the form of Lord
Shiva's consort Parvati. Stylised rather than natural, wasp-waisted
with unmistakably sensuous hips swaying in the stance known as
tribhanga or 'triple-bent', the figure's face shows some individual
features but is sufficiently mannered to be taken for a goddess, so
blurring the lines between what was royal and what was divine.
Her elongated left hand is lowered by her side with fingers pointing
downward in the *varada mudra*, a gesture that signifies a promise
to grant the devotee's wishes. Her right hand is raised in order to
grasp a (now missing) flower, most probably a lotus or blue lily.

Two possible portraits of a powerful and pious Chola queen. (Above, left) A Chola 'bronze' now identified as the tenth-century Chola queen Sembiyan Mayadevi, a statuette which probably came from her temple of Kailasanatha Svamin in the village named after her. (Above, right) One of the near life-size female figures set in niches in the walls of the Nageshwaram temple at Kumbakonam, dedicated to Shiva in the form of Nageshwara, the serpent-king.

In presenting herself to her devotees both as queen of the Cholas and (by implication) as consort to Lord Shiva, Sembiyan Mahadevi crossed the demarcation line between divinity and royalty, as if to make it clear that she herself should be regarded as quasi-divine. This was very much in accord with the Imperial Cholas' promotion of themselves as all-conquering kings or *chakravartin*, an ancient Sanskrit word that has its roots in the wheeled *chakra* and the chariot wheels of a conqueror that roll in every direction without meeting any resistance. Initially the Cholas had simply followed earlier models, taking their cue from the Gupta dynasty of kings who had earlier dominated Northern India and who had also seen themselves as all-powerful *chakravartin*. But precisely at the time of Sembiyan Mahadevi the Cholas dramatically upped the stakes by identifying themselves more intimately with Lord Shiva – and representing him in a striking and dramatic new form.

This leads us to another of the many temples with which our Chola queen Sembiyan Mahadevi was closely associated, albeit as restorer rather than builder, the Thillai Nataraja temple at Chidambaram, often spoken of by Tamil followers of Lord Shiva as the Golden Temple on account of its gilded roof – but also because of its supposed significance as the centre of the universe as occupied by Lord Shiva in the role of cosmic destroyer and recreator.

Chidambaram marks the penultimate step in the Cholas' northward advance towards the borders of Andhra, sited beside the most northerly of the many channels of the Cauvery River. What distinguishes this particular Shiva temple from virtually every other Shiva temple in India is its *murti*, the image of the deity that provides the main focus of worship. In the central shrine of virtually every Shiva temple you find a stone linga, a representation of the god in aniconic form which, as stated earlier, some

The great tank of the Nataraja temple of Chidambaram, a supreme example of Chola art and architecture spread over many centuries, as engraved by an unknown artist in the 1870s.

Hindus consider an emblem of generative power while others argue that it is no more than a symbol of the formless Lord Shiva. Either way, the linga is the prime image of Shaivism. But here at Chidambaram the presiding deity is Lord Shiva in anthropomorphic form, transformed through the malleable medium of copper alloy into a vibrant, free-standing male dancer. He is Kuttuperumal, the 'Lord of the Dance', or Adavallan, 'Master of the Dance', both derived from the same Tamil source: *Koothu*, dance (noun) and *aadu*, to dance (verb). In this form he is a manifestation of Shiva better known outside Tamil Nadu and Kerala in its Sanskrit form as *Nataraja*.

Today we take Shiva Nataraja, the cosmic dancer, for granted, because we have seen him so often in books, brochures and posters. But imagine how overwhelming, if not downright shocking, this new manifestation of Lord Shiva must have appeared when first shown to the public in procession, as a golden dancer with one foot raised and hair streaming across the firmament – an image so radical and so revolutionary that it could only have been made with powerful royal backing.

This was part of the repositioning of Lord Shiva by his royal devotees as supreme among the gods: Shiva reinterpreted as cosmic mover and shaker, in which role he performs the *tandavam* or *tandava ananda*, the divine dance, in order to create, maintain and destroy the universe in one cosmic cycle after another. Ringed by a circle of fire, the lord of yogis treads on the recumbent figure of Muyalakan (known outside Tamil Nadu as Apasmara), the dwarf demon of arrogance and ignorance. In his right upper hand he shakes his double-sided yogic drum, the *damaru*, to mark the passing of time, in his left he holds fire, symbolising the dissolving of the world. With one open hand on his left he protects humanity while the other lower hand out-stretched offers solace. In his headdress is a skull, representing both death and time. Entangled in his hair is the goddess Ganga, caught in Shiva's locks in her descent from heaven to water the earth.

The devotee who worshipped Shiva as Nataraja would not have missed the link between the cosmic-encompassing god and his royal representative on earth. Here was a manifestation fit for a dynasty of empire-makers and wheel-turning *chakravartin*.

This brazen manifestation of Lord Shiva as cosmic dancer took off in Tamil country in the ninth century and very quickly spread throughout the South. But it was not entirely original, being more in the nature of the apotheosis of a new way of representing Lord Shiva that had first appeared in stone under the aegis of the kings of two quite distinct Kannada-speaking dynasties of the western Deccan: the Early Chalukyas and the Rashtrakutas.

(Above, left) One of the earliest known Nataraja 'bronzes', possibly from the ninth century CE. It was long assumed to be Chola but recent analysis of its metal has now led to it being considered Pallavan in origin. (Above, right) A panel from the rock-cut Shiva temple on Elephanta Island, showing an early carving of Shiva as Nataraja. Detail from a stereoscopic photograph by James Ricalton, 1903. (Below) Dressed bronzes of Shiva Nataraja and his consort Shivakami carried in procession in a portable *mandapa*, or pillared pavilion, accompanied by priests bearing flowers and devotees carrying symbols of royalty in the form of parasols, fly-whisks and pennants. A pen and wash drawing probably from Trichy, c. 1820.

I made passing reference to the Early Chalukyas in Chapter 6 as enemies of the Pallavas. They first appeared in the middle of the sixth century to challenge the Brahmin Kadambas, who themselves have a claim to be founders of Karnataka as a distinct Kannada-speaking region with its own identity. These Chalukyas were most probably a hill tribe and they made a secure homeland for themselves in the mountains of the Western Ghats in an upper stretch of the Malapraha, one of the highest tributaries of the Krishna River, with their capital at Vatami (today Badami), where the town nestles under a wall of cliffs topped by a fortress. It was here on the steep escarpment between the town and the fort that the Early Chalukyas followed Buddhist example by digging into the yellow sandstone to create three rock-cut caves, each following the well-established pattern of a pillared verandah at the front that opened into a square chamber supported by more pillars.

The first of these caves, Cave 1, was dedicated to Lord Shiva, and of particular interest to us here because of the carving on the wall immediately to the right as you enter. At 5 feet in height and breadth, it is modest in comparison to what came slightly later at the far more ambitious rock-cut Shiva temple on Elephanta Island in Bombay Harbour, but it is generally considered to be the earliest portrayal of Shiva as Nataraja – because he is quite clearly dancing, with two arms held out in front and turned in at the elbows, the right hand turned outward with palm exposed, the left turned down and inward, and one foot poised on its toes, as if about to be dance in the posture of *ghurnita* or 'thinking' found in the Indian classic dance form known as Bharatnatyam that originated in the temples of South India. But there are more hands too, eighteen in all, arranged in a semi-circular fan around his body to suggest both multiplicity and motion, because this is the cosmic cycle.

Also to be found in the same chamber is another bas-relief

which is literally half Shiva and half Vishnu, in the fused composite known as Harihara. This rather nicely sets the scene for the second cave to be built, cut into the stone just above the first. This is largely given over to Lord Vishnu, as indeed is the third cave, Cave 3. This is the last, largest and most elaborately decorated of the three and it is the only one to carry a dated inscription, which names its consecration as taking place on the day of the full moon on the local calendar equivalent of 1 November 578.[4] This places it in the reign of the second of the Chalukya kings, Kirtivarman, which suggests that it was his successor Pulakeshin who was the Shiva-worshipping builder of Cave 1 and its prototype Nataraja.

From Badami, this prototype Lord of the Dance seems to have moved north, to the Ellora Caves and Elephanta. However, the later Early Chalukyas under the most successful of their rulers, the illustrious Vikramaditya II, avenged his forefathers by defeating their ancient enemies the Pallavas and taking over their capital at Kanchipuram, where he recorded his victory in Kannada on a pillar in the main hall of its Kailasanatha temple, dated to the year 732. A second Chalukyan incursion followed in 744, so presumably it was at this time that the concept of Shiva Nataraja migrated south to take root in Pallava country.

Recent studies have shown that the Shiva Nataraja's transmogrification from stone into metal may not have taken place under the Cholas, as previously thought, but by their southern vassals, the now weakened Pallavas. This is not to deny the Cholas credit for taking over this casting technique from the Pallavas and raising it to heights of perfection previously unknown in India, resulting in some of the most breathtaking works of religious art ever created. These Chola Natarajas were made to be seen. Although installed in the dark recesses of temples they were brought out daily and regularly conveyed in procession through the surrounding streets to the sound of music and drum. It can be argued that the elevation of Lord Shiva by his followers in the Tamil South to a position of supremacy within the Hindu pantheon went hand in hand with the promotion of Shiva Nataraja under the Cholas as the very embodiment of Chola supremacy, no longer frenzied as in the earlier stone carvings but as a calm, controlling ruler at the centre of a whirling cosmos.

Shiva Nataraja as we know him today owes a lot to the efforts of two early promoters of Indian art: the British art historian Ernest Havell, who first came out to India in 1884 to manage the Madras School of Art, and the Ceylon-born Ananda Coomaraswamy, a Brahmin scholar, art historian and Tamil nationalist who scandalised his contemporaries by marrying a succession of English, American and Argentinian wives but nevertheless made it his life's mission to educate Westerners about Indian art in general and Tamil art in particular.

After the break-up of the EICo in 1858 all the artworks in the Company's museum in Leadenhall Street had been divided between the British Museum and the Victoria and Albert Museum (V&A). According to the first official handbook to the V&A's Indian section, the Indian sculptures so acquired were without artistic merit and, for the most part, 'puerile and detestable'. The attitudes of British historians of India such as Vincent Smith, author of the first edition of *The Oxford History of India*, published in 1904, were equally dismissive – unless, of course, that art was perceived to have been influenced by Greek aesthetics.

Havell challenged these prejudices in his book *Indian Sculpture and Painting*, published in 1908. 'Indian art is essentially idealistic, mystic, symbolic and transcendental,' he wrote. 'I hope I have succeeded in showing that the Indian ideal is not, as archaeologists call it, a decadent and degenerate copy of a Graeco-Roman prototype; that Indian fine art is not, as an Anglo-Indian critic puts it, a form of artistic cretinism, but an opening into a new world of aesthetic thought, full of the deepest interest, and worthy of the study of all Western artists.'

According to Havell, one of the finest examples of Hindu sculpture was to be found in the Madras Museum. It was a Chola bronze of Shiva as Nataraja, 'remarkable, not only for extraordinary technical and decorative skill, but for the consummate art with which the abstract ideas of Hindu philosophy are realised ... It is wonderful how the movement of this bronze, in all its seeming naiveté, embodies the mystic ideal of divine ecstasy.'

Two years later Havell, Coomaraswamy and other like-minded individuals in England joined together to form the Indian Society, with the aim of promoting Indian art in Britain. Coomaraswamy then entered the debate with a now-famous essay, subsequently republished many times over, in *The Dance of Siva: Essays on Indian Art and Culture*, in which he proclaimed the best of Indian art to be universal. 'I do not mean to say,' he wrote,

> that the most profound interpretation of Śiva's dance was present in the minds of those who first danced in frantic, and perhaps intoxicated energy, in honour of the pre-Aryan hill-god, afterwards merged in Śiva. A great motif in religion or art, any great symbol, becomes all things to all men; age after age it yields to all men such treasures as they find in their own hearts. Whatever the origins of Śiva's dance, it became in time the clearest image of the *activity* of God which any art or religion can boast of.

In 2004 a gift from the Government of India was unveiled at CERN, the European Centre for Research in Particle Physics in Geneva, home of the proton-busting Hadron Collider. It was a 2-metre-tall statue of the Lord of the Dance, a quintessentially Tamil creation now widely regarded as the very image of Hindu India.

*

It is all too easy to get bogged down in Indian history as a multiplicity of dynasties of ruling kings come and go, and to end up with a bewildering list of names that mean very little and bring no sense of perspective. Sacrifices have to be made, so the reader must forgive me if I fail to give other dynasties of the western Deccan their due; for example, the Kalachuris, whose Shaiva king Krishnaraja, a contemporary of his royal neighbour the Chalukya king Kirtivarman, is the most likely candidate for the cutting of two of the greatest monuments of Western India: the vast rock-cut temple-cum-cave of Kailasa at Ellora, which has its own rather crudely cut Nataraja bas-relief, and the no less magnificently executed rock-cut cave-temple of Shiva on Elephanta. The latter has the usual Shiva linga at its heart but the shrine's real masterpiece is the massive Nataraja in a side-chamber. Although badly frayed by a combination of monsoon rainwater and Portuguese musket practice, enough has survived of the original to convey the god's superhuman energy and movement (see illustration on page 247).

Beyond a couple of passing references I have also said nothing about another of the Kannada-speaking dynasties, the Rashtrakutas, who under Raja Govinda III forced all four southern dynasties – Cholas, Pandyas, Cheras and Pallavas – to bend the knee in tribute, and whose son Amoghavarsha boasted that his father's horse had drunk from the icy streams of the Himalayas and his war elephants from the sacred waters of the Ganges, and yet apparently cared enough for the well-being of his subjects at a time of famine to sacrifice a finger to the goddess Lakshmi in a bid to bring rain, and who at the end of his life abdicated to become a Jain monk.

But the Imperial Cholas do cry out for more space, not least because they were the only rulers of India whose ambitions extended across the black waters of the *kala pani*. In the

Rijksmuseum van Oudheden in the university town of Leiden in Holland there is an unusual souvenir of the Dutch VOC's trading links with the Coromandel coast. It takes the form of twenty-four copper plates held together on a ring closed with the seal of the Chola kings: a seated tiger facing two fishes standing on their tails, flanked by two lamp-stands and topped by symbols of royalty in the form of a parasol and two fly-whisks. These so-called Leiden Plates had been found in the village of Anaimangalam, on the banks of a side-channel of the Cauvery, the Tellur, situated midway between Nagapattinam and Thiruvavur. They had been made by order of Raja Rajendra Chola and they recorded in a mixture of Sanskrit and Tamil various commitments involving land grants made by his late father Rajaraja Chola.

The royal seal of the Leiden Plates: twenty-four copper plates record-ing the terms of the funding of a Buddhist monastery by the Chola kings Rajaraja and his son Rajendra.

Using richly poetic imagery the king sets out at length the genealogy of his royal line and its many achievements. He then gives details of an order made by his father for the construction of a large Buddhist monastery, the *vihara* of Chulamanivarma at Nagapattinam, including its boundaries as determined by the circumambulation of a female elephant. The terms of the grant are set out in detail, including incomes to be derived from various surrounding lands and taxes, as well as various conditions that are to be kept, such as the maintenance of irrigation channels, tree-planting and the digging of wells. All this was being done by the Cholas as a favour to a distant neighbour, a Buddhist king of Srivijaya in faraway Java.

What these copper plates show is that two committed devotees of Lord Shiva in the persons of the Chola kings Rajaraja and his son Rajendra were happy to extend their patronage – or at the very least, their tolerance – to the local Buddhist community at Nagapattinam. These two Chola rulers felt confident enough to allow their subjects to worship as they pleased, and with good reason.

At the battle of Takkolam fought in 949 the Rashtrakutas had comprehensively thrashed the Cholas almost to the point of eclipse, only for them to bounce back with a vengeance within forty years with the accession to the Chola royal *gadi* or couch of Rajaraja in the year 985. His victories allowed the Cholas to expand northwards and eastwards to the point where they had effective control of an empire that extended all the way round the Bay of Bengal from Lanka to Sumatra. This was very much the work of a father and son team: the father being Rajendra Chola, the same ruler who celebrated his defeat of the Pala king of Bengal and Bihar by naming his new capital Gangaikondacholapuram; the son being his successor and for many years his co-ruler, Rajadhiraja Chola. The conquest of Bengal was just one in a series of military campaigns that began in 1002 with the crushing of his immediate neighbours, continued with the annexation of Lanka and the capture of its king with all his crown jewels in 1017, and culminated in the despatch from Nagapattinam in 1025 of a great armada of ships that led to the conquest of the kingdom of Srivijaya in Sumatra and the Malay peninsula, which won the Cholas 'a heap of treasures' and control of the sea-trade in that area. This Chola empire is something that Indian nationalists tend to overlook when they berate Britain for its imperialism!

The father gave thanks to Lord Shiva by building the mighty granite temple of Brihadishvara in Thanjavur. The son responded by building his own Brihadishvara temple in Gangaikondachol-apuram but had the courtesy to make its 180-foot-high main tower 10 feet lower than his father's. Both temples are now UNESCO World Heritage Sites. The latter temple has a notice stating that it remained undamaged from the time of its building in 1035 until the arrival of the British, who removed its stones to build a dam. Photographs taken by Alexander Rea in about 1890 before he oversaw the start of the temple's reconstruction show that its surrounding wall, two outer shrines and its entrance *gopuram* lay in ruins (see page 256). However, the damage had been done not by Rea's fellow Britons but by the resurgent Pandyas. In 1279 Raja Maravarman Kulasekara Pandyan I defeated the army of Rajendra Chola III and then set out to destroy the Chola capital, razing every building but the central temple itself. After that there is a no further mention of the Cholas in the records, although the name lingered on in folk memory.

Forty years after that last Chola defeat an entirely novel and devastating form of Islam manifested itself in Tamil country. It came in the form of the cavalry of Sultan Ala-ud-Din Khilji, ruler of Delhi. Threatened by Mongol raiders from the north-west, Ala-ud-Din had hit on a tactic that had been tried many times before in Northern India but never in the South. He embarked on

(Above) A poor-quality print of part of the Brihadishvara temple complex in Gangaikondacholapuram as it was when photographed by Alexander Rea in about 1890, showing the ruinous state of an outer shrine. (Below) The Brihadishvara temple as it is today, showing the fully restored *vimana* (spire).

a series of fund-raising raids that each year struck ever deeper into the Deccan and beyond.

In the autumn of 1310 one such force, under the leadership of a Hindu convert to Islam named Malik Naib Kafur, fought its way south into Chola country, looting the temples as it went. Their first target was the complex of the Chola Ranganath temple in Srirangam, which alerted the temple authorities at Chidambaram, who did their best to hide or disperse their most valuable treasures. But that best was not good enough. The subsequent pillaging of Chidambaram was recorded in pious and supposedly scandalised terms by Sultan Ala-ud-Din's Indo-Persian court poet Hasrat Amir Khusrao in his *Khaza'inul futuh* or 'Treasures of Victory':

> The stone idols, called Ling-i-Mahadeo [Shivalingas] which had been for a long time established in that place – to which the women of the faithful behave shamefully – these up to that time the kick of the horse of Islam had not attempted to break. [Now] the Mussulmans destroyed all the lingas. De Narain [Vishnu Narayan] fell down, and the other gods who had fixed their seats there, raised their feet so high, that at one leap they reached the feet of Lanka; and in that affright the lingas themselves would have fled, had they any legs to stand on.[5]

In their determination to secure whatever treasures might have been hidden away the invaders are said to have pulled down the temple's walls and dug up its foundations: 'Wherever there was any treasure in that deserted building, the ground was sifted in a sieve and the treasure discovered.'[6]

Malik Kafur then moved on to Madurai, where he stripped the famous temple of Meenakshi Amman of its golden roof and the golden image of the goddess. 'He destroyed the golden idol temple of Ma'bar,' wrote Malik Kafur's contemporary, the historian Zia-ud-Din Barni, 'and the golden idols which for centuries had been worshipped by the Hindus of that country. The fragments of the golden temple, and the broken idols of gold and gilt became the rich spoils of the army.'[7]

The final tally of gold bullion removed under Sultan Ala-ud-Din's orders from the South amounted to 96,000 maunds in weight, which could be anywhere between 1000 and 6900 tonnes. When paraded in triumph through the streets of Delhi, along with 612 captured elephants and twenty thousand horses, this booty created such a sensation that it passed into folklore within the Muslim world, eventually to be transformed by way of the *Arabian Nights* into Aladdin's Cave.

From time to time tangible evidence of Ala-ud-Din's impact on the South continues to come to light as farmers and construction workers stumble upon carefully buried temple deities, as happened in August 1987 when workmen renovating the temple of Tiruramanathesvara in Esalam village in South Arcot District, inland from Pondicherry, came across four layers of buried metal objects. These included a copper plate charter issued to the temple by the Chola king Rajendra in 1036, several bells, some ritual tripods and twenty-three bronzes of a variety of Shaiva deities, all of which had been carefully laid face down within a brick pit and covered with sand. The fact that they were not recovered soon after their burial would suggest that no one involved had lived to reveal the secret of their whereabouts.

The first Arab invader who led an army into Sind in 712 brought with him his own historians, who set down written accounts of his triumphs over the unbelievers and idolators in gloating detail. That pattern was followed by the many Muslim warlords who followed him into India. These historians most certainly exaggerated, and that has to be taken into account. But even if we discount 90 per cent of these stories, the sheer volume and consistency of these scores of histories extending over the best part of eight hundred years cannot just be wished away, even if they are politically awkward or are misused by those determined to present Islam in India as un-Indian. The painful fact is that some invaders did glory in devastating infidel places of worship and in enslaving infidels, and their historians followed suit. Here, for example, is Amir Khusrao expressing his satisfaction at the damage done to Madurai:

The orthodox Sunni victors had now piously compelled all false houses of worship to bow their heads on the prayer carpet of the ground and had broken all stone idols like the stony hearts of the worshippers. How clean the breast of those who broke with the greatest severity those contaminated stones, which Satan had raised like a wall before himself.

Precisely that same tone of bigoted self-satisfaction would later characterise the Portuguese chroniclers' accounts of their masters' wars up and down the Malabar coast, always fought (so they tell us) to the glory of God and the eternal damnation of the heathen.

By Zia-ud-Din Barni's account there were further raids on Madurai and elsewhere in the South in which more damage is said to have been inflicted. But when the third raid was carried out in 1323 its commander, the future Sultan Muhammad bin Tughlaq, stayed on to become governor of the new Muslim province of Ma'bar, nominally under the authority of the Sultans of Delhi. From then on Islam was present in the South as the faith of a ruling power.

By that time Cholamandalam's centuries of glory were a thing of the past. But the name persisted – to be Europeanised into Coromandel.

'The king of Cochin accompanied by his Nayers', reads the caption to this print from Abbé Prévost's *Histoire générale des Voyages*, published in fifteen volumes between 1746 and 1759. Prévost's 'Nayres' were the Nairs of Kerala, who regarded themselves a warrior people and acted accordingly. 'They are all gentlemen,' wrote Robert Johnson of the Nairs in his *Relations of the most famous kingdoms and commonweales of the world*, published in 1616. 'At seven years of age they are put to school to learn the use of their weapons, where, to make them nimble and active, their sinews and joints are stretched by skilful fellows and are anointed with the oil *Sesamus*. The French illustrator had obviously never seen an elephant, never mind an Indian.

9
MALAYA INTO MALABAR

British vessels anchored off Calicut, on the Malabar coast, engraved from a drawing by James Forbes, from his four-volume *Oriental Memoirs*, 1813.

MALABAR, n.p. The name of the sea-board country which the Arabs call the 'Pepper-Coast', the ancient *Kerala* of the Hindus ... applied, apparently, first by the Arab or Arabo-Persian mariners of the Gulf. The substantive part of the name, *Malai*, is the Dravidian term for 'mountain', in the Sanskritised form *Malaya*, which is applied specifically to the southern portion of the Western Ghauts, and from which is taken the indigenous term *Malayalam*, distinguishing that branch of the Dravidian language in the tract we call Malabar ... In the great temple inscription in Tanjore we find the region called *Malai-nadu*, 'the Hill Country' ... The affix *bar* appears attached to it first in the *Geography* of Edrisi (c. 1150) ... Arabic *barr*, 'a continent'.

Col. Henry Yule and A. C. Burnell, *HOBSON-JOBSON*,
A glossary of colloquial Anglo-Indian words and phrases, 1886

Cherthala is a fast-expanding township halfway along the long strip of land that runs northwards along the Malabar coast from Alleppey (Alappuzha) to Cochin (Kochi) to form a low-lying barrier between the sea and the lakes and waterways that form part of Kerala's famous backwaters. In Cherthala's northern outskirts is a nondescript crossroads now called Manorama Kovala. This was formerly known as Mulachi parambu, although today few people in the locality seem to have heard of it. The Malayalam word *parambu* means 'plot of land' and *mulachi* means 'breasted woman', so it means something like 'the home of the breasted woman'.

The Malabar coast has its share of horror stories but few are as arresting as the tale of the housewife of Cherthala who presented her cut-off breasts on a banana leaf to the tax-collector at her door. It is hard to dismiss this particular story as sensational myth because of the details: the tax man running away in shock, the woman bleeding to death from her wounds, and her distressed husband – almost uniquely in Indian history – throwing himself on to her funeral pyre. We know her name, her caste and the place where this happened, but not the exact date. However, this did not happen in the ancient mists of time but in the kingdom of Travancore just over two centuries ago. And even though this was a case of self-harm there was an aggressor involved – in the form of the local Brahmin community and the powers it then exercised.

To understand how the Brahmins of Malabar acquired that power we have to go back to their origins. Just as the Tamils have their founding father in the rishi Agastya, so the inhabitants of the Deccan's western seaboard have their counterpart in the person of Parashurama.

Parashurama has a more godlike background than Agastya, being the sixth avatar of Lord Vishnu. He is also more violent, as the wielder of a terrible fiery axe, *Parashu*, gifted to him by Lord

Shiva, with which he slays innumerable enemies of the gods. Like Agastya, Parashurama features in both the great epics of the *Mahabharata* and *Ramayana*, and in the former we are told how Parashurama rid the world of all the Kshatriyas, not once but twenty-one times over. He then claimed their lands for himself and performed the *ashwamedha yagna* (horse sacrifice) as a sovereign ruler, before handing the land over to the head-priests of the Brahmins for occupation. That is the basic story, which is elaborated further in a later text known as the *Brahmanda Purana*, which can be translated as 'the ancient text of the creation of the world'.

The Puranas were written at a time when rival devotional cults within the broadening church of Hinduism had just begun to compete for popular acceptance – an extended process usually associated with the Gupta era in Northern India (c. 320–550 CE). The *Brahmanda Purana* is reckoned to be among the last of the Puranas to be written, in about the sixth or seventh century. Here we are told that when India's western coast was swamped by the sea Parashurama challenged the god Varuna, who by now had changed from a Vedic deity with responsibility for social order into a god of oceans and rivers. Parashurama threw his mighty axe into the sea, which caused the land to rise up out of the water, but land so salty as to be barren. So Parashurama performed a ritual to summon Nagaraja, the king of the snakes, who covered the land with snake venom, which neutralised the salt and made it fertile. This newly recovered land – which to this day is referred to by some as Parashurama Kshetra, 'the land of Parashurama', stretching from Gokarna in Karnataka to the southern tip of Kerala – was gifted by Parashurama to the Brahmins, whom he brought down from the North to settle the land. Since Parashurama had killed off all the Kshatriyas, the Brahmins were left in sole control of the local population, whom they classed either as Shudras or those without caste.

(Above, left) The axe-wielding Parashurama, who recovered the Malabar coast for the Brahmins. Detail of a miniature from an album of drawings owned by Thomas Baber, Collector and Judge in the Malabar Province of the Madras Presidency from 1798 to 1838. He returned to England but then sailed back to India to settle in Tellicherry, where he died in 1843. (Above, right) The entrance of the Vadakkunnathan temple in Thrissur, said to be the first temple established in Kerala by Parashurama, built in classic Keralan architectural style, with tiled roofs and steep-sloped eaves.

The first Westerner to take note of this Malabari creation myth and the curious caste system that went with it was Johannes Nieuhof, an employee in the service of the Dutch VOC who took part in the assaults on Quilon and Cranganore (Kodungallur) over the winter of 1662–3 which finally broke the power of the Portuguese in the East Indies. Nieuhof stayed on as the VOC's local representative and to administer the pearl fishery at Tuticorin. One of his first duties was to negotiate a new trade agreement with the Rani of Quilon, which gave him the opportunity to observe the local culture at first hand.

'She had a guard of about 700 soldiers about her all clad after the Malabar fashion,' Nieuhof wrote in an account first published in Dutch and then half a century later in English as *Mr. John*

Nieuhof's Remarkable Voyages and Travels to the East Indies (1732), 'the Queen's attirement being no more than a piece of calico wrapt round her middle, the upper part of her body appearing for the most part naked, with a piece of calico hanging carefully round her shoulders. Her ears, neck and arms were adorned with precious stones, gold rings and bracelets, and her head covered in a piece of calico.' Both the queen and her guards belonged to a people Nieuhof called Nayros or Nairos – today usually written Nairs – which Nieuhof's English translator misinterpreted as 'negroes', giving rise to a number of highly misleading prints.

Pliny the Elder in his *Natural History* refers to 'Nerae' living in the 'Capitalis' mountains, which may well be a reference to the Nairs. Copper-plate land grants from the ninth century onwards mention local chieftains thought to be Nairs acting as witnesses to agreements between local rulers and Christian and Jewish traders. But they remain shadowy figures until the arrival of the Portuguese, by which time the Nairs had gained a fearsome reputation as warriors.

Having encountered the Nairs on the battlefield, Johannes Nieuhof was well aware of their fighting abilities. 'The Nayros are brought up to the war,' he wrote.

> They apply themselves from their infancy to the use of arms, and frequently fight together with swords and targets [round shields], which renders them infinitely active in that sport. They are the best wrestlers in the world, and are very nimble on foot. They attack their enemies quite naked, their privites only being covered ... The Nayros women are clothed in the same manner as the men, so that there is not the least distinction to be seen between boys and girls, till the breasts begin to appear in the last ... They bore holes through the ears of both boys and girls, which they fill up with palm-tree leaves rolled

together. These rolls they make bigger and bigger by degrees till the holes are extended to the utmost and ... they adorn them with gold, silver and jewels. Though the Nayros are very bold and brave, they are nevertheless very civil and meek in their conversation, according to the custom of that country.

What Nieuhof noted but failed to fully understand were two defining characteristics of Nair culture: polyandry and snake-worship. Elsewhere in India men of their status took several wives, but not the Nairs. 'Women in this point have got the start of the men,' Nieuhof noted, 'they being permitted to have three husbands at once ... As often as any of them come to visit her, he leaves his arms at her door, a sign that neither of the other two must come in, for fear of disturbing the first. From hence the poorer sort reap the benefit, for they have the use of the wife, yet contribute only a third part towards the maintaining of the family.' What Nieuhof had missed was that this was a matrilineal society, where it was the women who owned and inherited property.

As to snakes, Nieuhof noticed the particular devotion the Nairs paid to 'serpents', but then went on to say, quite wrongly, that they did so because they considered them 'as evil spirits, made by God to torment mankind for their sins'. He failed to grasp the significance in rural India of the *Naag*, in the form of the hooded cobra *Naja raja* with its potentially fatal bite, its annual shedding of its skin and its apparent disappearance and reappearance before and after the monsoon. Snake-worship is still practised in many corners of India but nowhere more so than in Kerala, where carved images of cobras can be seen at virtually every wayside shrine (see illustration), and where a number of temples are dedicated to Nagaraja, the king of the snakes, the most famous being the Mannarasala Sree Nagaraja temple at Haripad, on the coast south of Alleppey. Until quite recently most Nair households maintained a grove of trees in the south-western corner of their gardens for their cobra, which all members of the family revered and fostered as guardian and protector.

A typical Keralan wayside shrine with offerings in the form of snake-stones.

What Nieuhof also remarked on was Nair arrogance, how they saw themselves as warriors and behaved accordingly, being 'very haughty' and refusing to 'converse with any of the lower orders ... of which they are so cautious, that they will not so much as suffer any to approach them, for which reason, when they walk abroad they cry out aloud to the common people, "*Popoire*, keep back", for if any of these should touch a *Nairos*, he would certainly ruin him.'

Nieuhof's admiration was reserved for the Brahmins of the Malabar coast, who also considered themselves a class apart. 'Among the several sects of the Malabars, that of the Brahmans is most reverenced,' he noted, with undisguised approval.

> They are generally very wise, ready, active, modest and charitable, and strict observers of their promises. Some are priests, whose business it is to offer sacrifices to their idols. Some there are among them who addict themselves to natural philosophy and other sciences, but especially to astronomy, others to physic and pharmacy ... They have many books, which contain an account of their religious ceremonies, much resembling the ancient Greek and Roman fables. They eat neither flesh nor fish, nor any other living creature, and drink nothing but water, nor do they ever eat before they have washed and bathed themselves. They are forbidden to eat any thing but what has been prepared by one of their own sect, for they rather chuse to die than eat any thing touched by one of another sect.

The wives of these Brahmins led severely restricted lives and were expected to follow their deceased husbands on to the funeral pyre:

> When a Brahman happens to die, his widow is obliged, as a demonstration of her affection towards her deceased husband, to burn herself. This is commonly done under the noise of several musical instruments, to suppress the doleful outcries of the dying person, and in the presence of their next kindred. They may excuse themselves as to this point if they please, but then they are branded with infamy, their hair is cut off close, which they must not let grow to any length again. They are excluded from the society of other women, nor are allowed to marry again.

Nieuhof also had plenty to say about those he described as the 'vulgar sort', with the Paraiyars considered 'a wretched sort of slave'. Through his work with the pearl fishery Nieuhof knew these Paraiyars as pearl- and oyster-fishers, 'they being the best divers in the world, from which they are accustomed from their first infancy'. But they were also, in his view, 'a cowardly and deceitful sort of people, lying and deceit being so customary among them as not to be looked on as a sin'.

Ironically, Nieuhof was himself accused of illegal trading while in charge of the pearl fishery and was imprisoned for several months before returning home to Holland to write his memoirs. He later sailed for Madagascar and was never seen again.

The legitimacy of the Malabar caste order rested on two supposedly ancient texts: the *Kerala Mahatmayam* and the later *Keralolpathi* – dismissed by the British Collector of Malabar William Logan in the late-nineteenth century as 'a farrago of legendary nonsense having for its definite aim the securing of the Brahmin caste of unbounded power and influence in the country'.[1] Logan's remarks were aimed at one particular group of Brahmins known as the Nambudiris or Nambothris. They claimed Parashurama as their founding father and traced their ancestors back to sixty-five families drawn from the banks of the Narmada, Krishna and Kaveri rivers. After their arrival in the Malabar country they had established themselves in sixty-four exclusively Brahmin settlements, the most important being at Perumchallur, now better known as Taliparamba, in north Kerala.

The Nambudiris claimed to be the first Brahmins in the region, but it is more likely that they were preceded by others such as the Shivalli Brahmins, who claimed to have been brought south by the Alva kings in about the fourth century. The acutely caste-conscious Nambudiris looked down on the Shivallis and considered them as non-Brahmins, and the fact that they spoke Tulu, a language which Bishop Robert Caldwell described in his *Grammar* as 'one of the most highly developed languages of the Dravidian family', suggests that at the very least the first Shivalli immigrants had intermarried with the local Dravidian population.

It is likely that the Nambudiri Brahmins came to Malabar just as the first of the Hindu temples in Kerala were being built as part of that frenzy of religious activity that saw popular Hinduism evolve out of Brahminism, accompanied by the rise of the competing cults of Vishnu and Shiva. Their superior religious status combined with their greater learning ensured that the Nambudiris filled the most senior posts as temple custodians and as royal counsellors, so that by the end of the ninth century they were firmly established as the supreme religious arbiters in the area, with their own distinctive traits that set them apart from the rest of the local community. The *Keralolpathi* asserts that they were influenced by the great reformer Adi Shankara, and it does appear that the Nambudiris followed his example in regarding the existing Buddhists as heretics, and that as Buddhism went into freefall so they moved in to fill its place, in the process declaring the former followers of Buddhism to be *avarna*, or without caste.

As their temples grew in wealth and land ownership so the Nambudiris became increasingly powerful landowners under the local system of *janman*, by which, in return for a third of the crops, they granted the right to cultivate land to *kannikan*s, mostly made up of Nairs, who in turn granted peasant tenant-farmers known as *erumpattakkaran* the right to work the land in return for another third of the crop.

This remarkable power shift – the closest parallel I can think of is the great landowning Catholic monastic orders of medieval

'Namburee and Namburechee': a Nambudiri Brahmin and his wife,
one of thirteen watercolours of castes of the Malabar coast, c. 1828.

Europe – was well established by Johannes Nieuhof's time but
reached its apotheosis a century later in Travancore.

The kingdom of Travancore was largely the creation of one
man. When in 1729 twenty-three-year-old Raja Marthanda
Varma ascended the royal *gadi* of the ancient coastal kingdom of
Venad – afterwards Quilon – he was expected to rule as a mere
figurehead, the real power being shared between a group of Nair
nobles known as the Ettuveetil Pillamar or the 'Lords of the Eight
Houses', and the Nambudiri Ettara Yogam, the 'Council of Eight
and a Half', which managed the enormously wealthy and powerful
Padmanabhaswamy temple in Trivandrum (Thiruvananthapuram).

Working as an assistant to a member of the Council of Eight and a Half was a young man of humble origins named Ramayyan. Marthanda Varma spotted his ability, secured his services, and when his Dewan or Chief Minister died in 1737 he appointed Ramayyan in his place. The Dutch VOC was by now securely established up and down the Malabar coast in a number of trade enclaves from which they controlled the pepper export market in alliance with several local rulers. With his Dewan's help, Marthanda Varma set about destabilising this cosy and hugely profitable alliance.

From his base in Nagercoil, just west of Kanyakumari, Marthanda set out to win over the Lords of the Eight Houses. This provoked an attempt on his life which he survived, stabbing his assailant to death in the process. He responded by hanging forty-two Nair chiefs, branding four Brahmins on the forehead as outcastes and handing over all their wives and children to the local outcaste fishermen. This secured the allegiance of the Lords of the Eight Houses. He next launched an attack on the Nambudiri stronghold of Perumchallur which was garrisoned by its own warrior Brahmins. Those who survived were exiled. This action won the allegiance of the Council of Eight and a Half.

By 1741 Marthanda Varma had won control of the largest pepper-producing region on the coast, which put him on a collision course with the Dutch, culminating in 1749 in a battle fought 20 miles (32 kilometres) up the west coast from Kanyakumari at Colachel, where the Dutch had a fort. The Nairs broke the Dutch fighting line and captured twenty-five Dutch officers and men as the rest turned and ran. This was the first instance of an Asian power beating a European one in battle and it hastened the eclipse of Dutch power in India.

Marthanda Varma now built himself a new palace in the grounds of an old fortress at Padmanabhapuram, inland from

Colachel about 40 kilometres up the west coast from Kanyakumari. This fine old structure still stands, with two palaces
at its heart, one for the king and an even grander one for his
mother, in line with Nair custom. A secret underground passage
is said to have run from here to the fortress itself, standing on
an isolated hill half a mile to the south-west. Today the fort is
called the Uthayagiri Bio-Diversity Park and is under the care
of the Tamil Nadu Forest Department, but its former name was
Dillanai Kottai, or 'De Lannoy's Fort'. All but lost in the under-
growth are the remains of a small Dutch cantonment and the
roofless walls of a small church. On its floor, and now guarded
by iron railings, are the graves of the man who became known
as Valiya Kappithaan, or the 'Great Captain', together with his
wife and son. Topped by a coat of arms, the central gravestone
carries two inscriptions, one in Tamil and one in Latin, which
translates as:

STAND TRAVELLER!
HERE LIES EUSTACHIUS BENEDICTUS DE LANNOY:
who was commander of the general Travancore army
and for nearly thirty-seven years with the
greatest faithfulness served the King,
to whom by the strength and fear of his armies
he subjugated all kingdoms from Kayangulam to Cochin.
He lived 62 years and 5 months and died first day of June 1777.
May he rest in peace.

Eustachius de Lannoy is very much part of Travancore's story.
Marthanda Varma gave the captured Dutch soldiers the choice
of enslavement or enlistment in his army, so they duly enrolled.
Their commander was thirty-four-year-old Captain de Lannoy,
whose diligence in training the raja's bodyguard led to him being

The ruins of Eustachius de Lannoy's church below the walls of Uthayagiri Fort, near Nagercoil.

given charge of the rebuilding of the defences of the old fort at Padmanabhapuram. Eventually he became joint commander of the Nair forces, who were now taught to fight with muskets and gunpowder and to dress, drill and manoeuvre in the European manner. At the same time de Lannoy's Dutch officers employed their engineering skills in building forts and defences, in particular a line of fortifications in the north that became known as the Nedunkotta or 'Travancore Line'.

Scarcely acknowledged today, this 'Europeanisation' of Travancore's army and its defences was the decisive factor that enabled Travancore to take on and annex its neighbours to north and south and so secure for itself the pepper trade. With the defeat of the forces of the Zamorin of Calicut at Purakkad in 1756, Marthanda Varma became the ruler of a kingdom that stretched from Kanyakumari to just short of Cochin.

Immediately after his victory Marthanda Varma made his way to Trivandrum, and there surrendered his new kingdom to Sri Padmanabhaswamy in the form of Lord Vishnu reclining on the serpent Ananatha, pledging that henceforth he and his descendants would rule Travancore as Padmanabha Dasa, or servants of the deity. However, it was made clear to him by the temple authorities that in their eyes he was by caste a Shudra and, as such, forbidden to enter the innermost precincts of his own temple.

But there was an important precedent in the form of the ancient rite of *Hiranyagarbha yagna* or 'golden womb sacrifice' by which a non-Kshatriya ruler might acquire legitimacy by undergoing a purification ritual. Originally that practice had involved sacrifice but over the years this had been replaced by *mahadanam*, or 'the making of great donations', by which the unqualified ruler could buy Kshatriya caste status by making large donations of gold. A century and a half earlier, another local ruler named Udayavarman had done just that when the Nambudiris at his court had refused to perform the rites. Udayavarman had responded by importing 237 Shivalli Brahmin families from Karnataka who were less particular than the Nambudiris. After receiving generous gifts of gold, they had subjected the raja to the required purification rituals by which he attained the status of Kshatriya.

It seems that the Nambudiris had learned their lesson, because when Marthanda Varma asked for promotion they obliged – but at a price. As well as being required to have a life-size golden cow built, 'under which he was forced to creep in order to be freed of his sins', the raja had also to ritually cleanse himself in a vast pot of gold (see illustration) which was then broken up for distribution to every Brahmin in his kingdom, the bulk of it going to the Nambudiris. A precedent had now been set whereby every new ruler of Travancore would have to undergo at least one hugely costly *mahadanam* during his reign. This was in addition to other hugely costly ceremonies as the *thulapurusha danam*, in which the monarch was weighed on a large set of scales against an equal weight of gold, also distributed to the Brahmins.

(Above, left) The approach to the Padmanabhaswamy in Trivandrum, said to be the richest temple in India. Detail of a photograph taken by Zakaria d'Cruz, c. 1895. (Above, right) The raja prepares to cleanse himself in a giant gold pot, afterwards divided among the Brahmins.

It is recorded that in the course of one such *thulapurusha danam* ceremony conducted in 1850 around 22,900 *kalanju* of gold were distributed, of which the head priest of the Padmanabhaswamy temple and twenty-six officiating priests received 5731, Nambudiri lords 846, Nambudiri and Canarese Brahmins 4778, Tamil Brahmins 3666, Brahmin women and children 1243, other Brahmins 3707, and the rest 2867. One *kalanju* is roughly the equivalent of 3.2 grams, so over 73,000 grams or 2350 troy ounces were distributed.[2] If similar amounts of gold were donated at every *mahadanam* ceremony it is easy to understand how this led to the enrichment of the Brahmins and the growing impoverishment of the state.

This practice ended in 1850 when the then Governor of the Madras Presidency made an unofficial protest, warning the then ruling maharaja that if he continued to make these *mahadanam*s the Madras Presidency would intervene and he might well lose his throne. So the *mahadanam* ended – but not before Travancore had become a byword in India for caste prejudice and discrimination.

When Marthanda Varma died in 1758 he was succeeded by Kathika Thirunal Rama Varma, who became known as the Dharma Raja on account of his good government. He, too, had the sense to appoint two able administrators: as his *dalawa*, or Chief Minister, a Nair named Kesava Pillai, better known as Raja Kesavadas, and as his finance minister a wealthy Syrian Christian trader in timber and spices named Thachil Matthoo. With the addition of the Great General, this was a winning team that enabled the raja to repel the invading forces of Tipu Sultan of Mysore and to complete an ambitious construction project that saw Alleppey transformed into a major port and financial centre. At this same time the East India Company (EICo) became increasingly involved in the affairs of Travancore, initially as an ally in Travancore's war against Mysore and from 1795 onwards as its protector by formal treaty.

With the death of the Dharma Raja in 1798 Travancore's fortunes changed for the worse. The raja's successor, Balarama Varma, was a fourteen-year-old simpleton and a puppet in the hands of a Nambudiri Brahmin named Jayanthan Sankaran. At Sankaran's urging Raja Kesavadas was arrested and proclaimed a traitor, subsequently dying of poisoning. Sankaran now took over as *dalawa* and, in alliance with Thachil Matthoo, proceeded to undo all the good work done by his predecessors, introducing a series of punitive taxes levied on all sections of the community – except the Brahmins and the Syrian Christians.

These events coincided with the British assault on Tipu Sultan's capital at Seringapatam (Srirangapatnam) and the death of Tipu Sultan (of which more in the next chapter). A Hindu ruler was restored to the throne of Mysore as a minor, Tipu's recently won territories were divided up between the Company and the Nizam of Hyderabad, and Travancore and Cochin were recognised as independent but subordinate allies of Britain, with each required to accept a British Resident at court to act both as ambassador and adviser. The first of these Residents was Colonel Colin Macaulay, who had just emerged from the dungeons of Seringapatam after spending two years there as a brutalised prisoner-of-war.[3] No sooner had Macaulay taken up his post in Cochin than he was reporting back to the Governor-General that Travancore was being ruled by 'a triumvirate of ignorance, profligacy and rapacity'.

At this same time the Scots surgeon Dr Francis Buchanan was brought in from Bengal to survey the newly won territories of Mysore, Canara and Malabar.[4] His working brief was to explore these three territories with a view to their commercial potential, but he extended his enquiries to include the people and their customs, gleaning most of his information from local Brahmins.[5] 'The divisions of the Brahmans here are different from those found in Bengal,' Buchanan observed, noting also the fierce rivalry existing between the Shaiva Brahmins, who were followers of Shankara, and the Iyengar Brahmins, who were Vaishnavas and in many instances followed secular professions as well as filling nearly all the government posts: 'They are called *Sri Vaishnavum* and *A'ayngar*, and may be readily known by the three vertical marks, connected by a common mark on the forehead, connected by a common line above the nose, and formed of white clay. They abhor *Isvara* [Shiva], calling him the chief of the *Rakshasa*, or devils, and worship only Vishnu, and the gods of his family.' The remaining Brahmins were more easy-going, 'thinking Vishnu to be the father of Brahma, and Brahma the father of Siva'.

However, as Buchanan entered the Malabar country by way of the Palakkad Gap he observed a marked change in society. He was particularly struck by the prosperity of the local Brahmins, who were very comfortably settled in their own communities, called *agraharam*s, where their houses stood in two rows either side of a road running north and south, with a temple to the local deity at the centre and temples to Shiva and Vishnu at either end. 'They are the neatest and cleanest villages I have seen in India,' Buchanan noted. 'The beauty, cleanness and elegant dress of the girls of the Brahmans add much to the look of these places.'

The Nairs, by contrast, preferred to live in individual households in the countryside but were as well-turned-out as the Brahmins, even though both communities made a point of keeping each other at arm's length – and the rest of the population at an ever greater distance. 'The whole of these Nairs formed the militia of Malayala, directed by the Namburis, and governed by the Rajas,' observed Buchanan. 'Their submission to their superiors was great, but they executed deference from those under them with a cruelty and arrogance rarely practised but among Hindus in their state of independence. A Nair was expected instantly to cut down a Tiar, or Musua who presumed to defile him by touching his person; and a similar fate awaited a slave who did not turn out of the road as a Nair passed.'

But what most intrigued Buchanan about these Nairs was not their arrogance but their unconventional customs, enshrined in the practice known as *sambandham*. 'The Nairs marry before they are ten years of age ... but the husband never afterwards cohabits

with his wife,' is how Buchanan begins his account of the Nairs'
highly unusual management of their private lives, which included
their women extending their favours to Nambudiri Brahmins and
others of high rank:

> It is no kind of reflection on a woman's character to say, that
> she has formed the closest intimacy with many persons: on
> the contrary, the Nair women are proud of reckoning among
> their favoured lovers many Brahmans, Rajas, and other persons
> of high birth ... In consequence of this strange manner of
> propagating the species, no Nair knows his father; and every
> man looks upon his sisters' children as his heirs ... A man's
> mother manages his family; and after her death his eldest sister
> assumes the direction. Even cousins, to the most remote degree
> of kindred, in the female line, generally live together in great
> harmony; for in this part of the country love, jealousy or disgust
> never can disturb the peace of a Nair family.

For Nair women, *sambandham* with Nambudiris and royalty
was a matter of prestige and enhanced social status. Even so,
when Buchanan's three-volume account of his survey was published in 1807, his description of the sexual mores of the Nairs
caused something of a sensation.[6] One of his readers was a young
English aristocrat named James Lawrence, who got it into his
head that here on India's Malabar coast there was to be found a
paradise of free love. 'The Nairs are the Nobility of the Malabar
Coast, and affirm that they are the oldest in the world,' Lawrence
wrote in the introduction to his novel published in 1811 in France,
Germany and England under the title *The Empire of the Nairs, or,
the Rights of Woman: an Utopian Romance in twelve books*. 'It is the
privilege of the Nair lady to chose and change her lover ... The
mother only has the charge of the children; and even the *Samorin*

[Zamorin] and other princes have no other heirs than the children of their sisters. The name of the father is unknown to a Nair child; he speaks of the lovers of his mother, and of his uncles, but never of his father. Such are the Nairs.'

Lawrence's romance was intended to demonstrate the superiority of what he referred to as 'the Nair system of gallantry' over conventional marriage, 'in insuring an indubitable birth, and being favourable to population, to the rights of women, and to the active genius of men'. These ideals appealed to many young romantics in Europe, among them the poet Percy Shelley, who wrote to Lawrence declaring himself a convert to Lawrence's ideas and describing marriage as 'licensed prostitution'. But Lawrence's utopian vision of free love was, of course, a Western fantasy, for the reality was much darker. If a Nair woman was caught bestowing her favours on any person of lower caste than herself she was instantly declared an outcaste. Even more severe penalties were applied to the men, as Buchanan noted: 'A Nair man who is detected in fornication with a Shanar woman is put to death, and the woman is sold to the Moplays [Muslims]. If he have connection with a slave girl, both are put to death.'

Buchanan's survey never extended into Travancore, which explains why he remained unaware of the degree to which its Nambudiri Brahmins, in their determination to enforce their version of Hindu law on the local population, had turned themselves into local tyrants.

When the Nambudiris first arrived in Malayala they had found themselves in something of a pickle. By their own interpretation of *varna*, they could not intermarry with the local population because none were worthy of *kshatriya* or *vaisya* status. Even the Nairs, with their sexual habits and their snake-worship, were beyond the pale. Furthermore, the Nambudiris' own customs demanded that only the eldest son of the family be allowed to marry, and only within his own people. It was this that led them to take advantage of the Nair custom of *sambandham*, so that the Nambudiri men could enjoy sexual relations with the Nair womenfolk without being required to reciprocate or to acknowledge any ensuing offspring. As for the Nair men, they made the best of a poor bargain by acting as the Nambudiris' enforcers.

It was not simply that all those deemed to be *avarna* were forbidden to enter Hindu temples. Over the course of several centuries a series of increasingly restrictive measures were brought into Travancore law, all built around the notion of caste pollution, with the single aim of preserving the Brahmins – and, to a lesser degree, the Nairs – from contamination by the rest. Fixed distances of separation were set down, all in multiples of six paces, ranging from six paces from the nearest Brahmin for Nairs to seventy-two paces for those at the very bottom of the ladder, the Paraiyars and others. Nair men could wear moustaches but their inferiors could not, their women could wear silver jewellery but not gold, the rest none at all. Nor could the underclasses carry umbrellas, wear footwear, send their children to school, drink from the public wells, wear new clothes without first making them soiled, put up gates and walls round their houses or use tiles on their roofs. If they had to converse with a Brahmin they had to observe the correct distance, but also cover their mouths with their hands, remain bowed and not speak of themselves in the first person.

Then at some point in the late eighteenth century it was further decided that a number of these now well-established caste prohibitions should be taxable – that is to say, a prohibition could be avoided by paying a tax on it. It has been calculated that very soon after the start of the nineteenth century the ordinary people of Travancore were being required to pay as many as a hundred petty taxes, ranging from head tax, hut tax, marriage tax and taxes on the tools of one's trade to taxes on the family cow, goat or dog, wearing jewellery, staging festivals, and even growing moustaches. But most iniquitous of all was what became known as the breast tax, *mulakkaram*.

As noted by Nieuhof, Buchanan and other observers of the Indian social scene, both sexes in South India had since time immemorial limited their clothing to *lungi*s, *kaili*s or *mundu*s in the form of waist-cloths secured with a belt, with the more wealthy adding shawls on occasion, and jewellery being the key to demonstrating high status. But with the settling along the Malabar coast of Arab Muslims (the Mappilas), and the growth of their community in parallel with the Syrian Christians (known as Nazrani, or Nazarenes), the women of these two communities took to covering their upper bodies in accordance with the demands of their religions. Catholic and Protestant Christian conversions from the sixteenth century added to their numbers, and soon it became the norm for women of higher and middle social status to cover up. But when *mulakkaram* was written into law in Travancore it became obligatory for every Hindu woman of low caste or without caste to bare her breasts in public or pay the required tax. This was increasingly resented, not as an affront to modesty but because it very publicly defined someone's low status.

Among the communities most affected were the Nadars, Thiyyas and Ezhavas, many of whom plied the same trade: tending and tapping the sap of the palmyra palm to produce an unrefined sugar called jaggery and liquor in the form of toddy and arrack, hence their nicknames of 'toddy-tappers' or 'climbers'. The Nadars regarded themselves as a warrior people originating from Tamil Nadu, whereas the Thiyyas and Ezhavas both claimed that their ancestors had been brought from Ceylon at the request of a Chera king to establish coconut farming in Kerala. These claims support the theory that their forebears were Buddhists whose

NASSRAUNEES,
are the descendants of the original syrians, who migrated to this place at the time immamorial, and are presently
multiplieb into extent, living upon trades, and nasbandry.

A Syrian Christian couple, the caption reading in part,
'NASSRAUNEES are the descendants of the original Syrians who
migrated to this place at the time Immemorial'.

refusal to abandon their religion had led to their being declared
outcaste.

These three communities now found themselves increasingly
discriminated against. Large numbers of the Malabar Nadars
followed the example of the lower castes in Tamil Nadu by converting to Christianity, which meant that they were subjected to
fewer prohibitions. However, the bulk of the Thiyyas and Ezhavas
refused to follow suit and suffered accordingly. One of their

number was that *mulachi* or 'breasted woman' from Cherthala, the Ezhava by the name of Nangeli, wife of Chirukandan, who in response to the *parvathiyar*, or tax-collector, calling at her door presented him with her severed breasts on a banana leaf.

The story of Nangeli and her tragic self-mutilation is now widely represented as the signal act of defiance that led to the abolition of the iniquitous *mulakkaram* tax. But that is history as we would like it to be rather than what actually transpired. Now we must turn back to the government of Travancore under the ministry of the Nambudiri Brahmin Jayanthan Sankaran, which ended in a popular insurrection and his replacement as *dalawa* by the man who had led the insurrection: a Velir nobleman named Velayudhan Chempakaraman Thampi, popularly known as Velu Thampi Dalawa.[7]

Today Velu Thampi Dalawa is lauded with statues and a postage stamp as a great Keralan patriot, which indeed he was. But he was also a ruthless man, who saw to it that Jayanthan Sankaran and his sidekick, the Christian trader Thachil Matthoo, had their ears cut off and their properties confiscated. In his determination to balance the state's revenues Velu Thampi Dalawa appears also to have added to the taxes imposed by his predecessor.

Velu Thampi and the new British Resident, Colonel Macaulay, were now increasingly at loggerheads, both of them uncompromising characters used to having their way, particularly in their dealings with the weak-minded ruler of Travancore, Raja Balarama Varma. Velu Thampi's cost-cutting led to a mutiny of the Travancore army which required the intervention of the EICo's troops, which in turn led to the drawing up of a new treaty by which Travancore State was forced to accept British troops on its soil as well as having to pay a hefty annual sum to pay for the cost of the EICo's intervention. When Velu Thampi appealed to the British Resident to have the amount of this subsidy reduced he was refused and warned that retribution must follow if the payment was not made in full.

Velu Thampi Dalawa and the Dewan of Cochin now began to lay plans to expel the British from their respective territories and kill Colonel Macaulay in the process. Macaulay had by now established himself in the British Residency at Cochin, an imposing Dutch-built bungalow on stilts known as the Bolghatty Palace, today the centrepiece of a resort run by the Kerala Tourist Development Corporation. An assault was made on the Residency while Macaulay was having dinner but was so mishandled that Macaulay escaped uninjured.

Velu Thampi's response to this debacle was to write a letter of apology and offer his resignation.[8] However, in the meantime a company of the 12th Regiment of Foot (afterwards the East Suffolk Regiment) had been sent by sea to Travancore to help deal with the disturbances. While proceeding up the Malabar coast in a flotilla of small boats they were hit by a storm and dispersed. One boat containing a platoon of thirty-three men commanded by Sergeant-Major Tildsley was guided into harbour at Alleppey, but as soon as they came ashore the soldiers were overpowered and each man had his wrists broken with an iron bar. After several days of imprisonment without food or water they were 'tied back to back and thrown into a deep tank, and, of course, all drowned'.[9]

Admirers of Velu Thampi Dalawa have dismissed this incident along with the killing of local Christians as propaganda put about by Macaulay and others to blacken their hero's name. However, the regimental records of the 12th Regiment of Foot, backed up by the memoirs of its officers, show Macaulay's account to be substantially correct. Macaulay held the Dewan personally responsible for the 'atrocious murder', and declared that he would see him hanged. Now that he had nothing to lose, Velu

Thampi Dalawa published what became known as the Kundaran Proclamation, calling on all the people of Travancore to unite in driving out the EICo. 'It is the nature of the English nation to get possession of countries by treacherous means,' his proclamation reads in part.

> Should they attain ascendancy in Travancore, they will put their own guards in the palaces, *Sircar* [government] buildings, and the fort gates, destroy the royal seal, and other distinguishing marks, suppress the Brahmanical communities and worship in pagodas, make monopolies of salt and every other thing, measure up and assert themselves absolute rulers of waste lands, impose exorbitant taxes on paddy lands [ricefields], coconut trees etc, get low caste people to inflict heavy punishments for slight faults, put up crosses and Christian flags in pagodas, compel intermarriages with Brahman women without reference to caste or creed, and practice all the unjust and unlawful things which characterise *Kaliyuga* [the Dark Age].[10]

This stirring call to arms is why Keralans rightly honour the name of Velu Thampi Dalawa. It was answered by the disbanded Nair soldiery, who now rallied to his cause in large numbers. But Nair valour proved no match for the Company's better-disciplined troops, among them the men of the 12th Regiment of Foot, who took their revenge by surrounding the village where their comrades had been murdered and killing all its inhabitants, 'sparing neither young nor old'.

After Velu Thampi Dalawa's last remaining Nair troops had been defeated in battles near Nagercoil and Kollam he sought refuge in the Kali temple at Mannadi, inland from Quilon. As the Company's troops closed in he chose to die by his own hand rather than surrender. On the orders of Raja Balarama Varma of Travancore – who, no doubt, took his orders from Colonel Macaulay – Velu Thampi's body was taken to Trivandrum and hanged from a gibbet outside the city, an act condemned by Governor-General Lord Minto as 'repugnant to humanity and the principles of civilised governance'. Macaulay was censured and dismissed, but kept his pension. So ended what can quite justifiably be described as the first real Indian revolt against British rule in India, and on that ground alone Velu Thampi Dalawa deserves his honoured place in history.

The death of Raja Balarama Varma in 1810 without a male heir led to a struggle for succession which ended with his niece ascending the royal *gadi*: twenty-year-old Rani Gowri Lakshmi Bayi. Macaulay's successor as British Resident, Colonel John Munro, lost no time in supporting her claim to the throne, and very quickly positioned himself to become the queen's staunchest ally – as well as becoming perhaps a little too friendly with her younger sister. It says a lot for the young queen's character that when the Nambudiri Brahmins objected to Munro setting up an inoculation programme to combat the smallpox then raging in many parts of Travancore, she and her family were among the first to be vaccinated, and made sure that this was widely known.

Like his predecessor before him, Munro very quickly concluded that Travancore's government machinery was rotten from top to bottom, writing to his masters in Madras that 'No description can produce an adequate impression of the tyranny, corruption and abuses of the system, full of activity and energy in everything mischievous, oppressive and infamous, but slow and dilatory to effect any purpose of humanity, mercy and justice.'[11] The only answer, as he saw it, was to bring in an outsider. To do so was 'one of the greatest evils', he admitted,

(Above, left) Rani Gowri Lakshmi Bayi, queen of Travancore for three years and then regent up to her death in 1815. (Above, right) Colonel John Munro, British Resident in Travancore and Cochin from 1810 to 1819, as well as serving as Dewan in both kingdoms from 1811 to 1814.

but 'necessarily resorted to as a good, to mitigate the still more intolerable grievances of injustice and oppression'. So on Munro's advice Rani Lakshmi Bayi dismissed and exiled the serving Dewan and asked the Company to allow Munro to take his place. Accordingly, in 1811 the British Resident at Travancore and Cochin became also, and uniquely, the Dewan of both. This gave Munro virtually dictatorial powers which, to his credit, he exercised wisely.

I have seen it written that John Munro introduced the worst of Travancore's punitive taxes. The records show the opposite, that Munro instituted a series of reforms to the existing system of taxation which reduced tax levels while at the same time bringing in increased revenue to the royal treasury.[12] He abolished inheritance tax, capitation tax and forced labour, and stripped revenue collectors of their former judicial powers. He introduced a policing network in the form of *thanas* and *darogahs* (police stations and police chiefs) and set up a modern judicial system with a central court of appeal and eight *zillahs*, local courts each presided over by a triumvirate of three judges – a Nair, a Brahmin and a Syrian Christian – all with good salaries and set rules 'to be regulated according to the Hindoo *shasters* and usages'. Munro should also be given credit for the royal proclamation of 1812 that abolished the buying and selling of all slaves in Travancore and for measures introduced in 1815 that gave lower-caste tenant farmers such as the Ezhavas and Nadars greater rights.[13]

Here I must admit to a degree of partiality, because in 1810 John Munro married Charlotte Blacker, whose family are among my more distant ancestors. So the reader should be aware of unconscious bias in all that I have written concerning Munro. I should also point out that Munro was an ardent Christian Evangelical and a committed supporter of the Church Missionary Society, which under the leadership of William Ringeltaube and a Tamil Christian named Vedamanikkam was given permission to set up a church at Mailadi in south Travancore. Initially they enjoyed great success in attracting the more oppressed sections of the local Nadar toddy-tappers, the Shanars, who in addition to all the other taxes were having to pay an *enikanam* tax for the ladders and a *thalaikanam* tax for the rope-belts they used to climb the palmyra trees. 'There was a rush of 5000 Shanars upon me,' wrote the missionary Ringeltaube in a letter to John Munro in March 1818, 'who had been long waiting for an opportunity to shake off the poll-tax and services attached to their caste and which they hoped to effect by connecting themselves with me. But when they found that no temporal advantages were to be obtained, their zeal for the Protestant religion collapsed.'[14]

I suspect that it was on Munro's advice that in 1812 the queen issued a proclamation allowing Nadar converts to Christianity to cover their breasts with *kuppayam* blouses as worn by Syrian Christian women, followed two years later by a proclamation that exempted Syrian and other Christians from paying taxes for the maintenance of Hindu temples – steps that were deeply resented by the Brahmins and other sections of the community.

Munro was well aware of the religious sensitivities of the Brahmins, but also of their exactions. In a bid to reduce the power of the Nambudiris he recommended that the self-regulated Devaswom or 'property of God' bodies that traditionally administered each temple should all be taken over by the central governments of Cochin and Travancore, along with all their properties, and their revenues treated as part of the state's revenues. This was much resented in some quarters but in Travancore Munro's scheme was accepted and a Travancore Devaswom Board was set up to control most, but not all, of the kingdom's temples. In Cochin there was greater opposition and the process was only partially implemented, and not fully realised until 1916. Here, I would argue, lies the real source of the continuing animosity in religious circles in Kerala towards John Munro.

In 1813 the Travancore queen gave birth to a son and heir, but after the birth of a second son a year later her health deteriorated, and she died in 1815. Her eldest boy was duly anointed Raja Karthika Thirumal Rama Varma, with his older sister acting as regent during his minority after the death of their mother. Munro himself had stepped down as Dewan of Travancore and Cochin shortly before the death of Rani Lakshmi Bayi and was replaced by two of his assistants, thereby setting a valuable precedent whereby the Dewans of both kingdoms were imported from outside, usually in the form of highly educated and experienced Tamil Brahmins from the Madras Presidency.

I should like to have ended this brief account of Munro's eight years in Travancore by saying that when he embarked for Scotland in January 1819 he left its people in a happier state. But these were hard times, partly as a consequence of the Tambora volcanic eruption of 1815, east of Java, which disrupted weather patterns for some five years and had a devastating impact on much of Asia, leading to droughts, floods and widespread famines accompanied by cholera.[15] Travancore was as badly affected as anywhere, while the abuses of caste and the widespread use of the outcaste *avarnas* as slave labour, generally known as *oozhiyam vala* or 'labour without pay', continued almost unabated. The granting of rights to Nadar and Channar women converts to wear the *kuppayam* blouse created tensions which degenerated into increasingly violent confrontations provoked by gangs of higher-caste men assaulting women whom they considered to be exceeding their status by dressing up or wearing jewellery inappropriately. This culminated in a series of affrays in several regions of Travancore in 1858, the so-called Channar Revolt, that prompted the then Governor of the Madras Presidency Sir Charles Trevelyan to intervene, leading to the issue on 26 July 1859 of a royal proclamation granting every woman in the kingdom of Travancore the right to cover her breasts and wear such jewellery as she chose.

But that was by no means the end of it. Writing to a friend in 1860, the wife of a Christian missionary reported that 'A Nair can approach but not touch a Namboodiri Brahmin: a Chovan [Ezhava] must remain thirty-six paces off, and a Pulayan slave ninety-six steps distant. A Chovan must remain twelve steps away from a Nair, and a Pulayan sixty-six steps off, and a Parayan some distance farther still. A Syrian Christian may touch a Nair (though this is not allowed in some parts of the country) but the latter may not eat with each other. Pulayans and Parayars, who are the lowest of all, can approach but not touch, much less may they eat with each other.'[16]

Given the source of that statement, we should allow for exaggeration and bias. It was written at a time when a fierce ideological struggle was taking place for the souls of the Keralans, which would end in Kerala becoming the most religiously mixed, the most literate and arguably the most tolerant state in India – a quite extraordinary turn-around when one considers the state of affairs in Travancore at the start of the nineteenth century.

A key factor in kick-starting this great change was the spread of education among the Christian communities of Travancore and Cochin. According to the 2011 Census almost 88 per cent of the present population of Tamil Nadu are Hindu, with Christians and Muslims virtually neck and neck at 6 per cent each – whereas next door in Kerala nearly some 24 per cent of the population are Christians. The success of this combination of Christian conversion and education inevitably spilled over into the wider community, leading some members of the Hindu majority to ask questions of themselves, exemplified by the rise of the phenomenon that became Ayyavazhi, or 'path of the father': a religious cult built around a mystic who saw himself as a reincarnation of Lord Vishnu, and which today has an estimated ten million followers in South India.

Its creator was a frail young man popularly known as Ayya Vaikundar, born to a Nadar or Channar couple in Kanyakumari District in about 1810. Many stories are told about this remarkable young man. He was said to have walked in the sea and disappeared and then returned to life, and after a six-year period of extreme self-mortification to have acquired powers that enabled him to banish evil spirits. He preached that he had come to bring the present Kali Yuga or 'dark age' to an end, together with all its injustices, after which he would rule as a Dharma Raja. His fast-growing popularity with the masses led to his imprisonment by the Travancore Raj in about 1839 on the grounds that he was disturbing the social order, although he appears to have been released without charge. Vaikundar's abiding message was that the Kali Yuga could be brought to an end if people lived with dignity and self-respect. This fired the imagination of Travancore's oppressed underclasses and explains why he remains such an inspirational figure among the common folk to this day.

Vaikundar is said to have died in 1851 while still in his early forties, his body being entombed in the Swamithope *pathi*, the main temple of the cult, midway between Nagercoil and Kanyakumari. Every year in late January his followers celebrate his rebirth from the sea by gathering in great numbers to bathe beside the seashore temple of Tiruchendur.

By contrast, Kanjan Pillai, better known as Chattampi Swamikal, came from the upper end of the social scale, being the offspring of a Nambudiri father by a Nair mother. Born in 1853 and raised in modest circumstances outside Trivandrum, he had little formal education. He is said to have worked as a labourer and subsequently as a clerk before coming to the notice of a Brahmin who took him under his wing. He subsequently became a wanderer and mystic, travelling through Tamil Nadu exploring Christian and Muslim theology as well as studying under a number of *avaduta*s or Hindu sages. He returned to Kerala a committed reformer, joining with Narayana Guru, the son of an Ezhava peasant, to denounce the orthodoxy of the Nambudiris and the caste restrictions imposed by them.

Although as much religious as social reformers, these three Keralans each in their different ways helped to clear paths for the next generation of reformers – a generation dominated by the formidable Ayyan Kali, a member of the Pulayar 'untouchable' community who never learned to read or write yet led the first non-violent protests and organised the first mass demonstrations and strikes that blazed a trail for the great Mahatma, M. K. Gandhi.

Every road in Travancore had, in theory, been open to all since 1865. However, a subsequent legal ruling had made a distinction between public and private roads, allowing many temple authorities to claim that the roads closest to their temple were private, open to all, including Christians and Muslims, but not to the outcaste *avarna*s. It was this bizarre situation which led that remarkable Bengali reformer and intellectual Swami Vivekananda to declare in exasperation in 1897, 'Was there ever a sillier thing before in the world than what I saw in Malabar country? The poor Pariah is not allowed to pass through the same street as the high-caste man, but if he changes his name to a hodge-podge English name, it is all right; or to a Mohammedan name, it is all right. What inference would you draw except that these Malabaris are all lunatics, their homes so many lunatic asylums, and they are to be treated with derision by every race in India until they mend their manners.'[17]

Ayyan Kali's first act of public protest against this injustice took place in 1893 when he bought a bullock cart – the ownership of which was forbidden to untouchables such as himself – dressed himself in clothing traditionally worn only by Nairs and then rode the cart down a temple road closed to untouchables. Other such blasphemous and officially illegal acts of protest followed, often provoking violent retaliation, but by 1900 the Pulayars had won the right to use most roads in Travancore State other than those controlled by the most orthodox Shaiva temples.

By 1904 state education had been introduced in Travancore but untouchables continued to be refused admittance. In 1915 Ayyan Kali's efforts to enrol a Pulayar girl in a government school in Ooruttambalam, outside Trivandrum, were met by violent opposition from the local Nairs, who burned down the school to prevent it being polluted. Ayyan Kali responded by organising a withdrawal of labour by the local agricultural workers – said to be the first organised strike in South India – which ended only when the Government of Travancore agreed to pass legislation lifting all restrictions on access to education.

Two basic human rights still continued to be denied to the lower castes and untouchables of Travancore: freedom of movement and temple access. This led to what became known throughout India as the Vaikom satyagraha, taking its name from the temple town of Vaikom on the eastern banks of Vembanad Lake in central Travancore, its centre dominated by a long-established Shiva temple owned by a number of Nambudiri Brahmin families. Every road surrounding the temple grounds carried notice boards proclaiming the ban, with policemen on hand to enforce it.

After all efforts to get the ban lifted had failed, the Oxford-educated lawyer and Malayalam scholar Kavalam Pannikar, a Nair with a Nambudiri father, suggested that the Indian National Congress should show their interest, so as to make the issue a national rather than a local cause. Mahatma Gandhi became involved, and a date was fixed for what Gandhi termed a *satyagraha* or 'soul-force' demonstration in the form of a peaceful march by volunteers drawn from all communities.

On 30 March 1924 this first historic protest march duly took place, leading to the arrest and jailing of all the Ezhavas and Dalits who took part. More marches and more arrests followed, events becoming increasingly violent as Nairs and others weighed in to block the protesters. In April the Tamil reformer Periyar joined the marchers, together with his wife and followers, and they too were arrested and jailed. The elderly Narayana Guru also came to offer his support, only to quarrel with Gandhi over the issue of whether or not the scaling of the barricades erected by the police constituted an act of violence.

Mahatma Gandhi now appealed for all Nairs and Brahmins of goodwill to show their support, which led to a march of several thousand that entered Trivandrum on 12 November. A petition was then presented to the Queen Regent of Travancore asking for all the roads around Vaikom temple to be thrown open to all. Gandhi is said to have approached Rani Sethu Lakshmi Bayi directly to ask for her support but was rebuffed. He then spoke to her twelve-year-old son, the minor ruler of Travancore, Maharaja Chithira Thirunal Balarama Varma, and asked him if on attaining his majority he would allow access to all roads, to which he replied 'Of course'. A compromise was now arrived at by which a new road was constructed that allowed free movement along three sides of the temple approaches but not on the fourth. This was enough for Gandhi, who moved on to greater things, having established that *satyagraha* could serve as a potent weapon in the national freedom struggle.

Two Keralan reformers. (Above, left) Koyapalli Kelappan. (Above, right) Velathu Lakshmikutty, who led protests against a temple ban in 1952.

However, there still remained the equally hurtful issue of the ban on temple entry. This came to a head at the Guruvayur satyagraha of 1931, which was directed at the Krishna temple of Guruvayur near Thrissur in what was then British Malabar, maintained by Cennas Nambudiris, supported by Nair Panikkars but under the authority of the Zamorin of Calicut. But now the protests were headed by a group of Nairs led by Koyapalli Kelappan, first president of the Nair Service Society, which was formed in 1914 both to protect the interests of Nairs and to improve their behaviour. Widely known as the 'Keralan Gandhi', Kelappan twice began hunger strikes, but on each occasion was dissuaded from continuing by Gandhi himself. In response to these protests a Temple Entry Enquiry Committee was set up but concluded that allowing access to untouchables was 'likely to cause breaches of the peace'. So the protests and petitions continued, now including a significant number of influential Nambudiris involved in the freedom struggle. Finally, on 12 November 1936, the Travancore Temple Entry Proclamation was published in the name of Maharaja Chithira Thirunal Balarama Varma declaring that 'there should henceforth be no restriction placed on any Hindu by birth or religion on entering or worshipping at temples controlled by us and our Government'. The final barriers had at last come down in Travancore, although it was another ten years before the caste restrictions at Guruvayur were lifted by order of the Zamorin.

This chapter opened with an account of a brave woman's self-sacrifice. The role played by women in history is as underwritten in India as anywhere, so it is only right to end with a mention of another woman of Kerala whose part in its history has only recently been publicly recognised. Her name was Velathu Lakshmikutty and she died in 2013 at the fine old age of 102 (see page 297). In 1952 she organised and led a march by women against the Manimalarkavu temple in Velur, Cochin, which – unbelievable as it seems to us today – was still requiring *avarna* women like herself to attend the Manimalarkavu pooram spring festival with breasts exposed. The protest that she led finally brought that particularly shaming form of caste discrimination to an end, although it serves as a reminder that the oppression of the powerless by the powerful is far from being a thing of the past.

Other legacies of Kerala's unhappy dealings with caste injustice are slowly being resolved, one concerning the extraordinary wealth that had accumulated in the vaults of the Padmanabhaswamy Vishnu temple at Trivandrum.

As Independence approached in 1947 Travancore's Chief Minister, C. P. Ramaswamy Iyer, refused to accede to the Indian Union as most of the other Princely States were doing, believing that Travancore could go it alone on what he called the 'American model'. He encouraged the now elderly ruler, Maharaja Balarama Varma, to declare independence, leading to a violent uprising in the Alleppey region that was equally violently suppressed with the loss of several hundred lives. Iyer had to resign, and the maharaja then agreed that Travancore should join the Union. So in 1949 the two former kingdoms of Travancore and Cochin became a single state within the Indian Union, with the former Maharaja of Travancore taking on the largely symbolic role of governor. In 1956 this short-lived state became Kerala State, in the process gaining the district of Malabar but losing its four southernmost divisions to what became Tamil Nadu. In 1957 Kerala state's first communist government was elected to power and began a sweeping programme of reform under Chief Minister E. M. S. Namboodiripad, whose very name is an indicator of what huge shifts in attitude had taken place.

Throughout this period the royal family of Travancore retained managing control of the Padmanabhaswamy temple in the form of

a temple trust. This continued right up to 2009, when an elderly
Brahmin named T. P. Sundarajan filed a writ challenging the royal
family's authority over the temple. Sundarajan was a committed
if eccentric devotee who, according to the temple priests, had
frequently disturbed the sleeping Lord Vishnu by chanting loud
'wake-up' *shloka*s. Whatever his motives, Sundarajan's writ eventually led, in July 2011, to the Supreme Court appointing him a
member of a panel charged with drawing up a complete inventory
of the temple treasury, believed to be contained in six underground vaults. The contents of four of the six vaults were known
but not those of the remaining two, labelled Vaults A and B, which
had remained closed since the 1930s. Following objections made
by the temple authorities a divining service was conducted to
determine the will of Lord Vishnu. This revealed that if Vault B
was opened it would provoke divine displeasure and bring bad
luck to Kerala, so it was decided that Vault B should remain closed
for the time being, but that Vault A could be opened. This duly
took place in July 2011.

No official inventory has yet been published, but a combination
of off-the-record briefings and determined digging by journalists
has since revealed treasure on a scale that has made headlines all
round the world, seemingly confirming the temple's reputed status
as the richest in the world. The contents are said to include a 1-
metre-tall solid gold statue of Vishnu; a 5.5-metre-long gold chain;
a 500-kilogram gold sheaf; a gold veil weighing 36 kilograms; a
sixteen-part gold *anki* or ceremonial costume weighing almost
30 kilograms; a giant gold throne, studded with diamonds and
precious stones; at least three gold crowns similarly studded with
precious stones; hundreds of gold chairs; thousands of gold pots
and jars; 1200 chains of gold-coins; gold coconut shells studded
with precious stones; several sackfuls of gold artefacts, necklaces
and diadems, as well as diamonds, rubies, sapphires, emeralds

and other gemstones; several Napoleonic-era gold coins; and an 800-kilogram (1800 lb) hoard of gold coins that include Greek and Roman examples dating from 100 BCE onwards.[18]

Vault B remains unopened, but if an unofficial inventory made for the Travancore royal family back in 1931 is accurate, this is as full of treasure as Vault A. There are also rumours that two more vaults, G and H, have been located. In the meantime, arguments rage both in the papers and in the law courts as to who has a legal right to all this wealth: the Travancore royals, Kerala State, central government or the Padmanabhaswamy temple itself?

A Muslim mullah and his wife. From an album of castes and occupations from the Tanjore region, c. 1790.

10

TIPPOO'S TIGER

The Cheraman Juma Masjid at Kodungallur, Kerala, which has a claim to be the oldest mosque in India. This is the only surviving photograph of the mosque with its Keralan tiled roofs as it was in the 1950s before a more characteristically Islamic façade with twin *minars* was added.

With its pale green onion domes and its twin whitewashed *minars* the little mosque of Cheraman Juma Masjid, on the road leading south out of Kodungallur, looks much like every other mosque in Kerala. But open a few doors and you'll find that this is just a modern façade, a false front to a much older building, built in the traditional Keralan regional style found all the way down the Malabar coast from about the sixteenth century onwards.

The local imam welcomes us with a cheery greeting and hand-shake. He seems genuinely pleased to see non-Muslims such as ourselves and takes great pride in showing us around his mosque and its little museum. And he has every right to be proud, because this modest little building has a claim to be the oldest mosque in India. Its earlier predecessor may even have been raised during the lifetime of the Prophet, making it one of Islam's earliest mosques outside Arabia.

The Cheraman Juma Masjid takes its name from the local Chera kings, who became known collectively as the Cheraman Perumal, or 'great ones of the Cheras', one of whom who is said to have been so impressed with an early Muslim seafarer to his shores and his new religion that he quit his kingdom and sailed to Arabia, where he met and talked with the Prophet himself in Medina. He died on his way back and was buried in Salalah in present-day Oman, but before his death he asked a companion of the Prophet, Malik Bin Dinar, to spread the message of Islam in his homeland. Malik Bin Dinar then travelled through Kerala seeking permission from local Hindu rulers to set up a number of mosques before returning home, the first of these being the Cheraman Juma Masjid.

Arabs from what is now Oman and Yemen had been involved in the Indian spice trade for centuries as masters of the Indian Ocean, their navigators taking full advantage of the seasonal winds they called *mausim* (literally 'season', from which the English word 'monsoon' is derived by way of the Portuguese *mauçam*). In early summer, as the Indian interior began to heat up and draw in moisture-laden air from the Arabian Sea, they pointed their dhows towards the Malabar and Konkani coasts and let the wind fill their sails. Then as winter approached and the Indian land-mass began to cool, the winds reversed, allowing them to go home with their sails again filled – as well as their holds. Given these long-established trading links with the Malabaris and the rapid spread of Islam within Arabia it is more than probable that there were very early Indian converts to Islam among the colonies of Arab traders settled on the Malabar coast – where their descendants are to be found to this day. However, that an Indian ruler converted to Islam during the lifetime of the Prophet is more questionable. We simply do not know, although the traveller Ibn Battuta tells us that the rulers of the Maldives converted to Islam in the twelfth century. The first European account of Cheraman Perumal's conversion comes from a Portuguese named Duarte Barbosa, who came to Kerala in 1510 and recorded that these events had taken place six hundred years before the arrival of the Portuguese, which would place the conversion of Cheraman in about 898.

The name their Indian hosts gave these early Arab Muslim settlers was Mussulman Mappila, the first word derived from the Arab *Muslimeen*, 'those who submit', the second from the Tamil for 'son-in-law', which demonstrates that they were welcomed and found local wives. Thanks to the local caste prohibitions, the sea-faring skills of these Mappilas were much sought after, so much so that in later years the Hindu rulers known as the Zamorins of Calicut made it compulsory for every family of Hindu fishermen to give one son to Islam so that he could be trained as a sailor. The horses the Arabs imported were equally prized, as was the horsemanship they brought with them. Horses were always a rare and valuable commodity in India, being vulnerable to climate and disease, so that their stocks were constantly having to be replenished. As a result, the 'Arab' became a key element in the Indo-Arabian trade balance, and one of the oldest Muslim communities in South India are the Ravuttanas, a word derived from the Tamil for 'cavalryman', whose descendants can still be found in Madurai, Tirunelveli, Coimbatore, North Arcot and in the Nilgiris.

These Mussulman Mappilas were soon established along India's western seaboard as traders in spices and pearls, and as seamen and cavalrymen. The Islam they brought with them was inclusive and accommodating, very much in harmony with the theistic bhakti cult that was at this time emerging within early medieval Hinduism. To this day some Mappila mosques still incorporate what some more orthodox Sunni Muslims would consider to be unIslamic practices, suggesting that in earlier times their predecessors sought to fit in with their new environment.

Similarly, images of Kamadhenu, the wish-fulfilling cow widely venerated among Hindus, often show her with a crowned human female face and a peacock's tail, which some art historians attribute to the influence of popular Shia images of Al-Buraq, the heavenly steed upon which the Prophet made his famous night-time journey from Mecca to Jerusalem. But it might equally be the other way round. Either way, both creatures are much beloved as talismans of their respective faiths.[1]

Islam won many converts in South India among the downtrodden. Islam's egalitarian nature offered an escape from the rigid social order of orthodox Hinduism, and not only in the South. The British civil

(Above, left) Kamadhenu, the Hindu 'cow of plenty'. Detail from a gouache painting from Trichy, c. 1820. (Above, right) The heavenly steed Al-Buraq flying to Jerusalem. A popular print from South India, c. 1910.

servant and historian William Hunter spent many years in Bengal in
the middle decades of the nineteenth century and was one of the first
Englishmen to write sympathetically about the impact of Islam on
India, and what he had to say about conversions in Bengal can equally
be applied to other parts of India. 'It was not to force that Islam owed
its permanent success (in Lower Bengal),' he declared. 'It appealed to
the people, and it derived the great mass of its converts from the poor.
It brought in a higher conception of God, and a nobler idea of the
brotherhood of man. It offered to the teeming low castes, who had
sat for ages abject on the outermost pale of the Hindu community, a
free entrance into a new social organisation.'[2]

However, from the tenth century onwards a very different manifestation of Islam began to impact on the subcontinent, its tone set
by the many warlords who descended on Northern India by way
of Afghanistan in search of plunder and slaves while claiming to
be acting as servants of Allah, among them the Mongol Timur the
Lame.

After sacking Delhi with great slaughter in the year 1398, Timur
pondered on what he perceived to be his religious duty. 'I then
reflected that I had come to Hindustan to war against infidels,' he
wrote in his autobiography. 'I had put to death some *lacs* [1 lac =
100,000] of infidels and idolaters, and I had stained my proselytising sword with the blood of the enemies of the faith.'[3]

Again, we have to be extremely wary of such boasts, yet it is
hard to avoid the conclusion that Timur's concept of the 'proselytising sword' did indeed manifest itself in India to a degree, that
iconoclasm did take place and that slavery was endemic. There
was undoubtedly a slave trade into Central Asia, which is memori-
alised in the name given to the slave trail through the mountains
of Afghanistan to Samarkand and the Khanates. 'Upon this road
there is a mountain called *Hindu kush*, which means "the slayer
of the Indians",' noted the fourteenth-century Berber traveller

Ibn Battuta in his *Rihla*, 'because the slave boys and girls who are brought from the land of India die there in large numbers as a result of the extreme cold and the great quantity of snow.'[4]

However, context is everything and slavery has been a feature of virtually every society since the dawn of recorded history, with Hindu India no exception. The *Manusmriti* lists seven different categories of *dasa*, and Chanakya takes much the same line when setting out the rights of slaves in his *Arthashastra*. Islam recognised slavery as an outcome of *ghanim*, or 'spoils of war', and as a means of winning converts through manumission, or the freeing of slaves. However, in practice the second half of the Koran's well-known injunction to set free the bonds of the captive unbelievers[5] was frequently overlooked as slavery became increasingly institutionalised. Christian Europe has been rightly castigated for the genocidal West African slave trade into the Americas and West Indies but the scale of slavery under Islam bears comparison, even if it is far less well documented. In the Indian context, the enslavement of *dhimmi*s, or non-Muslims, progressed from being a weapon of war to an essential feature of the economy of the Delhi Sultanates and the so-called Slave Dynasty.[6]

In South India, the Deccan Sultanates of Ahmadnagar, Bijapur, Berar, Golconda and Bidar were all similarly dependent on labour forces of enslaved *dhimmi*s, a famous example being Malik Ambar, an Ethiopian slave purchased in the slave-market of Baghdad who rose to become commander of the army of the Sultan of Bijapur before switching sides to become the de facto ruler of what later became the city of Aurangabad. I have given these Sultanates scant recognition in these pages, but it should be noted that once they had been secured an extraordinarily cosmopolitan and pluralist culture tended to flourish within their borders, leaving their non-Muslim subjects free to practise their religion provided they paid the *jizya* infidel poll tax.[7]

Emperor Akbar (1542–1605) sought to prohibit the enslavement of Hindus conquered in the many wars fought under his authority, but his successors resumed the practice, most notably his great-grandson Aurangzeb, who codified it in his *Fatawa-e-Alamgiri*, the stifling impact of which I explore later in this chapter.

The advance of this more martial Islam from North India into the South meant that by the time the Portuguese began their depredations at the start of the sixteenth century the Mappilas had been joined by other Muslims, known locally as Pardesi, or 'strangers'. The Portuguese Duarte Barbosa, whose fluency in Malayalam led his employers to use him as an interpreter in their dealings with the rulers of Cannanore (Kannur) and Cochin (Kochi), observed that their Muslim communities were now made up of 'Arabs, Guzaratees, Khorasanis [Afghans, Turks and Persians] and Deccanis. They are great merchants, and possess in this place wives and children, and ships for sailing to all parts of the world with all kinds of goods.' He also observed that they had adopted the local dress code – but only to a degree: 'They go bare like the Nairs, only they wear, to distinguish themselves from the Gentiles, small round caps on their heads, and their beards are fully grown' (see illustration at the start of this chapter).[8]

But as the Portuguese set about securing for themselves both the spice trade and the shipping lanes, so the Pardesi element on the Malabar coast dwindled and the ancient links with Arabia were all but severed. The Portuguese also participated in the sale of Indian slaves, although not on the scale that had gone before, and their Dutch successors continued the practice. To its credit, when the East India Company took over Malabar Province in 1792 it banned the buying and selling of slaves, although the purchase of children in times of famine was exempted – and here let me raise a glass to the memory of Thomas Baber, judge and magistrate of Zillah North in Malabar, for acting against a certain Mr Murdoch Brown,

who had been given permission to buy Pulliar slaves from Malabar
to work on his pepper plantation in Anjarakandy on the grounds
that they were already 'by their own laws in a state of bondage'.
Back in 1767 the EICo had established a cinnamon plantation in
what is now Kannur District in Kerala (which is still in operation to
this day). This had been leased to Mr Brown, whose treatment of
his slaves became so brutal that Baber decided to intervene. Acting
without orders, in 1811 he raided the plantation and took away
seventy-six men, women and children, 'all of whom declared that
they had been stolen or forcibly carried away by Moplahs and others
from South Malabar, Cochin and Travancore, and transported to
Mr Brown's plantation at Anjaracandy'. Brown then laid a complaint
against Baber and won, with the court ordering that all the slaves
should be returned to him except for six of the children. However,
when the case reached the Supreme Court in Calcutta a year later,
the judgment was reversed and it was pronounced that 'Mr Baber
was fully justified in the measure he had adopted'.[9]

Thomas Baber's actions led to a ban on the import and sale
of slaves throughout the EICo's territories, even if the institution itself was only finally banned in India in 1843.[10] Ironically,
abolitionist pressure on slave-owners in Muslim states such as
Awadh was one of several reforming measures that contributed
to the great sepoy revolt of 1857. Of course, it can be argued that
the system of indentured labour introduced into India by the
British at this same time was simply slavery by another name.
And it could further be argued that slavery within Islam had one
distinct advantage over slavery by caste, which was that it held
out the prospect of liberty through conversion. But this raises
the tricky issue of forced conversion, because there is no question but that over the course of several centuries thousands of
Hindus, Buddhists and Jains had to face a choice between Islam
or enslavement and that many converted.

After Independence this issue of religious violence perpetrated by Muslim rulers and warlords became to all intents a taboo subject, with what were then the younger generation of historians such as Dr Romila Thapar and Dr Irfan Habib condemning what they saw as simplistic interpretations of the past and focusing instead on socio-economic factors – attitudes that infuriated some among the older generation of leading historians, such as Dr R. C. Majumdar, author of the monumental *History and Culture of the Indian People*, who condemned what he saw as the conscious efforts of his fellow historians to 'rewrite the whole chapter of the bigotry and intolerance of the Muslim rulers towards Hindu religion'. That argument rumbles on to this day.

In recent years there has been a conscious effort by some writers of history to highlight an aspect of Islam in India that was overlooked in the past, which is the hugely positive role in India played by the Sufi missionaries and saints, both in the North and the South. This is right and proper because it has corrected an historical imbalance. Sufism's most distinctive characteristics are its mysticism and its emphasis on ecstatic personal devotion – a devotion that overwhelmingly has been inclusive and open-hearted – and in this way it echoed and even embraced the parallel impact of Hindu bhakti. But Sufism was not always so tolerant, because it is also true to say that some of the most intolerant figures within Islam in India have been ardent Sufis or followers of Sufi saints. The Mughal emperor Aurangzeb was one such, choosing his grave so that it might be as near as possible to that of the Chisti Nizami Sufi saint Syed Zain-ud-din Shirazi.

Few Westerners visit the Heavenly City of Khuldabad these days. It lies just outside the city of Aurangabad, originally Khadke, which the young Mughal prince Aurangzeb made his headquarters when his father the Emperor Shah Jehan appointed him Viceroy of the Deccan in 1653. Aurangabad subsequently became the springboard for Aurangzeb's overthrow of his father and his many military campaigns against the Maratha highlanders of what is now Maharashtra. In Victorian times, European travellers setting out from Aurangabad for the famous rock-cut caves at Ellora would pause at Khuldabad to take in its silent, ruined landscape of domed tombs and its melancholy atmosphere of past glory. And with good reason, because this was India's Mecca, the *karbala* of Islam in the Deccan, a ghost city of the dead where some of its greatest saints and rulers lie buried.

In 1850 one of those visitors was the young English water-colourist William Carpenter, who lingered long enough to draw a sketch of the graveyard's most famous occupant, Emperor Aurangzeb, laid to rest here in 1707. His drawing (see page 313) shows Aurangzeb's grave very much as the emperor had ordered it to be: unmarked, without decoration, and open to the sky. That is not how it is today. That grand imperialist Lord Curzon deemed the tomb unfit for a ruler of India and twisted the arm of the Nizam of Hyderabad, who, being the richest man in the world, was happy to pay for the marble screen that surrounds the tomb today.

Aurangzeb's tomb at Khuldabad still attracts a stream of visitors, and why not, since he is revered by millions of Sunni Muslims. Despite his murderous track record, which included the deposi-tion and imprisonment of the emperor his father, the murder of his heretical, open-minded elder brother Dara – whose tragic story was recently re-enacted on the stage of London's National Theatre in Tanya Ronder's adaptation of Shahid Nadeem's moving drama *Dara* – and the disposal of other weaker brethren, to his many admirers the single-minded Aurangzeb was the greatest Muslim ruler India had ever known, the emir who imposed the steel frame of *Adl*, or 'divine justice' upon his empire.

Aurangzeb brought together five hundred Islamic scholars who followed the Hanafi school of jurisprudence to produce the landmark thirty-volume *Fatawa al-Hindiya* ('Islamic rulings on India'), better known throughout the Muslim world today as *Fatawa-e-Alamgiri*. This now became the main basis for the enforcement of sharia throughout South Asia and it remains a key source of precedent in the Muslim world east of Iran.

(Above) The hallowed Muslim cemetery of Khuldabad, outside Aurangabad. A line engraving by an unknown English artist who visited the site c. 1860. (Below) The unadorned tomb of Emperor Aurangzeb at Khuldabad, as drawn by the artist William Carpenter in 1850.

The *Fatawa-e-Alamgiri* conferred legitimacy on Aurangzeb's efforts to bring his Muslim subjects into line, first by crushing the deviant Shia kingdoms of Bijapur and Golconda, outlawing *ziyarat* – the popular custom of venerating the graves of Sufi saints – and banning alcohol, music, gambling, prostitution, fireworks and other corrupt practices. Although he spent the last twenty-five years of his life in hugely expensive and ultimately fruitless military campaigns to subjugate and hold the Deccan, he himself lived a life of increasing saintliness, shunning all fripperies in favour of the study of the Holy Koran, making copies of the same in his own hand and embroidering prayer caps for sale in the bazaar.

But it has to be said that in seeking to enforce his sharia Aurangzeb made life harder for India's majority *dhimmi* population – non-Muslims who under Islamic law should have been protected persons. In April 1669 a general order was issued for the destruction of Hindu and Jain temples and their replacement by mosques, along with a ban on public worship and the restriction of Hindu festivals. In practice, these orders were rarely implemented and were less damaging than Aurangzeb's reimposition in 1679 of *jizya*, the infidel tax that had been abolished by his great-grandfather Emperor Akbar more than a century earlier. This was followed by a Hindu pilgrim tax and further bans on Hindus travelling in palanquins, on elephants or on horseback. Hindus who converted to Islam were given four rupees per male and two rupees per female. So it went on, year by year, despite the arguments of his ministers, although it is true to say that Aurangzeb's impact was far great in the north than it was south of the Narmada.

Aurangzeb had hoped to turn Aurangabad into the centre of Islamic culture in Asia, the Indian equivalent of the Damascus of the Umayyads or the Cordoba of the tenth-century Caliphate of Al-Hakam. In the event, the octogenarian emperor's last years were spent in the saddle as he rode from one battlefield to another, his state all but bankrupt, the once mighty edifice of the Mughal dominion falling about his ears. After his death in March 1707 his empire imploded. Marathas, Sikhs, Persians and Afghans, to say nothing of the British and the French, moved in to fill the power vacuum. Aurangzeb's conquests of Golconda and Bijapur had brought the last of the five Deccan Sultanates under Mughal rule but as his empire splintered his local viceroys seized the opportunity to make themselves masters in their own lands, with the Nizam of Hyderabad to the fore. As Aurangzeb's descendants continued to squabble among themselves the last of their authority drained away, culminating in the blinding of Aurangzeb's great-great-grandson Shah Alam II by a mad Afghan warlord in 1788.

Aurangzeb's uncompromising forty-nine-year rule is one of those hot potatoes no one wants to touch – except those who have chosen to metaphorically wrap themselves in the saffron-coloured robes traditionally associated with self-sacrifice within Hinduism and who subscribe to the ideology of Hindutva – about which I have more to say in my last chapter. It is precisely because these ideologues have made Aurangzeb's intolerance and Muslim iconoclasm a central pillar of their faith that those opposing them are so reluctant to go near the subject. To my mind, this silence does India's Muslim minority no favours, because it ignores the seismic shift within Sunni Islam that Aurangzeb helped along, whereby power shifted from the secular authorities to the clerics, the *ulema*, with far-reaching consequences.

That process had begun in the wake of the sacking of Baghdad, the capital of the Islamic world, by the Mongols in 1258. In response the theologian now known to his admirers as Shayk-ul-Islam Ibn Taymiyyah called upon all Muslims to return to the pure Islam of *al-salaf al-salih*, the 'pious forefathers', meaning the Prophet and his companions. Ibn Taymiyyah's narrow reinter-pretation of Islam is what gave the green light for today's Salafis, Wahhabis and all their offshoots.

The failure of the Mughals and their Muslim allies in India to stand up to the Marathas of the Deccan, leading to Delhi being sacked twice within the space of two years – first by the Marathas in 1737 and then by the Persians in 1739 – led to similar heart-searching among Muslim clerics, among them a student of theology named Shah Waliullah, whose father Shah Abdul Rahim is said to have played a major role in the compilation of Emperor Aurangzeb's *Fatawa al-Hindiya*. Shah Waliullah travelled to Arabia in search of answers and returned home fired with Ibn Taymiyyah's vision of a return to first principles. Coincidentally, he studied in Mecca and Medina at precisely the same time as another student of theology, Muhammad ibn Abd al-Wahhab from Arabia. Muhammad al-Wahhab's story is well known: how he formed an alliance with a minor tribal Bedouin chief that led ultimately to the founding of the Wahhabi-based kingdom of Saudi Arabia, and, from 1979 onwards, the widespread export of that fundamentalist creed very largely thanks to Saudi Arabia's petro-dollars. Shah Waliullah's legacy in South Asia is barely known about in non-Muslim India, let alone in the West, but has been equally far-reaching.[11]

Shah Waliullah returned to his father's seminary in Delhi, Madrassa-i-Rahimiya, and from there set out to reform Islam in India. In 1760 he wrote to the new ruler of Afghanistan Ahmad Shah Durrani, calling on him to return India to Islam. Ahmad Shah duly took up the invitation, leading to the battlefield of Panipat, north of Delhi, where over a hundred and fifty thousand Hindu Maratha warriors are said to have died. This was a catastrophe for the Marathas, who were by now masters of Western India and had been poised to take control of Northern India. The disaster at Panipat cleared the way for the EICo to extend its rule beyond Bengal and Bombay, and in South India it allowed Hyder Ali and his son Tipu Sahib to expanded the territories of Mysore.

Hyder Ali claimed descent from the Prophet Muhammad's Quareshi tribe but was more likely a descendant of one of the many Afghans who had followed the Mughals into India. As an officer in the army of the Hindu raja of Mysore, he had shown himself to be so capable a leader that he was given command of the army, after which it was only a small step to ruling Mysore in the raja's name. He then set out to secure control of the Malabar country with its coastal ports and its profitable spice plantations. North Malabar was won in 1766 and Cochin a year later, but Hyder Ali and his equally capable son Tipu then found themselves constantly at war with the Nairs, whose obstinacy they met with ever-increasing brutality. Hyder's determination to ally himself with the French in India then brought him into conflict with the EICo, leading to what became known as the Second Anglo-Mysore War of 1779-84. With his father's death in 1782, Tipu stepped into his shoes and continued Hyder Ali's policy of expansionism by attacking the kingdom of Travancore.

The first obstacle that Tipu's army encountered was the fort at the river-crossing of Kuttippuram, north of Thrissur and Cochin, where the two-thousand-strong Nair garrison was starved into surrender, forcibly circumcised and made to complete the ceremony of conversion by eating beef. Hindu and Jain temples were fired on Tipu's orders and cattle slaughtered in the temple premises.[12] As word of Tipu's actions spread, towns and villages were abandoned and refugees began to flee south. A Portuguese missionary named Fra Paulino da San Bartolomeo, then based in Cochin, afterwards set down an account of what he was told (albeit hearsay):

That barbarian Tipu Sultan tied the naked Christians and Hindus to the legs of elephants and made the elephants to move around till the bodies of the helpless victims were torn to pieces. Temples and churches were ordered to be burned down, desecrated and destroyed. Christian and Hindu women were forced to marry Mohammadans and similarly their men were forced to marry Mohammadan women. Those Christians who refused to be honoured with Islam, were ordered to be killed by hanging immediately. These atrocities were told to me by the victims of Tipu Sultan who escaped from the clutches of his army and reached Varappuzha, which is the centre of Carmelite Christian Mission. I myself helped many victims to cross the Varappuzha River by boats.

Tipu took great exception to what he regarded as the 'obscene practices' of the Nairs, whose sexual mores he considered to be 'more shameless than the beasts of the field'. In 1788 he issued a proclamation ordering the Nairs to forsake their sinful practices, with the threat that he would 'honour the whole of you with Islam' if they failed to obey him. The Nairs' response was predictable, provoking Tipu to issue an order to his army commanders that became known as 'The Order of Extermination of the Nayars'. Soon he was able to write that he had achieved a great victory in Malabar and that over four hundred thousand Hindus had been converted to Islam – although, as always, we should deduct at least one zero, and possibly two. However, Tipu's triumph was short-lived. His attack on Travancore brought in the armies of the EICo in alliance with the Nizam of Hyderabad. Tipu was forced to sue for peace and the outcome was that the districts of North Malabar, Salem, Bellary and Anantapur were all ceded to the EICo's Madras Presidency.

To the British public Tipu Sahib was now represented as the epitome of the oriental despot, a bogey-man whose hatred of the British placed him on a par with Napoleon and made him just as dangerous. But what particularly caught the public imagination was Tipu's obsession with tigers. By ancient custom Indian rulers had always identified themselves with lions as symbols of royalty, but for Tipu it was the Bengal tiger. According to one of his British opponents on the battlefield, 'He had adopted as his emblem of state, and as a species of armorial bearing the figure of the royal tiger, whose head and stripes constituted the chief ornament of his throne and of almost every article which belonged to him.' So Tipu's banners bore Persian characters shaped into tiger masks, his throne included a number of golden tiger heads, his weapons and possessions carried tiger motifs and stylised tiger stripes, and his soldiers wore tiger liveries. Among the collection of manuscripts found in Tipu's extensive library[13] after his death was a manuscript in Persian that became known as 'Tippoo Sultaun's Dreams', in which the highly superstitious Tipu had recorded in his own hand thirty-seven of his dreams, revealing his preoccupation with tigers as instruments for the extermination of *kaffir*s, or 'infidels', with himself as the chief tiger.

But what quickly came to be seen as the most sensational and the most notorious of all Tipu's tiger-based possessions was 'Tippoo's Tiger': a mechanical pipe-organ that when cranked emitted the growls of a tiger and the screams of its victim. This had been built to Tipu's orders to celebrate the killing by a tiger of the son of General Sir Hector Munro, the man who had vanquished Tipu and his father Hyder Ali in battle in 1781.

For the EICo, the tipping factor was not so much Tipu's continuing belligerence as his friendship with England's enemy France and his employment of French military advisers. That could not be allowed, and Napoleon's invasion of Egypt in 1798 gave Governor-General Sir Arthur Wellesley enough grounds to invade Mysore with his local ally, the Nizam of Hyderabad, culminating in the storming of Seringapatam (Srirangapatnam) in 1799 and the death in arms of Tipu, the Tiger of Mysore.

Tipu's death on 4 May 1799 was the signal for looting on a staggering scale as the victors awarded themselves vast sums in prize

MECHANICAL TIGER MADE FOR TIPPOO SULTAN.
India Museum.

(Above, left) 'Tippoo's Tiger', first displayed in the EICo's museum in 1808 and now one of the more curious treasures of the Victoria and Albert Museum. (Above, right) A miniature of Christopher Baldock in his cadet's uniform painted just before he sailed for India aged sixteen. (Left) Baldock's silver medal, issued in gold, silver or lead, according to rank, to all those who fought (on the winning side) at Seringapatam in 1799.

money from Tipu's treasury as well as jewels from the royal apartments. That treasure helped to bankroll not only the EICo in its continuing rise to power in India but also many members of the British aristocracy.

One of the first of my forebears to seek his fortune in India took part in the assault on Seringapatam and it made him a rich man (see illustrations). Eighteen-year-old Ensign Christopher Baldock's share of the prize money as the most junior British officer present was £1000 – the equivalent today of at least £80,000 – which he doubled overnight in a game of cards. We still have Christopher's silver medal in the family, as well as a copy of a letter written by his daughter describing the aftermath of the storming of Tipu's fortress, part of which reads as follows:

After the battle he [Christopher Baldock] was ordered to go into a tower to guard a part of the vast treasure taken from

Tippoo Saib. He told my mother that he stood all night in the very centre of the tower, close all around him were small bags of a sort of calico tied up at the mouth. They reached up to his armpits. He stood there all night trying to keep awake with both arms spread out on the bags. He had barely room to stand in the middle ... All the young officers receiving so much prize money, had nothing better to do than to gamble. One night he went with the others to a neighbouring tent & played [with cards]. He had no clear recollection of any thing till the next morning very early still he was awakened by his *khansomma* [steward], a faithful man whom he kept all the time he was in India. He told this servant to count the money & take some of it. The man counted it & found nearly £2000. By a strange turn of luck my father had all but doubled his prize money.

During my travels in the Bangalore region I was frequently surprised to hear local people speaking warmly of Tipu. I could understand why local Muslims admired him, even to the point of veneration as a saint and martyr. But what I found mystifying was that Tipu Sahib should be seen by wider sections of the general community as a patriot who fought and died in a vain attempt to halt British imperialism in India.

After 1799 the EICo's policy of annexing local states was abandoned in favour of subsidiary alliances, by which the remaining Hindu kingdoms or Muslim-ruled areas in the South had accepted the suzerainty of the British monarch while remaining largely independent of the Government of India. These included the Hindu kingdoms of Mysore, Coorg (Kodagu), Travancore, Cochin, Pudukkottai and the tiny Maratha princedom of Sandur, the almost equally small Shia Muslim state of Banganapalle, and the Sunni Muslim state of Hyderabad and Berar – the second largest of all the Indian princely states and the richest, even if those riches were largely confined to its ruling Nizam and his nobility (see Map 8).

The main losers in Tipu's defeat and death were the Mappilas, many of whom had cast their lot with him and had been rewarded with land taken from Kodava, Nair and Nambudiri Brahmin landlords, which they were now forced to return with interest. The good relations that had long existed between them and their non-Muslim neighbours were replaced with enmity and suspicion on both sides. To make their plight worse, those now living under EICo government found that the rules of land ownership had changed. The Jenmi landlords, largely made up of Nairs and Brahmins, now became absolute owners of the land, free to charge their Kanakkaran tenant-farmers as much rent as they could exact from them. These Kanakkaran then did the same with the peasant cultivators who worked the land, the Verumpattakkaran,

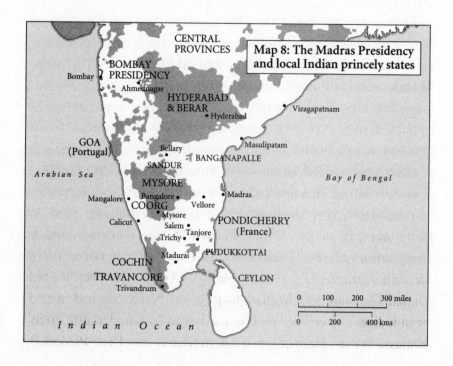

Map 8: The Madras Presidency and local Indian princely states

mostly made up of Mappilas and Hindus of the Ezhava cultivator caste – with inevitable consequences.

The great uprising of 1857 which the British called the Sepoy or Indian Mutiny had relatively little impact on South India. We should remember that there was at this time no overarching sense of national 'Indian' identity, especially so south of the Narmada, so that the war in the North was of no great concern to those in the South, who had their own loyalties. Yet it was the scattered Sunni Muslim community in India that had the strongest sense of shared identity, and in the wake of 1857 their religious leaders now began to ask themselves the same question that Shah Waliullah's son Shah Abdul Aziz had asked himself half a century earlier: how could Islam defend itself against the steady advance of British and Christian imperialism?

Two very different responses emerged, both claiming to be the authentic voice of Sunni tradition. The traditionalists argued for a return to pure Islam, 'Arabisation' and separatism. They found their first champions in Maulvi Nazeer Husain of Delhi and Siddiq Hasan Khan of Bhopal, founders of the Ahl-i-Hadith 'the Way of the Traditions (of the Prophet)' movement, which was Wahhabi in all but name. But these Ahl-i-Hadiths soon found themselves outflanked by a much more focused group of separatists led by Rashid Ahmad Gangohi and Muhammad Qasim Nanautwi, two former students of the Madrassa-i-Rahimiya. In the great uprising of 1857 they and a number of students and teachers from the Madrassa-i-Rahimiya had refused to ally themselves with Emperor Bahadur Shah in Delhi and had briefly set up their own Muslim theocracy outside Delhi at the village of Thana Bhawan. They had soon been broken up, with a number of survivors fleeing to Arabia. However, Rashid Ahmad Gangohi and Muhammad Qasim Nanautwi had stayed on in hiding – to emerge nine years later to co-found a little 'Arab' madrassa in the village of Deoband, in what is now Uttar Pradesh.[14]

With its uncompromising, separatist interpretation of Islam, the
Deobandi creed ought to have withered on the vine. But a significant proportion of India's Muslims, finding themselves increasingly
isolated and denied opportunities for advancement, rallied to its
clear-cut laying down of the law. By the end of the nineteenth century alumni of the original Dar-ul-Ulum Deoband madrassa had
gone on to found more than a dozen allied madrassas in India, and
what had begun as a tiny Arabic seminary in Deoband had become
a source of Islamic pronouncement to rival that of the ancient Al-
Azhar University in Cairo. Today Dar-ul-Ulum Deoband is the
headquarters of the pan-Islamic Deobandi movement, with many
scores of Deobandi madrassas across the world. By my count there
are eight such madrassas in South India: two in or near Hyderabad,
two in or near Vellore, and one each in Chennai, Bangalore, Salem
and Kollam.

Not all former students of the Madrassa-i-Rahimiya followed the
traditionalist path, among them the aristocrat Syed Ahmad Khan,
judge, intellectual and social reformer. His extensive contacts with
the British as a government official led him to conclude that if the
Muslims in India were to preserve their identity they had to learn
to compete with the West on equal terms. In 1875 he founded
the Mohammedan Anglo-Oriental College at Aligarh in what is
now Uttar Pradesh, with the aim of giving potential leaders of
the Muslim community an Islamic education that was thoroughly
modern and fully integrated with the rest of the community.
Osmania University, established in 1918 in Hyderabad, is founded
on the same liberal principles, described as 'seeking to achieve
an intellectual synthesis of oriental and occidental learning of the
best that has been thought of and said, both in the East and in the
West ... and the creation of an academic and social environment in
which "National Integration" is not a nebulous idea but a tangible
reality'. Both universities produce some of India's top graduates of

Sir Syed Ahmad Khan, knighted in 1888 for services to the Government of India, which allowed his critics to brand him a tool of the British.

both sexes – in striking contrast to Dar-ul-Ulum Deoband, where the all-male students still follow an introverted and separatist eighteenth-century Arabic curriculum centred on the Koran and its exegesis.

With the formation of these three institutions – Aligarh College, Dar-ul-Ulum Deoband and Ahl-i-Hadith – a struggle began for the hearts and minds of India's Muslims, one in which the modernisers proved unable to match the appeal of the traditionalists and separatists. But the latter did not have it all their own way. In the 1890s a fourth institution entered the debate, founded by a Hanafi cleric named Ahmed Reza Khan Barelvi in response to Ahl-i-Hadith and Deobandi attacks on the popular practice of venerating the shrines of saints and praying for their intercession. This quasi-Sufi move-ment became known as Barelvi Islam and became hugely popular throughout the subcontinent, so that in South India divisions began to emerge between the traditionalists and the modernisers, both groups led by Sayyids claiming direct descent from the Prophet through his daughter Fatima.

The modernisers took their lead from a line of Sufi preachers that went back to Sayyid Ahmad Jalauddin, who had emigrated from Bukhara to Malabar in the sixteenth century to play a leading role in the spread of Sufi teaching throughout India. The traditionalists looked for leadership from a very different group of Sayyids who came to be known in Malabar as Thangals, a local honorific applied only to Sayyids.

The first of these Thangals was the Islamic scholar Sayyid Alavi Mouladaveel Thangal, whose house and tomb in Mambaram, south of Calicut, are now important places of pilgrimage for Sunni Muslims in South India. His arrival in Calicut from Yemen as a young man in about 1770 marked the beginnings of increased conservatism within the Muslim community in South India. As Sayyids, he and his successors were considered religiously supe-rior to the long-settled Mappilas and they came to be accepted as the leaders of the Muslims in the region, with their heartland at Mambaram and other centres at Malappuram, Ponnai and Calicut. More significantly, they were far more fundamentalist in their thinking than their predecessors, being influenced by the opposi-tion to all form of perceived innovation emerging in central Arabia that its critics called Wahhabism.

Portrayals of Muslim women in South India up to the middle of the nineteenth century show them following local styles of dress, usually with their hair covered but never their faces concealed. As a general rule, only high-born women, Hindu as well as Muslim, then followed the patriarchal custom of purdah or *ghunghat*, remaining in seclusion indoors and veiling their faces in public. This was more marked in the north and in the Sultanates south of the Narmada, but now even in the South this began to change as Muslim women from all sections of society increasingly began to follow suit.

After Sayyid Alavi Mouladaveel Thangal's death in 1845 his only son, Sayyid Fazal Pookoya Thangal, returned to Malabar

A watercolour showing three couples in the Madras Presidency, two Muslim and one Hindu. But which is which? The men can be identified by their style of dress but not the women. The man on the left holding a rose is listed as a 'Nabob Khandan', a Muslim zamindar or landowner from the upper ranks of society. The man on the right holding a betel-nut case is described as a 'tamboolie lubay' or Muslim betel-nut (areca) seller from the lower ranks. The man in the middle is named as a 'Tanjore razabut', a Hindu Rajput of the Kshatriya caste. From a volume of thirty watercolours of castes and occupations from the Tanjore region, c. 1830.

in 1849 after several years of self-imposed exile in Mecca, where the Wahhabis had recently been overthrown and dispersed by the Ottoman powers. He was seen by the British authorities as a 'fanatical ostentatious Wahabee of considerable influence', a view subsequently shared by a Saudi historian who has described him as 'highly influenced by the thoughts of Muhammad bin Abdul Wahhab' from his years in Mecca.[15] He now presented himself as the champion of the Mappila peasantry in their struggles against their Hindu landlords by issuing a fatwa that made it a religious duty for all Muslims to make jihad against their oppressors.

Isolated acts of violence now began to occur, nearly always involving a group of Mappila cultivators turning on a Jenmi landlord and killing him. These outbreaks became increasingly serious, leading the British authorities in 1852 to deport Sayyid Fazal Pookoya Thangal to the Yemen. The British administrator who had ordered his exile, Henry Conolly, Collector and Magistrate of Calicut, was then murdered in his bungalow by the Sayyid's followers. Further outrages followed, all ruthlessly put down by the authorities. Disturbances in 1896 in Chembrasseri and Mancheri ended with the shooting dead of ninety-two Mappila rioters.

A generation later another Thangal, Sayyid Sanulla Makti Thangal of Malappuram, assumed leadership of the radicals, initially to counter what he saw as the growing influence of the Christian missionaries among the Mappila community. However, he became increasingly troubled by the failure of local Muslims to recognise the advantages of modern education. To this end, he devoted much of his life to spreading the message of education, while also taking on both the Christian missionaries and those among his own people who were urging Muslims to turn their backs on all things unIslamic. The Sayyid was also far ahead of his time in recognising that women in the Muslim community could equally be empowered through education, citing the example of the Prophet's young wife Ayesha. His name is frequently cited as a supporter of the Mappilas' armed struggle against the British but all the known evidence suggests the opposite: that while remaining a fierce critic of British rule, Sanulla Makti Thangal nevertheless opposed armed struggle against the ruling power, with a particular dislike of the growing trend among the Mappilas to deliberately seek martyrdom by killing a Hindu landlord.

Sayyid Sanulla Makti Thangal died in 1912 and so never lived to see the outbreak of the First World War and the rise of the Khilafat separatist movement that convulsed the Muslim population in India. The movement eventually ran out of steam as Turkey moved towards secularism and the abolition of the caliphate. Even so, in Malabar it led to the setting up of local Khilafat Committees whose prime aim was nothing less than an independent Muslim nation in Malabar. This inevitably created tensions between the Muslim Mappilas and the Kerala Provincial Congress Committee, dominated by Tamil Brahmins and Malabar Nairs. Despite these differences, the central All-India Khilafat Committee joined with the Hindu-dominated Indian National Congress in 1920 in a nationwide civil disobedience campaign that became known as the Non-cooperation Movement. In March of that year Mahatma Gandhi addressed a Khilafat meeting in Bombay and declared it incumbent on all Muslims to rebel against the British government in India and to follow their religious leaders. Gandhi intended his speech to be taken as referring to his allies the Ali brothers and their platform of non-violence, but in Malabar his speech was seen as an endorsement of their local religious leadership and their local aims.[16]

I am puzzled by the extent to which what followed is represented in some quarters as part of India's freedom struggle against the British. I share the majority view that it was primarily about land – that what the British authorities termed the 'Mopla outrages' of 1920–21 were at heart a desperate attempt by Mappila tenant farmers and landless labourers to destroy the existing landlord system by killing Nair and Nambudiri landlords, a movement that rapidly escalated into widespread acts of terrorism directed at the non-Muslim community in general.

Initially, the Mappilas had considerable success. In August 1921 the police attempted to arrest a number of Khilafat members gathered in the Mambaram mosque in Tirurangadi, among them the imam, Haji Ali Musliyar (see illustration), whose family had played a leading role in several earlier Mappila uprisings in which his grandfather and an elder brother had been killed. A large crowd of Mappilas prevented the police from making any arrests, but the police station itself was then attacked, leading the police to open fire. A Mappila uprising followed, which over the next few weeks spread to more than half a dozen districts. Police stations were seized, government buildings occupied, and in the districts of Ernad and Valluvanad a Muslim state was declared. In August 1921 Haji Varian Kunnath Kunjahamma, of whom very little seems to be known, took over the rebellion's leadership from Ali Musliyar and issued a promulgation that no harm should come to any non-Muslims and that there should be no looting – orders that often went unheeded. By the time law and order had been restored by heavy-handed military intervention some six hundred Hindu and Christian civilians had been murdered and somewhere between 2337 (the official figure) and 10,000 (the unofficial estimate) Mappila rebels killed, at a cost of forty-three troops dead.

The government was in no mood to show mercy. Haji Varian Kunnath Kunjahamma was among an unknown number of prisoners who were tried by a military tribunal and shot by firing squad in the Kottakumo fort in Malappuram. Haji Ali Musliyar was one of a dozen leaders who were sentenced to death and hanged.

(Above, left) The Mappila leader Haji Ali Musliyar, sentenced to death for treason and hanged in Coimbatore Jail on 17 February 1922. (Above, right) Captured Mappila rebels under armed escort, 1921.

At least twenty thousand Mappilas were deported to the penal colony in the Andaman Islands. A regime normally so scrupulous in keeping records and statistics signally failed to produce reliable figures of the human cost of the Mappila revolt, giving rise to wild exaggerations on both sides. A conference summoned by the Zamorin of Calicut subsequently passed a resolution condemning the government's attempt to minimise the crimes committed by the rebels, which it summarised in highly emotive terms:

Brutally dishonouring women, flaying people alive, wholesale slaughter of men, women and children, burning alive entire families, forcibly converting people in thousands and slaying those who refused to get converted, throwing half dead people into wells and leaving the victims to struggle for escape till finally released from their suffering by death, burning a great many and looting practically all Hindu and Christian houses in the disturbed areas ... cruelly insulting the religious sentiments of the Hindus by desecrating and destroying numerous temples in the disturbed areas, killing cows within the temple precincts, putting their entrails on the holy image and hanging skulls on the walls and the roofs.[17]

Traumatic as the Mappila insurrection was for Malabar's non-Muslim population, its impact on the Muslims in South India was far more devastating, and is still being felt to this day in terms of a reluctance in some quarters to engage with the rest of the community. Had the modernisers won the battle for Muslim hearts and minds the situation might well be different, but it was the traditionalists who emerged triumphant, in part because of fears over the prospect of Hindu majority rule with the approach of Independence but also because of the continuing rise of peaceful but separatist Deobandism.

In India today two thirds of its Sunni Muslim population are Barelvis who are essentially hostile to the Deobandis' ultra-conservative model. Both communities reject violence and are in many respects model and loyal citizens. Yet the temptation to follow the Deobandi model of separatism remains, and for any minority to seek to live separate lives divorced from the mainstream is essentially destabilising for both parties, the majority community quite as much as the minority.

It is a sad fact that while Kerala regularly comes top of the state league tables in such areas as literacy, healthcare and the elimination of poverty, it is the Muslim community, making up just over a quarter of Kerala's population, who lag behind when it comes to such areas of social development as birth rates, infant mortality and numbers working abroad in the Gulf. Continuing links with Saudi Arabia and the Yemen have brought about a degree of 'Arabisation', which manifests itself in increased conservatism in dress and attitudes, and growing intolerance towards anything that could be considered as insulting to the Prophet, as in the case of the assault that took place in the Ernakulam District in 2010 on a Christian professor of Malayalam. His crime was to have set an exam question based on a university-approved text that offended a Muslim extremist group calling itself the Popular Front of India. Equally shocking was the outcome: the dismissal of the professor from his post at the Mahatma Gandhi University for 'offending the religious sentiments of a community'. The professor's wife subsequently committed suicide.

But such tragedies have to be put in context, which is that in Kerala as elsewhere in India many Muslim communities live very much as Dalits lived in earlier times, isolated from the mainstream and constantly subjected to small provocations and threats. From time to time these provocations lead to retaliations that often escalate into wider violence in which the Muslim minority invariably comes off worst.

This is not a very reassuring note on which to end this brief foray into Islam in South India – but history should never be reassuring.

The goddess Meenakshi, the three-breasted warrior-queen, as carved in stone at the end of a long passage known as Trimul Naik's Portico or Puthu Mandapam, in Madurai's Meenakshi Amman Kovil temple. Now the centre of a bustling bazaar complex, the Puthu Mandapam was built in the 1630s by Raja Thirumalai Nayak as a summer abode for the goddess Meenakshi and her spouse, Lord Shiva as Sundareshvara. Her missing left hand originally held a lotus. From an album of forty-one prints by the pioneer photographer Edmund Lyon in 1868.

ENDNOTE:
HISTORY AND ANTI-HISTORY

The Pandyan virgin goddess Meenakshi, 'queen of Madurai', marries
Lord Shiva, with Lord Vishnu presiding. The Divine Marriage is hugely
popular in South India, re-enacted at the Meenakshi Sundareshvara
temple and at other temples as part of the annual Panguni Uttiram festival. An ivory carving probably made in Madurai in 1766.

I began this personal history with a Preface, so I shall end with an
Endnote.

The goddesses of Hinduism come in many forms but only one
of them has ever had three breasts – and I say 'had' rather than
'has' because one of the three disappeared when she first set eyes
on the god she was to marry. The goddess in question was named

Meenakshi, or 'fish-eyes', because those eyes of hers were said to
be fish-shaped. Her name carries less weight north of Hyderabad,
but turn about and the further south you travel the bigger she
becomes – and nowhere bigger than in Madurai, which is very
much her city.

Madurai takes its name from the Sanskrit word *madhura*, or
'sweetness', as a consequence of the divine nectar showered
on the city by the god Shiva as he shook his matted locks. It is
undoubtedly an ancient city – if not quite as old as some would
want it to be – and at its centre is the great temple complex of
Meenakshi Sundareshvara, from which the surrounding streets
radiate outwards, like the spokes of a cartwheel. The temple is
the hub around which the city revolves, and it has always been so.
From the early days of the Pandyas onwards no ruler dared rule
without first seeking legitimacy from the temple's prime deity,
Meenakshi.

Of all the thousands of temples dedicated to Lord Shiva, this
temple stands alone in giving equal space to his female *shakti* –
not Parvati, Uma, Kali, Durga, Chamunda or any of the usual *devi*
suspects, but a local girl. Three-breasted Meenakshi grew up to
become a mighty conqueror, a warrior-goddess, but could find no
one worthy to be her partner – until she attacked Lord Shiva's
abode on Mount Kailas. She overcame Shiva's army of elemental *bhoothagana*s and even subdued Shiva's bull Nandi, but the
moment she caught sight of Shiva himself she was overwhelmed
by love, and knew then that he was her destined husband –
whereupon her middle breast vanished. All the gods attended
their wedding but, according to local legend, refused to partake
of the feast until Shiva had danced for them, for which he took
on the form of Nataraja, the Lord of the Dance, to perform the
cosmic dance now famous throughout India and abroad thanks to
its vibrant portrayal in Chola bronze.

You could interpret Meenakshi's story as symbolising the process by which a powerful Dravidian female deity – a mother goddess or fertility goddess that may even have had her origins in a local warrior-queen – was absorbed into the fast-growing cult of Shiva in about the fourth or fifth century. However, what concerns us here is the tale told of three-breasted Meenakshi as a three-year-old. In that form she is said to have made three appearances: first to her parents out of a sacrificial fire, then to the seventeenth-century Tamil poet Kumaraguruparar when he presented his devotional poem *Meenakshi Amman Pillai Thamizh* to the public;[1] and finally to a British administrator named Rous Peter. That third appearance is said to have taken place about two decades after the EICo had taken over the administration of what the British termed the Carnatic from the Nawab of Arcot in 1801. It then became part of the official duties of the Collector and Magistrate of Madurai to act as the *thakkur* or civil guardian of the Meenakshi temple to ensure its smooth running.

One such *thakkur* was Rous Peter, a Cornishman from England whose father was the Member of Parliament for Bodmin – and whose unusual Christian name suggests that he was a red-head. He landed at Fort St George, Madras, in July 1801 aged sixteen, and after two years' training and language study was posted to Trichinopoly (Trichy), where he spent three years as an assistant to the District Collector. In 1807 he was moved to Madurai, where he remained for the rest of his life. In 1812 he was promoted Collector and Magistrate of Madurai, an all-powerful post he held for sixteen years.

According to local legend, Rous Peter always began his daily round by riding to the temple on horseback to pay his respects, and over time he became a devotee of the goddess. He reduced local taxes and became so popular with the area's inhabitants that when the *Tanjore Division Gazetteer* was updated in 1914 its author noted that 'vernacular ballads are still being sung in his honour'. According to these folk songs, Rous Peter was sleeping in his bungalow when he was woken by a three-year-old girl with three breasts who dragged him by the hand out of his bungalow, whereupon it was struck by lightning and burned to the ground. The girl then ran into the Meenakshi temple and was not seen again.

In gratitude for his deliverance Rous Peter made an offering to the temple in the form of a pair of golden stirrups studded with rubies. Refusing to return to England on retirement, he died in Madurai and, in accordance with his wishes, was buried in the local Christian church but with his face turned towards the Meenakshi temple. In support of this story there is the evidence of the pair of jewel-encrusted golden stirrups, still to be seen in the temple treasury and regularly brought out whenever the *murti* of the goddess Meenakshi is carried in procession through the town.

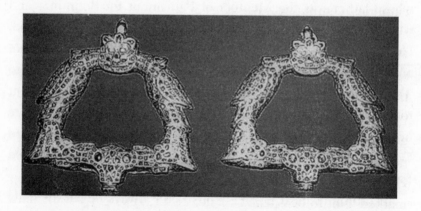

The pair of jewel-encrusted golden stirrups presented to the Meenakshi temple by the EICo administrator Rous Peter in the 1820s.

But there are other versions of the Rous Peter story. One is set down in the *Madurai District Gazetteer* of 1906, which tells us that Peter 'lived in princely style, was of a most bountiful disposition (both the Meenakshi temple and the Alagarkovil possess valuable jewels which he gave them) and did great things in ridding the hills around Kaunivadsi, Periyakulam and Bodinaykkunur of the elephants which in those days infested them and the country below. The people nicknamed him "Peter Pandya". He died in Madurai on 6 August 1828 and was buried in the heart of the town outside the then Protestant church.'

Government records show that Rous Peter did indeed secure a reduction in local taxes, as well as granting further reductions to no fewer than fifty-two villages. But then the story changes. The gift of stirrups was indeed a thank-offering – not for being rescued by a three-year-old goddess but 'for an escape from an elephant he had wounded'. And now the story begins to grow darker: 'The wildest stories about Rous Peter's end are current in Madurai and it has been stated in print that he was charged with defalcation [embezzlement] and, when a commissioner came down to make enquiries, committed suicide.'

Dig deeper still and you find that on being appointed Collector, Rous Peter began to draw freely on the government's purse as if it were his own. He built himself a palatial bungalow and lived the life of a prince, so much so that by 1819 he was in such a financial pickle that he asked his accountant to take what was left in the government treasury and use it to speculate, resulting in even greater losses. He then wrote out a statement apologising to the EICo for what he had done, which he placed in a sealed envelope marked 'Not to be opened till my death', apparently contemplating suicide. In the event another nine years passed before Peter's death, by his own hand, on 6 August 1828.

In the inquiry that followed it was discovered that Peter had squandered away huge sums of government money 'to the amount of between £70,000 and £100,000' – somewhere in the region of £5 million to £8 million by today's reckoning. Five members of his staff were imprisoned, and his estate, including a great many jewels, was sold to pay off part of the debt. 'So ended a life of extortion, cruelty and immorality by suicide,' noted a contemporary who got caught up in the scandal.[2]

So here are two accounts of the same man: one familiar to hundreds of thousands of devotees of the goddess Meenakshi and to readers of Wikipedia; the other virtually unknown except to the few who have checked the facts.

These include the fact that throughout the EICo's Madras Presidency local administrators in the form of commissioners, collectors and magistrates presented gifts to the temple deities at major festivals in the name of the *Sircar* (government), often in the form of shawls, a tradition derived from the Muslim custom of rulers presenting *khilat*, or robes of honour. These same administrators also attended such festivals as representatives of the Sirkar, just as they also sat on temple management committees. One of Rous Peter's contemporaries next door in Travancore State was Colonel John Munro, whose place in Travancore's history has been recounted in Chapter 9. Munro is known to have presented 'a gaily decorated horse' and 'a big circular gold-plated umbrella with green glass stones suspended all around the frame' to the Padmanabhaswamy temple in Trivandrum,[3] as well as a pair of golden bangles to the Mahadeva temple at Chengannur, where Lord Shiva's *shakti* in the form of Bhagavathi is said to be subject to a monthly menstrual cycle. Here the local myth is that Munro laughed at this belief and stopped the funds that supported the monthly *Tripootharattu* rites performed by the temple's Nambudiri Brahmin priests. His wife then started to bleed incessantly and continued to do so until Munro was informed that this was a punishment for his insult to the goddess. Only when Munro had promised to set up a trust to fund the *Tripootharattu* did the bleeding stop, whereupon Munro presented the golden bangles in gratitude. All I can add to this is that John Munro had married Charlotte Blacker two years before he came to Travancore and that their first child was born in Scotland five years later.

This practice of British officials making presentations to temples continued for many years but went into decline following protests from Christian missionaries that this was pandering to idolatry. One of the earliest of these protestors was Charles Shubrick, Collector and Magistrate of Chingleput (Chengalpattu), who gained some notoriety in the 1850s for refusing on religious grounds to present a ceremonial shawl to the presiding deity at the Varadharaja Perumal Vishnu temple in Conjeeveram (Kanchipuram) – this despite the fact that a century earlier Robert Clive (the notorious 'Clive of India') himself had presented an emerald necklace to that same deity, today known as the Makarand ('nectar') necklace and still worn by the *murti* on all ceremonial processions.

Another form of now popular mythology relating to British involvement in religious affairs presents the local administration in the role of vandal or robber. One such example comes from the magnificent Chola temple in Chidambaram, dedicated to Lord Shiva as the cosmic dancer Nataraja. This was at one time staggeringly wealthy, thanks to centuries of royal patronage and donations of land, money and jewellery, much of it originating from the war booty of the Imperial Cholas. As related in an earlier chapter, this made the temple prey to raiders, but if you go on the temple's website you will learn that this treasure was stolen by the British:

During the British era, they took over many temples because of the enormous amount of wealth attached to them and all the jewellery has completely disappeared today. They say that a huge amount of the British funding for World War II came from Indian temples. Lands were also taken over and distributed, so the temple has become poor and unmanageable now.

These are the words of Sadhguru Jaggi Vasudev of Coimbatore, respected yogi and yoga-teacher, and leading light of the Isha Foundation. The Sadhguru is the inspiration behind the very laudable environmental initiative known as Project GreenHands, which over the course of three days in 2004 planted more than eight hundred and fifty thousand saplings in 6284 locations in Tamil Nadu, involving no fewer than a quarter of a million volunteers, and which has since set up greening movements and plant nurseries in Tirupur, Karur, Madurai, Dindigul and Trichy.

If the Sadhguru were to re-examine the issue of Chidambaram he would find that initially the British authorities in the Madras Presidency were reluctant to get involved in temple affairs for fear of giving religious offence. However, they then accepted that as the new ruling power they had a duty to provide some level of financial aid to make up for the shortfall brought about by the loss of revenue from previous royal patrons. In 1814 John Wallace, Collector of Tanjore, reported that 993 temples in his Collectorate were each receiving thirty-seven thousand gold pagodas from the Madras Presidency Government. But at the same time, Wallace was receiving complaints from pilgrims about 'undue exactions' by the temple authorities and the misuse of endowments. He was also having to mediate in temple disputes, chiefly involving quarrels over access between Vatakalais and Tenkalais, the northern and southern branches respectively of Tamil Vaishnavism.

Wallace recommended that the management of temple finances and some temple affairs should be brought under the control of a government-appointed Superintendent. As a result, the Madras Government became embroiled in temple management to a ridiculous degree. In 1834 we find Robert Nelson, Assistant Collector of Tanjore, complaining that as part of his official duties he was expected to provide all the main temples with 'coolies' to draw their *rathas* – the great chariots that carry *murtis* of the temple deities in procession during the major festivals. Almost unbelievably, Tanjore's most important festival alone required no fewer than thirty thousand such coolies, and in that particular year the two principal festivals had coincided with a harvest season affected by heavy rains so that much of the grain had been lost.[4] The outcome was that in 1841 the EICo's Board of Directors in London ordered all three Presidency governments to withdraw from 'interference in the management of all Native religious institutions'.

However, continued complaints of temple mismanagement and caste discrimination finally led the Madras Presidency Government to take the view that temples were places of public worship and not the property of the Brahmins who ran them. Accordingly, under the Religious Endowments Act of 1863 all control of temple properties and revenues passed to temple boards made up of government-appointed trustees overseeing local committees of temple appointees. This secular control was further strengthened in 1923 by the setting up of Hindu Religious and Charitable Endowments Boards, each made up of a president and commissioners nominated by government. After Independence each state within the Indian Union further extended this policy, so that today no religious leaders are directly involved in temple management. It was only at this post-Independence stage that state governments felt sufficiently empowered to appropriate temple assets, chiefly in the form of land.

As for the Chidambaram temple, the presiding priests there have always been Podu Dikshitars, a Brahmin sub-caste who only marry among themselves and are found nowhere else in Tamil Nadu. It is greatly to their credit that they were among the first Brahmins to open their temple doors to all Hindus irrespective of caste. Indeed, the Chidambaram temple is one of the few Shaiva temples in South India that allows access to non-Hindus to all but the innermost temple precinct. However, it is equally a fact that no inventory of the temple's treasures was ever produced to the authorities. From the 1920s onwards scores of Chola bronzes began appearing on the market as art collectors and foreign museums began to appreciate their inspired artistry – and their value. The very finest of these were the Nataraja Shiva bronzes, many of which are believed to have been associated with the Chidambaram temple, as related earlier. Reader, you must draw your own conclusions as to how such treasures came on to the market.

I could list many more instances of such revisionism, some trivial and others rather more serious. The two examples I have cited both happen to involve South Indian temples and the British administration, but such misrepresentation of the past, wilful or through ignorance, appears to me to extend right across the board, not only on the internet and the media but also in some academic circles (and, as I emphasised in my Preface, history writing should never be taken at face value without asking where it's coming from). But the real issue, surely, is our natural preference for comforting mythology over uncomfortable history. This is as much an issue in the US and the UK as it is in India, but India, I believe, is something of a special case.

India has a vast and truly wonderful corpus of mythological literature that extends far beyond the *Mahabharata* and the *Ramayana* to include thousands of lesser-known works in Sanskrit, Tamil and other languages, all set within religious frameworks, whether

Vedic, Brahministic, Shaiva, Vaishnava, Buddhist or Jain. This corpus is far richer and far more varied than the entire mythologies of Europe put together. Indeed, what we have in the British Isles is so pitiful that we have had to borrow most of our mythology from our continental neighbours and from the classics of Greece, Rome and the Levant, so that their gods have become ours.

But that is only half the picture, because what Britain had from an early age is historiography – again, entirely thanks to the Classical world.[5] That is rather a crude comparison, but my point is that just as the one culture has elevated the historical at the cost of the mythical, so the other has done the exact opposite.

This apparent difference in national attitudes was first noted by South India's Robert Caldwell, who observed that 'It is a singular fact that the Hindus, though fond of philosophy and poetry, of law, mathematics, and architecture, of music and the drama, and especially of religious or theosophical speculations and disquisitions, seem never to have cared anything of history. The original meaning of the word "history" is investigation, and the Hindus never appear to have cared to investigate.'[6]

That remarkable Italian philosopher Roberto Calasso has more recently stated much the same thing in highlighting the differences between the classical Western mode of thinking and the Vedic thought that continues to underpin much of Hindu society to this day:

For a Westerner trained in philology, it is hard to think of anything more frustrating than Indian history. Quicksand in every direction. Dates and figures never certain. Here the centuries move back and forth as months do elsewhere ... There is no point in looking for help from historical events, since there is no trace of them. Only texts remain: the *Veda*, the Knowledge, consisting of hymns, invocations, incantations in verse, of ritual formulas and prescriptions in prose ... The Arya ('the nobles', as Vedic men called themselves) ignored history with a disdain unequalled in the annals of any other great civilisation.[7]

I can vividly recall my first encounter with this Vedic hangover. I had long wanted to visit the traditional sources of the Ganges at Badrinath and Gangotri in the Garhwal Himal, and that opportunity became available to me in 1979, when the Indian Government relaxed some of its prohibitions against foreigners approaching its border with Tibet. Because photographer Richard Cooke and I were the first foreigners to be allowed in we were treated with justifiable suspicion when we arrived at the starting point of our trek, which was the check-post at Uttarkashi. Here we were joined by a well-spoken official who announced that he would be coming with us, 'purely as a fellow-traveller, you understand'.

This would have been fine had it not been for the determination of this gentleman to lecture us on the glories of ancient India and the decadence of the West. He began by taking us through every twist and turn in the story told in the *Ramayana* of how the Bhagirathi River – which we were then following to its source – got its name. So we heard all about King Sagar and how his sixty thousand sons in their search for the sacrificial horse required for the *Ashwamedha yagna*, the ancient Vedic horse sacrifice, had disturbed the sage Kapila as he sat in meditation, causing the sage to open his eyes and blast the sons to ashes. For their unquiet souls to ascend to Swarga (heaven) their ashes had to be immersed in the waters of the sacred Ganga River, which then flowed only in Swarga and not on earth. We learned how the good King Bhagirath, in order to make this possible, had retired to the mountains to perform the arduous meditation known as *tapasya*, which he did for a thousand years until Lord Brahma granted his wish to bring the Ganga to earth. We learned how Lord Shiva had caught the river's falling waters in his matted locks – the Himalayas – and so brought the mighty Ganga to earth, making it possible for Bhagirath to immerse his ancestor's ashes in its sacred waters.

It is a captivating myth, inspiring one of the most audacious sculptures ever created, carved thirteen centuries ago across the face of two huge boulders at Mahabalipuram (Mamallapuram). But for us two twentieth-century trekkers this was only the first of many tales forced on us by our companion, who became increasingly dogmatic with each story told. The breaking point arrived on the third day after our companion had waxed at length about Lord Vishnu and the weaponry he had invented for the Hindu nation: jet aircraft, flying saucers, lasers and the atomic bomb – all Indian inventions. We had had enough, and while our unwanted companion dozed after tiffin we quietly packed and double-marched away from him – to no purpose, since he had us arrested on our return to Uttarkashi. He was, I should explain, a Brahmin deeply committed to his faith, and exhibiting precisely those characteristics that have both preserved Hindu India and held it captive.

This was my first encounter with what was at that time a comparatively rare species: the ideologue who lives in denial of the real – as opposed to the mythical – past.

Readers familiar with my earlier books will know that I have argued that the modern era of Indian historiography and Indian studies began with the British Raj. As I have defined it earlier, imperialism is the exploitation of one people by another but it is also a two-way street, and one of the by-products of British rule in India was cross-fertilisation and the importation of new ideas – perfectly encapsulated in the person of one man and the institution he founded: the jurist Sir William 'Oriental' Jones and the Asiatic Society of Bengal.

Founded in Calcutta on 15 January 1784, the Asiatic Society
of Bengal was Asia's first learned society, modelled on the
Royal Society in London (of which the present president, Sir
Venkatraman Ramakrishnan, just happens to be a Nobel Prize-
winning scientist born in the temple city of Chidambaram in
Tamil Nadu). At the Asiatic Society's inaugural meeting William
Jones read out a thirty-three-page *Discourse* that he had prepared on his voyage out to India, a 'grand and stupendous' plan
to enquire into man and nature in general and Asia in particular. Fluent in thirteen languages and capable of understanding
another twenty-eight, Jones was the very epitome of the European
Enlightenment, the new way of looking at the world that the
German philosopher Immanuel Kant defined in the year of Jones's
arrival in India as 'the emancipation of the human consciousness
from an immature state of ignorance'.

This emancipation came about in Northern Europe as the
result of a combination of factors ranging from capitalism and
printing presses to coffee-houses and journalism. It was one of
those rare moments of conjunction in human history when a para-
digm shift in reasoning takes place. Ancient Athens experienced
just such a shift at the time of Sophocles, Plato and Aristotle in
the fifth century BCE, and so did the *mahajanapada* of Magadha
in Northern India at much the same time, spearheaded by such
thinkers as Vardamana (better known as Mahavira), founder
of Jainism, Gautama Sakyamuni, founder of Buddhism, and
Kakkhali Gosala, founder of the Ajivika movement, which at one
time rivalled the other two heterodoxies.

What all these thinkers had in common was their determination to apply pure reason in the pursuit of knowledge, even if that
meant challenging long-held beliefs. I do not believe it to be an
exaggeration to say that in 1784 this 'emancipation of the human
consciousness' returned to India.

Whichever side of the Orientalist argument you take, the fact remains that through their enquiries, translations, publications and exchanges of ideas, Jones and his fellow Orientalists made possible a diffusion of knowledge that had hitherto been confined to privileged elites and closed circles of initiates, or not even known at all. In doing so, these Orientalists initiated a process of revitalisation that had far-reaching consequences in India. One of the chief instruments for this revitalisation was Calcutta's Fort William College, an institution that has been described by the late Professor G. P. Deshpande of Jawaharlal Nehru University as 'the single most important intervention that colonialism made in the cultural life of India in the last two centuries'.[8] Scarcely less influential was Madras's Fort St George College, where young British probationer administrators and officer cadets rubbed shoulders with local language teachers and scholars. The outcome was that increasingly Western-educated and more politically aware sections of the populace began to challenge the status quo; not only British colonial rule but also religious orthodoxy of every sort, whether imported or local.

I began Chapter 3 with a description of the great statue of the poet-sage Thiruvalluvar which stands on the larger of the two islets offshore at Kanyakumari. But the other, smaller islet also has its memorial: a small temple built to commemorate the Bengali aristocrat Narendranath Datta, better known as Swami Vivekananda. It was here on this rock that the young revivalist sat and meditated for three days in December 1892 before hitting upon what he believed to be the solution for resolving India's ills. This was not, as is so widely believed today, a plan to unite India politically, but a project he termed 'our Work' that would unite Indian spirituality with Western liberty and practicality.[9]

'At Cape Comorin, sitting in Mother Kumari's temple, sitting on

SWAMI VIVEKANANDA
·The Hindoo Monk of India·

(Above) A postcard of Swami Vivekananda posing in saffron robe and turban, produced in 1893 to publicise his participation in the Chicago Parliament of the World's Religions.

the last bit of Indian rock, I hit upon a plan,' was how Vivekananda described his thinking to a fellow swami.

> We are so many *sanyassins* wandering about and teaching the people empty metaphysics. It is all madness. Did not our *Gurudeva* [his teacher Shri Ramakrishna] use to say 'An empty stomach is no good for religion'? That these poor people are leading the life of brutes is simply due to ignorance. We have for all ages been sucking their blood and trampling them under foot ... We as a nation have lost our individuality, and that is the cause of all mischief in India. We have to give back to the nation its lost individuality and raise the masses.[10]

This raising of the masses was to be achieved through their

education and their liberation. India had to be liberated, not just from British rule but from itself:

> The present Hindu society is organised only for spiritual men, and hopelessly crushes everybody else ... Our ancestors freed religious thought, and we have a wonderful religion. But they put a heavy chain on the feet of society, and our society is, in a word, horrid, diabolical. Liberty is the first condition of growth. Just as man must have liberty to think and speak, so must he have liberty in food, dress and marriage and in every other thing, so long as he does not injure others ... No priestcraft, no social tyranny! ... None deserves tyranny who is not ready to give liberty.[11]

Ten months after his visit to Kanyakumari Swami Vivekananda was speaking for India at the Parliament of the World's Religions in Chicago, an ambitious three-week event staged to bring together all the world's faiths. Although never officially credited as a delegate, Vivekananda dominated the proceedings with his forceful personality, his fluency in English and his sheer charisma. Over the course of five lectures at the parliament and subsequently in his lecture tours in the United States and Europe he presented an image of Hindu India that had far-reaching consequences, initiating a process of rebranding by which the West's view of a land mired in superstition was replaced by a perception of India as a country of unique spirituality based on ancient truths.

This rebranding included the deliberate softening of some of the cruder edges of Hinduism as perceived by its critics in the West. For example, at the Paris Congress of the History of Religions in 1900, Swami Vivekananda denounced as ridiculous the views of the previous speaker, the distinguished German Sanskritist Dr Gustav Oppert, who had declared the shivalinga to be 'the phallic emblem of the male'. He then explained that this 'thoughtless' view had emerged in India 'in her most degraded times, those of the downfall of Buddhism', and that the real origins of the shivalinga lay in the *yupa-stambha*, the sacrificial post of the Arya, quoting a hymn in the *Atharva-Veda* describing the *stambha* as 'beginningless and endless', representing the eternal Brahman.[12] This divorcing of the shivalinga from its origins as a phallic fertility symbol became increasingly accepted at a time when Victorian-style prudery over matters of sex was becoming the norm among the fast-growing Indian urban middle classes, the new opinion-makers.

The Swami's trail-blazing promotion of India overseas made him a great (and deserved) hero in his homeland, where his idiosyncratic reinterpretation of aspects of Hindu Vedanta, such as yoga and transcendental meditation, led to a new appreciation of Hinduism and of Indian nationhood that extended right across the political and social spectrum, from Mahatma Gandhi, who declared Vivekananda a great defender of Hinduism, to Vivekananda's fellow Bengali, the freedom-fighter-to-be Subhas Chandra Bose, who proclaimed him 'the maker of modern India'. Vivekananda's sudden death at the age of thirty-nine robbed India of a blazing genius whose ability to inspire is still felt today.[13]

Swami Vivekananda was perhaps the most striking presence in a Hindu revivalist trend that was sweeping across India at this time hand in hand with nationalism. But also coming to the fore was another movement that was greatly influenced by Enlightenment thinking, best represented by the Tamil rationalist and humanist E. V. Ramasamy, better known as Periyar. Because he died in 1973 at the ripe old age of ninety-four we tend to think of Periyar as a relatively modern figure, but he was only sixteen years younger than Vivekananda, having been born into the mercantile Balija caste in Erode in what was then the Madras Presidency in 1879.

After experiencing Brahminical discrimination at first hand while on a pilgrimage to Benares, Periyar became a militant atheist, arguing with ever-increasing fervour that Hinduism was an imaginary faith that promoted the superiority of the Brahmins at great cost to the Shudras and Dalits. Some of his actions – such as his frequently stated belief that continuing British rule was preferable to *Swaraj*, or 'self-rule', if that meant government by a Hindi-speaking Congress; his burning of a picture of Rama as a symbol of Arya domination of the Dravidians; his statement that 'He who invented God is a fool, he who propagates God is a scoundrel, he who worships God is a barbarian'; or even his suggestion that Hindus who found themselves marginalised should consider converting to Buddhism, Christianity or Islam – would today get him into very hot water.

Periyar's ardent Tamil nationalism combined with his atheism and his anti-Brahminism won him many admirers. Some of those same admirers, however, turned to violence, which led considerable numbers of Brahmins in Kerala and Tamil Nadu to make the decision to pack their bags and migrate out of Tamil country. Today only 3 per cent of the population in those two states are Brahmins – to my mind, a great loss to the South. For all the privileges they awarded themselves and for all the discrimination that this engendered, the Brahmins were and still are a quite extraordinary phenomenon, not just as keepers of the Vedic flame over millennia but as a small cadre of largely unsung intellectuals, scientists and healers whose learning brought great lustre to their culture. Consider, for example, the extraordinary work of the medieval astronomers and mathematicians of Kerala between the fourteenth and sixteenth centuries who, among other achievements, invented calculus a couple of centuries before their counterparts in Europe, the tragedy being that they kept these advances to themselves.[14]

(Above, left) A postage stamp celebrating the rationalist and humanist Tamil reformer E. V. Ramasamy, better known as Periyar, whose
Self-Respect Movement campaigned for the human rights of the
depressed classes in South India. (Above, right) A postage stamp
showing the revolutionary V. D. Savarkar, who coined the word
Hindutva, showing in the background the cellular prison on the
Andaman Islands penal colony where he spent many of his twenty-
seven years in jail and exile in the 1920s and 1930s.

The other side of Periyar was his work as a social reformer,
which led to the creation in 1925 of his Self-Respect Movement,
formalised in 1952 with such laudable aims as

to allow people to live a life of freedom from slavery to anything against reason and self-respect; to do away with needless
customs, meaningless ceremonies, and blind superstitious
beliefs in society; to put an end to the present social system in
which caste, religion, community and traditional occupations
based on the accident of birth, have chained the mass of the
people and created 'superior' and 'inferior' classes ... and to
give people equal rights; to completely eradicate untouchability
and to establish a united society based on brother/sisterhood;

to give equal rights to women; to prevent child marriages and marriages based on law favourable to one sect, to conduct and encourage love marriages, widow marriages, inter-caste and inter-religious marriages and to have the marriages registered under the Civil Law.[15]

By contrast, in Maharashtra, Gujarat and the so-called 'cow-belt' of the Gangetic plains it was the more orthodox and high-caste reformers who began to find their voice, men like the ascetic Dayananda Saraswati, born in Kathiawar, who founded the Arya Samaj Hindu movement as a force for Hindu reform, promoting education and equal rights and condemning such blights as child marriage and the caste system. It was Dayananda who first called for *Swaraj*, and who first used that term in calling for 'home rule' for India. But it was also Dayananda who, in his determination to rid Hinduism of what he regarded as idolatrous accretions, called on Hindus to reject Western secular values and return to the golden age of their ancestors under the slogan 'go back to the Vedas' – a vision of the Vedic past that infuriated such scholars as the philologist Professor Max Müller, who wrote of Dayananda:

> To him not only was everything contained in the *Vedas* perfect truth, but he went a stage further, and by the most incredible interpretations succeeded in persuading himself and others that everything worth knowing, even in the most recent inventions of modern science, were alluded to in the *Vedas*. Steam-engines, railways, and steam-boats, all were shown, at least in their germs, to the poets of the *Vedas*, for *veda*, he argued, means 'Divine Knowledge', and how could anything have been hid from them?"[16]

In 1881 Dayananda published a pamphlet entitled *Gokaru-nanidhi*, or 'Ocean of mercy to the cow', in which he declared the killing of cows to be anti-Hindu, leading to the formation of numerous cow-protection societies that increasingly assumed anti-Muslim, anti-British and Hindu nationalist overtones. Here Dayananda and the religious revivalists were greatly assisted by the popular prints published by the aristocrat, artist and publisher Ravi Varma, born into a Koil Thampuran family which by tradition produced the consorts for the princesses of the royal family of Travancore. A talented artist in his own right, Varma set up a lithographic printing press in 1894 at the suggestion of the then Dewan of Travancore. As well as popularising prints of his own paintings the Varma press mass-produced colourful images of Hindu deities. It was not the first press to do so – similar presses had preceded him in Calcutta (Kolkata) and Poona (Pune) – but the effect was to make religious art accessible to the man and woman in the street for the first time and on a wide scale.

Dayananda Saraswati died in 1883 but his reimagined past resurfaced in the 1920s as part of the Freedom Struggle's efforts to reclaim Indian history from British colonial bias and, before that, from the triumphalism of Muslim historiography. It followed the discovery of the buried brick city of Mohenjo-Daro (see Chapter 2) and the dawning realisation that this was just part of a widespread urban and farming culture that pre-dated India's known early history by fifteen thousand years and more.

The discovery of the Harappan Civilisation came as a godsend to the ideologues of the nascent Hindutva, or 'Hindu-ness', movement, an ultra-nationalist pressure group succinctly characterised by Professor Romila Thapar in a recent newspaper interview as 'a kind of syndicated Hinduism ... borrowing from Western models to create an organised, ecclesiastically run religion which might be used politically in a fascistic way to deny India's traditional plurality'.[17] The man who coined that word Hindutva was

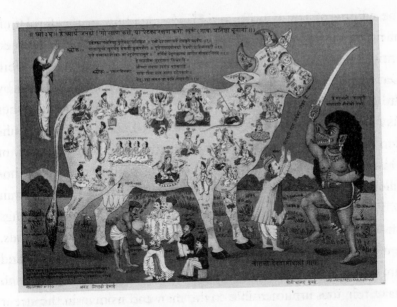

One of Ravi Varma's immensely popular coloured lithographs, entitled *Chorsai devata auvai gaya*, or 'The cow with eighty-four gods'. It shows a good Hindu holding up his hands to prevent the demon Ravana from killing the sacred cow, while a cow-keeper nourishes a group of citizens of all ranks with milk.

the indefatigable revolutionary Vinayak Damodar Savarkar, a Marathan Chitpavan Brahmin who had distinguished himself at the age of twelve by leading his schoolmates in an attack on his local mosque during Hindu-Muslim disturbances in the Nasik region in 1895. While studying law in London – where he met and profoundly disagreed with M. K. Gandhi – Savarkar examined the Italian nationalist Giuseppe Mazzini's role in the liberation and creation of modern Italy as well as the sepoy mutiny and uprising of 1857, leading to the publication in 1908 of his *History of the War of Indian Independence*, which was immediately banned by the British authorities.

Savarkar now set out to wage his own war of independence,

based on a vision of India as a Hindu nation made up of a Hindu
race and a Hindu culture, as set out in his *Essentials of Hindutva* –
written in 1923 in the penal colony of the Andaman Islands while
serving out one of his many extended jail sentences – later republished as *Hindutva: Who is a Hindu?* Savarkar had as many critics
as followers, then as now, but it is often forgotten that his uncompromising Hindu nationalism was equally uncompromising on the
injustice of untouchability, which he regarded as a great blot on
Hindu history, arguing that its eradication was essential for Hindu
unity: 'To regard our 70 million co-religionists as "untouchables"
and worse than animals is an insult not only to humanity but also
to the sanctity of our soul ... Untouchability should be eradicated
not only because it is incumbent on us but because it is impossible
to justify this inhuman custom when we consider any aspect of
dharma.'[18]

The revelation of Harappa made it possible for Savarkar and
his disciples to present the Indo-European origins of the Arya
and their migration into India as a colonial plot, a fiction created by the colonial British to claim family ties between Indians
and Europeans. One of the first proponents of this argument
was another Maharashtrian, M. S. Golwalkar. In the 1930s this
university-educated *sanyasi* rose to become head of the pro-Hindu
and anti-Muslim political party Rashtriya Swayamsevak Sangh,
or 'National Volunteer Organisation', better known as the RSS.
'We Hindus,' he proclaimed, 'have been in undisputed and undis-
turbed possession of this land for over 8 or even 10 thousand years
before the land was invaded by any foreign race.'[19]

That this sectarian view of Indian history did not catch on is
largely because of the determination of two secularist politicians
at opposite ends of the social scale: the Old Harrovian Kashmiri
Brahmin patrician Jawaharlal Nehru and the outcaste-born
Maharashtrian Bhimrao Ambedkar, the first ever 'untouchable' to

gain a university education. Both men found themselves increasingly at odds with M. K. Gandhi's vision of a *Ramrajya*, a model of government which harked back to a golden age as celebrated in the *Ramayana* when Lord Rama returns from exile to rule over Ayodhya.

For the Mahatma, the ideal national flag of an independent India was that which had emerged from the meeting of the All India National Congress at Vijayawada in what is now Andhra Pradesh in 1921, when a local activist from Machilipatnam, an ex-soldier turned geologist named Pingali Venkayya, produced a design that showed a *charka* or spinning-wheel superimposed upon two horizontal bands of red and green, Hindus and Muslims respectively – modified by Gandhi with the addition of a white stripe in the middle signifying purity. This tricolour and *charka* was adopted as the official flag of the National Congress in 1931 but came to be seen as having communal undertones. In July 1947, with Independence fast approaching, a new design was hurriedly agreed upon without Gandhi's approval, in which the *charka* was replaced by a *chakra*, representing dharma and the moral law as promulgated by Ashoka Maurya centuries earlier.

In the event, the Mahatma's tragic murder at the hands of a religious bigot on 30 January 1948 ended all talk of *Ramrajya* in Government circles. However, in the years that followed the distinction between history and politics began to blur as Prime Minister Nehru and the Congress Party embarked on a nation-building project with the entirely laudable aim of creating a stronger sense of national unity.

They did this in part by building up the Freedom Struggle into a quasi-sacred national epic to rival the *Mahabharata* and the *Ramayana*. Every new nation from ancient Rome through to the United States of America has drawn strength from just such foundation myths, and so it has been in India. But, to my mind, it has come at a price. Firstly, it was necessary to present what had gone before as a period of unmitigated oppression, and the Indian peoples as having been united against that oppression. The papering over of any cracks that challenged this simplistic view of the past or threatened the social cohesion of the present achieved its apotheosis in 1982 when India's National Council for Educational Research and Training issued a directive requiring school texts to gloss over sensitive issues such as sectarian conflict, declaring categorically, for example, that 'Characterisation of the medieval period as a dark period or as a time of conflict between Hindus and Muslims is forbidden'. This well-intentioned but misguided instruction played directly into the hands of the Hindutvatistas – by which I mean those disciples of Savarkar, Golwalkar and the RSS and all its offshoots – who saw it as proof of a Marxist-Muslim-Imperialist plot directed against their Hindu India.

A second consequence of this quasi-sanctification of the Freedom Struggle is that it was done to the near exclusion of much else. I would not for one minute wish to downplay what was by any standard an epic and glorious chapter in India's history, achieved through much personal sacrifice, but it is just that: a chapter. And like all chapters in India's history it deserves to be examined as scrupulously as other chapters and not set above all else. The effect has been to stifle historical inquiry, resulting in what strikes me as widespread ignorance about India's real as opposed to its imagined past – and perhaps even a preference for that imaginary India over the real, living one.

Ignorance of the past is what has allowed the revisionism that Golwalkar and his colleagues in the Hindutva movement initiated almost a century ago to re-enter the public consciousness, thanks to more recent proponents of Hindutva history such as the late Sita Ram Goel, a former Marxist turned publisher and polemicist.

Goel argued that the present generation of India's historians, in alliance with Nehruism, secularism, Marxism and media bias, are conducting an 'experiment with untruth', through the 'systematic distortion' of India's history by suppressing the true facts about the cultural damage inflicted on India by militant Islam and evangelical Christianity.[20]

Goel has many admirers both at home and abroad. Indeed, it is a striking feature of the Hindutva movement that some of its most vociferous proponents are Hindus who have settled overseas in Britain and the United States.

In Britain these views appear to have found an articulate champion in the well-known media figure Pandit Dr Raj Sharma, founder and vice-president of the Hindu Priest Association (UK). If you read Dr Sharma's report *The Caste System*, published in 2011 under the auspices of the Hindu Council UK, you will learn that it was the British who invented the caste system in order to subdue the Indian populace, and that the Orientalists who first translated and published the great Sanskrit classics did so as part of 'a strategy by the East India Company and other foreign parties in India to penetrate the Hindu Indian psyche by interpreting the Vedic scriptures ... [so as to] better manipulate the Indian populace, thereby facilitating the "divide and rule" policy more effectively'.

That policy, according to Dr Sharma, included the propagation of the myth of the Aryan invasion. This myth, Dr Sharma tells us, was developed in 1848 by 'Maximillian Muller ... a highly-paid German employee of the East India Company in order to deny any political or moral basis to the Hindu claim for independence from British rule. For, under this theory, Hindus too were as much foreigners in India as were the British. This theory was not openly challenged for over 120 years so that many Indians were duped into believing they were descendants of a superior foreign civilisation. Such an imperialist hypothesis was

designed to ensure the British were allowed "legitimate" political rights over India on the same grounds as Hindus, all being
foreigners.'[21]

The German Sanskritist Dr Max Müller was never an
employee of the EICo but for many years Professor of
Comparative Philology at Oxford University and directing editor
of the monumental fifty-volume *Sacred Books of the East* series
published by the Oxford University Press between 1879 and
1910, which included English translations of the Upanishads,
the Laws of Manu, the *Bhagavadgita*, the *Institutes of Vishnu*, the
Satapatha Brahmana, the *Grihya Sutras*, the *Vedanta Sutras*, the
Vedic Hymns and the *Atharva-Veda* – works produced for a world
readership and translated for the first time by such lackeys of
the British Raj as Georg Bühler, Hermann Oldenberg, Hermann
Jacobi, Julius Eggeling, Julius Jolly and George Thibaut. Is
Pandit Sharma aware that from August Schlegel – Europe's
first professor of Sanskrit – onwards scores of German scholars
have been proud to describe themselves as Indologists and
Orientalists?[22] I'm glad to say that many of Max Müller's works
are still in print in India, so perhaps Pandit Sharma is familiar
with his lecture 'What can India teach us?' in which he champi-
oned Indian culture in the following terms:

If I were asked under what sky the human mind has most fully
developed some of its choicest gifts, has most deeply pondered
on the greatest problems of life, and has found solutions [for]
some of them which well deserve the attention even of those
who have studied Plato and Kant – I should point to India.
And if I were to ask myself from what literature we, here in
Europe, we who have been nurtured almost exclusively on the
thoughts of Greeks and Romans, and of one Semitic race, the
Jewish, may draw that corrective which is most wanted in order

to make our inner life more perfect, more comprehensive, more universal, in fact more truly human, a life, not for this life only, but a transfigured and eternal life – again I should point to India.[23]

The Hindutvatistas' chauvinist, sectarian repackaging of the past now threatens to become mainstream thinking. In many instances it comes from seemingly authoritative sources and therefore demands to be taken seriously – and never more so than when it comes from well-respected religious figures. One such is the very personable Gaudiya Vaishnava guru Swami Bhakti Vijnana Giri, best known as Giriraj Swami, who teaches at the Sri Narasingha Chaitanya Ashram on the banks of the Kaveri in Tamil Nadu as part of ISKCON (the International Society of Krishna Consciousness), better known as the Hare Krishna movement. Born Glenn Phillip Teton in Glencoe, Illinois, Giriraj Swami is the author of *Myth of the Aryan Invasion*, which he concludes by asking 'why this ugly vestige of British imperialism is still taught in Indian schools today? Such serious misconceptions can only be reconciled by accepting that the Aryans were the original inhabitants of the Indus Valley region, and not a horde of marauding foreign nomads. Such an Invasion never occurred.'[24]

This indigenist or 'out of India' theory, which holds that the Arya were descendants of the Harappans and that the Indo-European language group had its origins in India, is the fastest-growing element of Hindutva revisionism. But equally troubling is the belief that foreign ideas have polluted Indian culture, as exemplified by the remarks attributed to the present Culture Minister, who at an RSS meeting in September 2015, spoke of his government's determination to 'cleanse every area of public discourse that has been westernised and where Indian culture and civilisation need to be restored – be it the history we

read or our cultural heritage or our institutes that have been polluted over years'.[25]

Many of my readers will, I know, be well aware of this Hindutva
encroachment of the past and will be as troubled as I am. But for
those who are new to this issue, let me explain that as long ago as
1972 that most distinguished historian Romila Thapar,[26] doyenne
of the history department of the Jawaharlal Nehru University,
spoke out on All India Radio against Indian historians 'serving,
consciously or unconsciously, the larger cause of nationalism',
describing the negative impact of this historical revisionism as
enormous: 'The ancient period became the golden age. The
antiquity of Indian civilisation was pushed back by dating the
Vedic literature to 4000 BC or even earlier. In order to emphasise
the national unity of India since the earliest times generalisations
were made on the history of the subcontinent, essentially in the
perspective.'[27]

Thirty years later Professor Thapar found it necessary to
return to the issue in more specific form. 'History as projected by
Hindutva ideologues,' she wrote,

> which is being introduced to children through textbooks and
> is being thrust upon research institutes, precludes an open
> discussion of evidence and interpretation. Nor does it bear any
> trace of the new methods of historical analyses now being used
> in centres of historical research. Such history is dismissed by
> the Hindutva ideologues as Western, imperialist, Marxist, or
> whatever, but they are themselves unaware of what these labels
> mean or the nature of these readings ... Engineers, computer
> experts, journalists-turned-politicians, foreign journalists posing
> as scholars of Indology, and what have you, assume infallibil-
> ity, and pronounce on archaeology and history. And the media
> accord them the status.[28]

Since then the pressure from the Hindutva right has, if anything, intensified, as exemplified by the reception given to Professor Wendy Doniger's hefty 779-page book *The Hindus: An Alternative History*, published in 2009. This was the product of years of study and research by one of the world's leading and most respected Sanskritists, written in part so that those outside the Hindu tradition could, in Doniger's words, 'come to learn about it and admire the beauty, complexity and wisdom of the Hindu texts'.[29] Doniger's writing style is folksy and she has never been afraid of enthusing about what she has termed the 'glorious sexual openness' of some Sanskrit texts.

But this frank speaking led to protests from Hindutva organisations both in America and India, culminating in a lawsuit brought against the publishers, Penguin India, by a member of the RSS on the grounds that Doniger had violated his religious feelings under Section 295A of the Indian Penal Code. Under mounting pressure, Penguin India withdrew the book from sale, although I am pleased to report that the book is once more available in most bookshops.

It is not just Professor Doniger's work that is demonised. The scholarship of other respected North American academics is also under attack, most notably Steve Farmer, Richard Sproat and Michael Witzel on account of their work on the Harappa Civilisation and their painstaking deconstruction of some of the claims made by the 'out of India' theorists. So, too, are those academics who are deemed to have insulted a nationalist hero, as in the case of the American academic James Laine and his book on the seventeenth-century Maratha warlord and ruler Chhatrapati Shivaji.[30] When published in India in 2003 the book was interpreted by some hotheads as insulting to their prime Maharashtrian hero. An Indian historian who Laine had thanked in his acknowledgements was beaten up, and the renowned Bhandarkar Oriental Research Institute in Pune, which had also had the misfortune to be thanked by Laine, was attacked and its library vandalised by a large mob calling itself the Sambhaji Brigade, made up of members of the youth section of the right-wing Maratha Seva Sangh. In November 2016 the Sambhaji Brigade announced that it was to become a political party – open to all except Brahmins!

The abuse now regularly heaped on both homegrown and foreign scholars who write about Indian history serves as a warning to all that India's religious differences and rivalries are like so many powder kegs waiting for someone to light this or that fuse. Fear of the consequences has made an ass of the law as it now exists in India – for which Indians may thank or curse the British, depending on where they stand on the issue of free speech.

Fear of giving religious offence under the notorious Section 295A of the Indian Penal Code has made a mockery of Article 19 of the Indian Constitution, which gives all persons the right to freedom of speech and expression subject to 'reasonable restrictions'. It has led to a situation whereby vast tracts of India's known history are either placed off limits or simply tiptoed over. Any zealot can now silence a writer of fiction or fact by complaining that his religious feelings have been hurt.

Nor is this an issue that Indians south of the Narmada can feel complacent about, because this is precisely what happened to the Tamilian author Perumal Murugan in January 2015: he was forced to make an abject apology to a local pressure group which declared itself offended by something he had written four years earlier in a historical novel. They complained to the local authority, who ordered the novelist to apologise. Writers in India and abroad rallied to support Murugan but not a single Indian politician, to my knowledge, spoke out against this abuse of power and the threat to free speech it posed. The latest news is that in July 2016 the Madras High Court issued a judgment that there was nothing obscene in the novel. It went on to remind the authorities that it was their duty to uphold freedom of expression and not pander to mob demands. It further advised that those who professed themselves hurt by the contents of a book should avoid reading it.[31] I'm glad to hear that Mr Murugan has recently resumed his profession.

Far more alarming than the wrong done to Mr Murugan is the killing of the Kannada scholar M. M. Kalburgi, who was shot dead on his doorstep in his home state of Karnataka on 30 April 2015. Kalburgi was a Brahmin and a Lingayat, a member of a popular devotional sect within Shaivism that rose to prominence in South India in the thirteenth century, its followers distinguishable by the *ishtalinga* necklaces they wear as a symbol of the deity. Although founded as a reforming movement that rejected caste, Brahminical authority and ritual within Hinduism, the Lingayat community has now become a powerful – and, on occasion, intolerant – force within Karnataka State politics.

Some years ago Kalburgi was forced by the Lingayat religious authorities to make a public recantation of some allegedly derogatory references he had made about the founder of the movement, the twelfth-century philosopher and statesman Basava. More recently, in 2014, Kalburgi was alleged to have made critical remarks about idolatry at a seminar in Bangalore, leading to a case being registered against him by the Vishva Hindu Parishad and other religious groups on the grounds that he had outraged their religious feelings under Section 295A of the Indian Penal Code. Kalburgi was given police protection but later asked for it to be removed.

His murder follows the shooting dead in Pune two years ago of Narendra Dabholkar, who was seeking to get a law passed in the Maharashtra Assembly to prevent the exploitation of people through superstition. In February 2015 Dabholkar's rationalist colleague Govind Pansare, a committed left-winger and writer, was similarly murdered in Kolhapur. To my knowledge, no one has yet been charged for their murders.[32]

Three secularist intellectuals murdered between 2013 and 2015 for
their allegedly anti-Hindu views: (from left to right) Govind Pansare,
Narendra Dabholkar and M. M. Kalburgi.

I grew up in India unconscious of the diversity around me, but
in my parents' house in 1947 my ayah or nanny was a Christian
Khasi, the cook a Buddhist, the head of the staff a Muslim and the
rest of the staff a mix of Hindus from the plains and animists from
the hills, with – I'm sad to say – the lowliest posts being filled by
'sweeper' outcastes. They were a microcosm of India itself, and
there were at that time a great many doom-mongers among my
parents' generation who prophesied that once the external authority represented by people like my father was withdrawn that
Indian macrocosm would quickly disintegrate into its constituent
parts. It didn't happen, and now as India celebrates seventy years
of independence I can only marvel at how that seemingly fragile
democracy continues to prosper and how the Indian Constitution
still holds firm despite all the divisive forces.

However, the arrival of the digital age and electronic media has
given rise to what is now being described as a 'post-truth' society
in which fact and fiction occupy the same space, leaving it entirely
up to the reader to sort out the one from the other. The populist
anti-intellectualism with which the Brexiters won the argument in

Britain's recent national referendum on the European Union, with a leading politician boasting that 'People in this country have had enough of experts', and the way in which a multi-millionaire fantasist seemingly incapable of separating truth from lies has been elected President of the United States, strongly suggests that the well-known maxim[33] 'Everyone is entitled to their own opinions, but not to their own facts' no longer applies.

Yet even in the face of these massive failures of reasoned democracy, the bottom line remains, which is that society is invariably diminished when falsehood goes unchallenged. Both in Britain and in the United States of America we the people are now having to face the consequences of failing to do just that. I hope – and believe – that India can do better.

The Republic of India is a truly astonishing experiment in democracy on the grand scale. Consider these bare statistics: the European Union, from which the British people are now set on divorcing themselves, is made up of twenty-eight member states with a total population of just over 500 million speaking twenty-four official languages and some fifty minority and 'immigrant' languages. India is made up of twenty-nine states and seven union territories with a total population of over 1.3 billion, made up of over 2000 ethnic groups speaking 122 major languages and more than 1600 minority languages. Yet it holds together. What an achievement!

In all my travels across India, now extending over seventy-seven years, I have never once been assaulted, or robbed or even been verbally abused. Official indifference, yes, when it comes to banks and getting permits, but in every other circumstance I have always been met with the unfailing kindness of strangers and India's proverbial and fully deserved tradition of hospitality. That surely speaks volumes for the kind of nation that Gandhi, Nehru, Ambedkar and their colleagues built.

As a child of India, I take comfort in the knowledge that this motherland in which I dare to claim a stake has plenty of wise heads, first-rate historians and courageous journalists prepared to stand firm against the pick-and-choose anti-history-makers.[34] Long may such bastions of free speech be allowed to go about their business unconstrained.

ACKNOWLEDGEMENTS

Many kind people went out of their way to help me in a variety of ways during my researches and in my writing. So protracted has this process been, with so many stops and starts, and so forgetful have I become over the last few years that some names that should appear here have either been lost or simply forgotten. My humblest apologies to those so unwittingly omitted, along with my thanks. This will include a great many local enthusiasts, amateurs and professionals alike, who share that same spirit of enquiry that drove the first Orientalists.

Toby Sinclair took the time to read my manuscript at an early stage, William Dalrymple, David Loyn and John Bynner each read sections, and all made invaluable suggestions. Dr Cameron Petrie was kind enough to make valuable comments and corrections arising from his work on the Harappan Civilisation. However, my greatest debt here is to two first-rate historians, Professor Emeritus Kesavan Veluthat, late of the Department of History at the University of Delhi, and Dr Crispin Branfoot, Reader in the History of South Asian Art and Archaeology at the School of Oriental and African Studies in London. Both were good enough to go through my manuscript at a late stage and take the time to make numerous suggestions and, indeed, corrections of fact. I am enormously grateful to both of them for bringing their scholarship to bear on my work and for saving me from making a complete ass of myself. I have done my best to answer their criticisms and concerns, but the responsibility for the finished article is mine alone and no one other than myself should be held responsible.

Next, my thanks to those kind persons who have allowed me to publish one or more of their photographs taken in the field. They include: the distinguished epigraphist Professor Iravatham Mahadevan who also allowed me to quote from his work *Tamil Epigraphy*; anthropologists Christa and Günter Neuenhofer from Germany; Christian Luczantis of SOAS; Dr Shanti Pappu of the Sharma Centre of Heritage Education; Jibu Rajan from Trivandrum; Siddeshwar Prasad from Karnataka; Sharat Sunder and Dr Ajay Sekhar from Kerala; Nigal Kalathil and Dr B. Jambulingam from Tamil Nadu; Professor Anand Ranganathan of JNU and *Newslaundry*; and the photographer Richard Davies in the UK.

My special thanks also to: polymath and publisher Dr Roberto Calasso, his translator Richard Dixon and the publisher Farrar, Straus and Giroux for giving me permission to quote two extracts from *Ardor*; Professor George L. Hart and poet and scholar Dr Hank Heifetz and Columbia University Press for giving me permission to quote two extracts from their work *Four Hundred Songs of War and Wisdom: an Anthology of Poems from Classical Tamil*; teacher and writer on Buddhism Stephen Batchelor and Riverhead Books for giving me permission to quote from *Verses from the Center: A Buddhist Vision of the Sublime*; and poet and teacher Andrew Schelling and White Pine Press for giving me permission to quote from *Dropping the Bow: Poems from Ancient India*.

Among the many other scholars, academics and local experts

to whom I owe thanks for assisting in a variety of ways, from offering scholarly advice to local expertise, are: Dr Alison Ohta, Ed Weech and Nancy Charley at the RAS; Dr Richard Blurton, Joe Cribb and Dr Robert Bracey at the British Museum; Dr Susan Strong, Dr Nick Barnard and Dr Rosemary Crill at the V&A; John Falconner and Dr Jennifer Howes at the British Library; Dr Shailendra Bhandhare at the Ashmolean Museum; Professor John Coningham at the University of Durham. Also Harry Marshall, Douglas Rice, J. M. Kenoyer and R. H. Meadow. In Germany: Professor Harry Falk, Dr Monika Zin and Dr Julia Hegevald.

In India: Nirmala Lakshman, Mahima Jain and their colleagues at *The Hindu* newspaper group in Chennai; Dr Naman Ahuja, John Elliott, Shantum Seth, Parvati Menon, V. K. Ramachandran and Madhura Swaminathan, Timeri Murari, Dhananjay Chavan and Shyam Syamaprasad. Also that polymath and most generous of hosts Aman Nath, who so kindly offered us the hospitality of the palaces, forts, mansions and homes along the Coromandel and Malabar coasts which he and the late Francis Wacziarg so lovingly restored to become part of his Neemrana 'non-hotels' group – specifically, Hotel de l'Orient at Pondicherry, the 'Bungalow on the Beach' at Tranquebar, and Le Colonial and the Tower House at Cochin.

Iain Hunt at Little, Brown very kindly read my first draft and made many useful suggestions before my manuscript was delivered to his successor as editor, Nithya Rae, whose own background experience and professional skills proved invaluable. Thank you, too, to Linda Silverman for securing permissions for the illustrations, and to John Gilkes for his superb maps. My gratitude, also, to Tim Whiting, commissioning editor at Little, Brown, whose faith in me has been sorely tried over the years but whose unwavering support has sustained my belief that there is still a place for history writing in modern publishing. These same sentiments can equally be applied to Vivien Green, who has stood by me through storm and sunshine for all these years as literary agent and friend.

My last word of thanks goes to my fellow travellers, for their usual forbearance and their company: Richard Davies from time to time and my beloved wife Liz.

NOTES

PREFACE: A HEALTH WARNING TO THE READER

1 *The Observer*, 'State of the Nation' Survey 2015, carried out by Opinion Research, published 19 April 2015.

INTRODUCTION: SOMETHING ABOUT MYSELF

1 YouGov January 2016. My thanks to Dr Shashi Tharoor, author of *Inglorious Empire: What the British Did to India*, 2017, for drawing the poll to my attention.

2 See Charles Allen, *Kipling Sahib: India and the Making of Rudyard Kipling*, 2007.

3 Quoted by musician and historian Mark Lindley in his paper 'Changes in Mahatma Gandhi's views on caste and intermarriage', unsourced and undated.

4 Exact figures for Brahmins in Tamil Nadu are hard to come by, with estimates ranging from 1 per cent to 6.75 per cent, hence my approximation.

5 For example, *Inglorious Empire: What the British Did to India* by that engaging Congress Party politician-cum-historian Shashi Tharoor, which is essentially the case for the prosecution, brilliantly argued.

6 Professor Romila Thapar, 'The Aryan Question Revisited', lecture delivered at the Academic Staff College, Jawaharlal Nehru University, 11 October 1999.

CHAPTER 1: THE INDIAN PLATE

1 William Sykes, 'Inscriptions of the Boodh caves near Joonur', *Journal of the Royal Asiatic Society*, Vol. IV, 1837.

2   Robert Bruce Foote, *Prehistoric and protohistoric antiquities of India*, 1916.
3   T. J. Newbold, 'On some ancient mounds of scorious ashes in Southern India', *Journal of the Royal Asiatic Society*, Vol. VII, 1843.
4   Raymond Allchin, *Neolithic cattle-keepers in South India: a study of the Deccan mounds*, 1963.
5   D. Q. Fuller, R. Korisettar and P. C. Venkatasubbiah, 'Southern Neolithic cultivation systems: a reconstruction based on archaeobotanical evidence', *South Asian Studies*, Vol. 1, 2001.
6   *The Hindu* newspaper, 6 November 2007.
7   Robert Caldwell, *A political and general history of the district of Tinnevelly*, 1881.
8   There are numerous theories as to the origins of the name but I am persuaded by the arguments of the Tamil-born French historian J. B. Prashant More in his book *Origins and Development of Madras*, 2014. Similar arguments rage over the origins of the more recent name Chennai.
9   Samuel Purchas, *Purchas His Pilgrimage, or Relations of the World and the Religions observed in all Ages and Places discovered, from the Creation unto this Present*, 1613.
10 Edgar Thurston, *Castes and Tribes of Southern India*, Vol. III, 1909. Thurston drew on the earlier work of M. Ratnaswami Aiyar, 'Kanikkars of Travancore', *Indian Review*, 1902.
11 However, it would be incorrect to state that all these hill-dwellers were among India's earliest immigrants, as Thurston and his peers believed. Research by Professor Sumit Guha and others has shown that reverse migration also occurred in South India in which later arrivals regressed into the hills in the medieval era. S. Guha, *Environment and ethnicity in India 1200–1991*, 1999.
12 They became bipedal, developed a layer of subcutaneous fat, changed body shapes to become more streamlined in water, lost much of their body hair, grew special bones in the ear found only in regular swimmers, protected their new-born babies with a special layer of grease found only in aquatic mammals, learned to close the trachea and hold their breaths thus gaining the ability to speak, grew bigger brains and lived longer. See Elaine Morgan, *The Aquatic Ape*, 1982, and *The Aquatic Ape Hypothesis*, 1997; and Philip Tobias, *Water and Human Evolution*, 1998. See also more recent studies by Michael Crawford, William Archer and Mark Verhaegen.
13 Recent research can be found in C. V. Murray-Wallace and C. D. Woodroffe, *Quaternary sea-level changes: a global perspective*, 2014.
14 C. Clarkson, M. Petraglia, R. Korisettar et al, 'The oldest and longest enduring microlithic sequence in India: 35,000 years of modern human occupation at the Jwalapuram Locality rockshelter', *Antiquity*, Vol. 83, 2009.

15   P. Mellars, K. C. Gori, M. Carr et al, 'Genetic and archaeological
      perspectives on the initial modern human colonization of southern
      Asia', *Proceedings of the National Academy of Sciences of the USA*, 110
      (26), 2013.

CHAPTER 2: THE KNOWLEDGE

1   This is to entirely ignore the oldest archaeologically verifiable city on
      the Indian subcontinent: Mehrgarh, immediately south of one of the
      main gateways into India from the west, the Bolan Pass, which sug-
      gests links with other early urban communities to the west in places
      like Ur, Uruk, Eridu and Jericho. Excavations at Mehrgarh show that
      by about 6800 BCE a farming community was settled in mud-brick
      dwellings and engaged in pioneering that revolutionary transition from
      hunter-gathering and nomadic pastoralism to settled cultivation, plac-
      ing them among the world's earliest farmers.
2   Charles Masson, *Narrative of Various Journeys in Balochistan, Afghanistan
      and the Panjab*, 1843.
3   In fact, Banerji was beaten to it by a young Italian linguist named
      Luigi Pio Tessitori, who in 1919 recovered three Harappan seals at
      the now well-known site of Kalibangan on the southern banks of the
      Ghaggar River in Rajasthan. However, luck was not on Tessitori's
      side. He caught the prevalent Spanish flu and died in Bikaner in
      November 1919. Excavations began in earnest at Kalibangan only
      in 1960 but little was published on the Kalibangan excavations until
      2003 – a foot-dragging repeated all too often at other archaeological
      sites. See Nayanjot Lahiri, *Finding Forgotten Cities: How the Indus
      Civilization was Discovered*, 2012.
4   Sir John Marshall, *ASI Annual Report 1923-34*, 1934.
5   A number of cuneiform tablets excavated in Iraq refer to trade links
      with a country named Meluhha or Melukhkha which has been taken
      to refer to the Harappans. Some scholars have linked the word to the
      Sanskrit *mleccha* ('foreigners'), while others have suggested a link with
      the Dravidian word *mel akam*, meaning 'high country', which seems
      perverse considering that the great cities of the Harappans were mostly
      confined to the plains. Even so, the significance of the name Meluhha
      has in recent years been elevated to a ridiculous degree.
6   A recent much-touted claim for a seal depicting the rear end of a horse
      has been shown to be based on a combination of photoshopping and an
      over-active imagination. Similarly, a number of supposed horse skel-
      etons have been shown to be linked to the Indian wild ass. See Michael
      Witzel and Steve Farmer, 'Horseplay at Harappa', *Frontline*, Vol. 17,
      Issue 20, Sep-Oct 2000, with subsequent articles, including their review
      of N. Jha and N. S. Rajaram, *The Deciphered Indus Script*, 2000.

7   E. J. H. Mackay, 'Excavations at Mohenjodaro', *Annual Report of the Archaeological Survey of India: 1928–29*, 1929.

8   B. and R. Allchin, *Origins of a civilisation: the prehistory and early archaeology of South Asia*, 1997.

9   Jonathan M. Kenoyer, 'The master of animals in the iconography of the Indus tradition', in D. B. Coutts and B. Arnold (eds), *The Master of Animals in Old World Iconography*, 2010.

10 My thanks here to Dr Cameron Petrie, co-director of the Land, Water and Settlement Project at the University of Cambridge and Banaras Hindu University. See also G. R. Schug, *Bioarchaeology and climate change: a view of South Asian Prehistory*, 2011; L. Gosian, P. D. Clift, M. G. Macklin et al, 'Fluvial landscapes of the Harappan Civilisation', *Proceedings of the National Academy of Sciences*, May 2012; and Y. Dixit et al, 'Abrupt weakening of the summer monsoon in northwest India 4,100 years ago', *Geology* 42 (4), 2014.

11 As far as the archaeological record is concerned, post-Harappan India underwent a virtual black-out that lasted for almost a millennium. Even the two phases of so-called Black and Red Ware (BRW) and Painted Grey Ware (PGW) pottery-making that span this Indian Iron Age culture are remarkably feeble in their artistry.

12 It is also found among the Romani or 'Gypsy' peoples who migrated westwards out of India about a thousand years ago – a striking but rare example of westward migration most probably initiated by the captivity of musicians and armourers who were serving as camp-followers to conquered Rajput armies.

13 The research threw up some anomalies. Three Adivasi tribal groups tested – the Chenchu and Valmiki in Andhra Pradesh and the Kellar in Tamil Nadu – as well as the Manipuri hill people in Eastern India, and 13 per cent of Sinhalese in Sri Lanka were found also to have low but still significant proportions of Haplogroup R1a1a in their genetic makeup. These anomalies have been cited in support of the 'out of India' theory advanced in some Indian circles, which argues that the Indo-European language family had its origins in India. The alternative – and, to my mind, more convincing – explanation is that these isolated genetic pockets represent outriders of the Arya advance who were swallowed up by their host communities.

14 P. A. Underhill, N. M. Myres, S. Rootsi, M. Metspalu, L. A. Zhivotovsky, R. J. King, J. Roy, A. A. Lin, C. E. T. Chow et al, 'Separating the post-Glacial co-ancestry of European and Asian Y chromosomes within haplogroup R1a', *European Journal of Human Genetics* 18 (4), 2009.

15 Roberto Calasso, *Ardore*, Edizione S.p.A. Milano, 2010 (tr. Richard Dixon, *Ardor*, Allen, Lane, 2014, pp.3-6).

16 See, for example, *R-V* 7.21.15.

17 For example, animal and fire sacrifices loom large in both the Avesta and the *R-V*. In Early Iranian the term is *yasna*, in Sanskrit it is *yajna*.

18 D. D. Kosambi, *Ancient India*, 1965. See also A. Basham, *The Sacred Cow*, 1989, and more recently D. N. Jha, *The Myth of the Holy Cow*, 2001.

19 There were, of course, dogs in India and a dog's paw mark has been found in bricks at Chanhu Daro, but no evidence of domesticated dogs.

20 B. Debroy, *Sarama and her Children: the Dog in Indian Myth*, 2008.

21 In *R-V* 7.55 one of these watch-dogs is praised as 'master of the house', even though his barking irritates the household. 'Be on thy guard against the boar,' runs verse 4, 'and let the boar beware of thee. At Indra's singers barkest thou? Why dost thou seek to terrify us? Go to sleep.' R. T. H. Griffith, *The hymns of the Rigveda*, 7.55.2-5, 1889.

22 For my datings of the Vedas I have drawn mostly on Irfan Habib and V. K. Kumar, *The Vedic Age*, 2003.

23 H. H. Wilson, *The Vishnu Purana: a System of Hindu Mythology and Tradition*, 1840.

24 Griffith was for many years principal of Benares College before retiring to the hill-station of Kotagiri in the Nilgiri mountains, where he made many of his translations and where he died in 1906.

25 R. T. H. Griffith, The *hymns of the Atharvaveda*, 1895.

26 R. T. H. Griffith, *The hymns of the Rigveda*, 10, 90, 11-12, 1889.

27 C. E. Gover, 'The Pongol festival in Southern India', *Journal of the Royal Asiatic Society*, New Series Vol. V, 1870.

CHAPTER 3: AGASTYA'S COUNTRY

1 M. Ariel, in a letter in *Journal Asiatique*, Nov–Dec 1849, quoted in G. U. Pope, *The sacred Kurral of Tiruvalluva Nayanar*, 1886.

2 See Thomas Trautmann, *The Madras school of Orientalism: producing knowledge in colonial South India*, 2009.

3 Tamil grammars had earlier been printed in Germany and in Danish Tranquebar in 1738. See Stuart H. Blackburn, *Print, Folklore and Nationalism in Colonial South India*, 2003. My thanks to Dr Crispin Branfoot for drawing this to my attention.

4 J. W. McCrindle, *The Commerce and Navigation of the Erythræan Sea; being a translation of the Periplus Maris Erythraei*, 1879.

5 Unusually, Kamban was not a Brahmin but an *Uvachchar*, a sub-caste of temple servants whose traditional role was to blow the conch and chant verses in Tamil.

6 According to press reports in December 2015, what is believed to be a sixth-century version has been discovered tucked into a *purana* in the library of the Asiatic Society of Bengal, Kolkata. This would make it by far the oldest extant version, although no formal announcement has been made to date.

7   William Carey and Joshua Marshman, *The Ramayuna of Valmeeki, in the original Sungskrit, with a prose translation and explanatory notes*, 1806-10.

8   In recent years this line 'Mahendra, planted in the sea' has been taken literally by some, who see it as further evidence of the Great Inundation.

9   R. T. H. Griffith, *The Ramayana of Valmiki*, Book IV, Canto 41, 1870-75.

10 Nachinarkiniyar, *Payiram*, Porul. 34.

11 K. R. Subramanian, *The origin of Saivism and its history in the Tamil land*, 1929.

12 Quoted in E. F. Irschilk, *Politics and social conflict in South Asia: the non-Brahmin movement and Tamil separatism 1916-19*, 1969.

13 No direct reference to Agastya exists in Sangam literature, but much has been made in recent years of one ambiguous word in Poem 201 of the *Purananuru* discussed earlier, in which its composer praises a Velir ruler of Kodumbalur (between Madurai and Tiruchirappalli) named Irungovel, *'slayer of tigers'*, whose dynasty is descended from Lord Krishna. He refers to him as a descendant of forty-nine generations of Velirs whose ancestor ruled over a distant walled city called Turuvai and who sprang from the *tadavu* of a 'northern sage'. That word *tadavu* is usually translated as 'pit', as in a ceremonial fire-pit, but with some stretching can be read as a 'clay pitcher', which would identify this 'northern sage' as Agathya.

CHAPTER 4: JAINS AND SANGAMS

1   See S. N. Sadasivan, *A Social History of India*, 2000.

2   Mackenzie in a letter to Sir Alexander Johnstone, quoted in Kavali Venkata Ramaswami, *Biographical sketches of Dekkan poets: being memoirs of the lives of several eminent bards, ancient and modern*, 1829.

3   Colin Mackenzie, 'Extracts of a journal by Major C. Mackenzie', *Asiatick Researches*, Vol. 9, 1809. See also Jennifer Howes, *Illustrating India: the Early Colonial Investigations of Colin Mackenzie (1784-1821)*, 2010.

4   Francis Buchanan, *A Journey from Madras through the countries of Mysore, Canara, and Malabar, performed under the orders of the most noble the Marquis Wellesley, governor general of India, for the express purpose of investigating the state of agriculture, arts, and commerce; the religion, manners, and customs; the history natural and civil, and antiquities, in the dominions of the rajah of Mysore, and the countries acquired by the Honourable East India Company*, 1807.

5   H. H. Wilson, *Mackenzie Collection: a Descriptive Catalogue of the Oriental Manuscripts, and other Articles illustrative of the Literature, History, Statistics and Antiquities of the South of India; collected by the late Lieut-Col. Colin Mackenzie*, 1828. The rest of the collection went to the EICo's London headquarters, and was afterwards broken up, so that today the

contents are divided between the British Library, the British Museum and the Victoria and Albert Museum.

6   Margaret Stevenson, *The Heart of Jainism*, 1915.

7   First published in English translation by Hermann Jacobi in 1884, as the twenty-fourth book in Max Müller's *Sacred Books of the East* series.

8   Although these German philologists' reliance on Digambara sources was at the expense of the rival Svetambara sect, which initially distorted the picture.

9   Albrecht Weber, *Indische studien*, 1885.

10 Benjamin Lewis Rice, *Inscriptions at Sravana Belgola, a chief seat of the Jains*, 1889. Also *Epigraphia Carnatica*, Vol. II, 1895.

11 P. Sclater, 'The Mammals of Madagascar', *The Quarterly Journal of Science*, 1864. I must here acknowledge my debt to Sumathi Ramaswamy, Professor of History at Duke University; in particular her book *The Lost Land of Lemuria*, 2004, a lucid, comprehensive and objective study on which I have drawn heavily.

12 Ernst Haeckel, *The History of Creation*, 1876.

13 Charles D. Maclean, *Manual of the Administration of the Madras Presidency*, 1885.

14 Here I am indebted to Sumathi Ramaswamy, *Passions of the Tongue: Language Devotion to Tamil India 1891–1970*, 1997, and Paula Richman, both for her own work and the essays edited by her in *Many Ramayanas: the Diversity of a Narrative Tradition*, 1991.

15 J. D. Milliman and J. P. Lie, 'Step-like rise of post-glacial sea levels and geological implications', *OCEANS 2003, Proceedings*, Vol. 3, 2003.

16 Alexander Rea, 'Prehistoric antiquities in Tinnevelly', *ASI annual report* 1902–3, 1904.

17 E. Iniyan, 'Burial and funerary culture of ancient Tamils', *International Journal of Social Studies and Humanity*, Vol. 5, No. 1, 2015. And B. Sasiskaran et al, 'Adichallanur: a prehistoric mining site', *Indian Journal of History and Science*, 45.3, 2010.

18 The poem's opening couplet compares the letter 'A', *akara* (the first letter of the Brahmi alphabet), to the Tamil noun *pakavan*. The English missionary George Pope, founder and for many years headmaster of Bishop Cotton School, Bangalore, in his English translation of the *Tolkappiyam*, published in 1886, translated *pakavan* as 'primal deity'. Jains have no problem with the concept of a supreme being in the form of a liberated human soul, but they reject the concept of a god or supreme creator. If *pakavan* refers to a non-human deity then the *Tolkappiyam* could not have been the work of a Jain.

19 George L. Hart and Hank Heifetz, *Four Hundred Songs of War and Wisdom: an Anthology of Poems from Classical Tamil, the Purananuru*, 1999.

20 Robert Caldwell, *A Comparative Grammar of the Dravidian or South Indian Family of Languages*, 1856.

21   Not to be confused with either the pioneer Tamil scholar and collector of manuscripts U. V. Swaminatha Iyer or the well-known Dewan of Travancore State V. S. Subrahmanya Iyer.

22   Iravatham Mahadevan, *Early Tamil Epigraphy, from the Earliest Times to the Sixth Century B.C*, 2003.

23   Iravatham Mahadevan interviewed by T. S. Subramanian for *The Hindu* newspaper's magazine *Frontline*, 4 July 2009.

CHAPTER 5: BUDDHISTS AND ROCK-CUT CAVES

1   My own view is that Chanakya's *Arthashastra* would have been among the first documents to be written in Brahmi, since it was an entirely secular work and Chanakya was ideally placed to get it done.

2   K. Rajan and V. P. Yatheeskumar, 'New evidences on scientific dates from Brahmi script as revealed from Porunthal and Kodumanal excavations', *Pragdhara*, 21-22, 2013.

3   Most recently, Nayanjot Lahiri, *Ashoka in Ancient India*, 2015.

4   Sharada Srinivasa and Srinivasa Ranganathan, *India's Legendary Wootz Steel: An Advanced Material of the Ancient World*, 2004.

5   The word dharma, which Ashoka used repeatedly in all his inscriptions, had its origins in the Vedas, where it stood for the cosmic laws underpinning the universe and by extension the proper ordering of society. Within Hinduism it covers a wide range of meanings, from the correct performance of rites to caste rules. For Buddhists it means the universal truths as contained in the teachings of Buddha Sakyamuni. Ashoka, however, gave the word an entirely new spin, by promoting it as a code of ethics, a 'moral law' that he wished all his subjects to follow, irrespective of their religions.

6   Ven. Shravasti Dhammika, *The Edicts of King Asoka*, 2009.

7   Harry Falk, *Asokan Sites and Artefacts*, 2006.

8   Harry Falk, 'Remarks on the Minor Rock Edict of Asoka at Ratanpura', *Jnana-Pravaha Research Journal* XVI, 2013.

9   There is a strong case for Emperor Ashoka's Suvarnagiri being the hilltop upon which the present Bellary Fort now stands, believed to have been built over the remains of a Buddhist stupa – the 'golden hill' from which he sent out his scribes and stone-carvers north, south, east and west during his South Indian tour. The case is further strengthened by the fact that when the Erragudi MRE was first discovered by a mining engineer in 1928 a set of Ashoka's major rock edicts were also found carved on several rock surfaces higher up on that same hilltop. Only here at Erragudi have two sets of Ashokan edicts been found on the same site.

10   R. L. Mitra, 'Beef in Ancient India', *Indo-Aryans*, 1881.

11   My special thanks to the independent scholar Virchand Dharamsay,

author of *Bhagwanlal Indraji: the First Indian Archaeologist*, 2012.

12 Andrew Stirling, *An account, geographical, statistical and historical, of Orissa proper, or Cuttack*, 1822.

13 *Epigraphia Indica*, Vol. XX (1929-30), 1933.

14 Ibid.

15 Only with the rise of the Vishnu cult does Shri become Lakshmi, whereupon she is relegated to the role of benign consort and goddess of wealth and prosperity, required to follow Vishnu as faithful wife through all his avatars (except that of the Buddha).

CHAPTER 6: SATAVAHANAS AND ROMAN GOLD

1 W. Sykes, 'Inscriptions of the Boodh caves near Joonur, communicated in a letter to Sir John Malcolm, G. C. B., President of the Bombay Literary Society', *Journal of the Royal Asiatic Society*, Vol. IV, 1837.

2 W. H. Schoff, *The Periplus of the Erythraean Sea*, 1912.

3 *Akananuru*, poem 149, verses 7-11, as translated by P. Meile, 'Les Yavanas dans l'Inde tamoule', *Journale Asiatique*, 232, 1940, quoted in Lionel Casson, *The Periplus Maris Erithraei*, 1989.

4 E. J. Rapson, *A Catalogue of Indian Coins in the British Museum: Coins of Andhra Dynasty, the Western Ksatrapas, etc*, 1990.

5 The Maharashtrian polymath and eminent Indologist Ramakrishna Gopal Bhandarkar, whose name lives on in the Bhandarkar Oriental Research Institute in Pune, believed the word should be translated as 'protector of the Brahmans'.

6 Andrew Schelling, *Dropping the Bow: Poems from Ancient India*, 1992.

7 See Rea's ground-breaking *A Forgotten Empire: Vijayanagar*, published in 1900, the opening sentences of which still have the power to thrill, despite their author's anti-Muslim bias, e.g. 'When Vijayanagar sprang into existence the past was done with for ever, and the monarchs of the new state became lords or overlords of the territories lying between the Dakhan and Ceylon ... And yet in the present day the very existence of this kingdom is hardly remembered in India ... Even the name has died out of men's minds and memories, and the remains that mark its site are known only as the ruins lying near the little village of Hampe ... '

8 A. H. Longhurst, *The Buddhist antiquities of Nagarjunakonda*, Madras Presidency, 1938. In his report Longhurst also commented that 'the ruthless manner in which all the buildings at Nagarjunakonda have been destroyed is simply appalling. This cannot represent the work of treasure-seekers alone since so many pillars, statues, and sculptures have been wantonly smashed to pieces.'

9 From Li Rongxi's translation of 'The Life of Nagarjuna Bodhisattva Translated from the Chinese of Kumarajava', *BDK English Tripitaka 76-III, IV, V, VI, VII Lives of great monks and nuns*, 2002.

10   See Stephen Batchelor, *Verses from the Center: a Buddhist Vision of the Sublime*, 2000. Nagarjuna's teaching was built around the twin concepts of *sunyata*, or 'emptiness', referring to the 'emptiness' of inherent existence, and *Pratiyasamutpada*, or 'dependent origination', the chain of causes which result in the endless cycle of rebirth and suffering, but which can be broken by attaining liberation and nirvana. No less important is his clarification of the 'two truths' doctrine in the Buddha's teaching, the idea that there is *samvrti satya*, 'superficial truth', and *paramartha satya*, 'ultimate truth', the latter being that all is emptiness. In Batchelor's words: 'To experience emptiness is not a descent into an abyss of nothingness but a recovery of the freedom to configure oneself as an intentional, unimpeded trajectory through the shifting, ambiguous sands of life.' Batchelor writes: 'Nagarjuna's *Mulamadhyamakakarika* served as a catalyst to trigger the chain of events that was to revolutionize Buddhist tradition ... He opened up the possibility of tradition being animated as much by contemporary voices as by reference to ancient discourses and encyclopaedia. The key to Nagarjuna's *Verses* lies in his understanding of emptiness as inseparable from the utter contingency of life itself. Moreover, the emptiness experienced by easing one's obsessive hold on a fixed self or things is declared by Nagarjuna to be the Buddha's middle way.'

11   B. Subrahmanyam et al, *Buddhist Circuits of Andhra Pradesh*, 2011; Peter Skilling, 'New discoveries from South India: the life of the Buddha at Phanigiri', *Arts Asiatiques*, Vol. 63 (1), 2008.

12   See M. Arunchalam, *The Kalabhras in the Pandyan country*, 1979.

13   Tanlin, *Treatise on the Two Entrances and Four Practices*, c. 575. Quoted in Hutan Ashrafian, *Warrior Origins: the historical and legendary links between Bodhidharma, Saholin Kung-Fu, Karate and Ninjutsu*, 2014. See also Father Heinrich Dumoulin's classic *Zen Buddhism: a History*, revised ed., 2005.

14   Bodhidharma's links with kung fu begin with a manual supposedly written by him entitled *Yijin Jing* or 'Muscle Training Classic'. Research by Chinese scholars in the 1960s concluded that this was the work of a Taoist priest named Zining written in 1624. Bodhidharma the martial arts master only entered the public domain with the publication of a picaresque novel called *The Travels of Lao T'san*, published in 1907 by a Chinese author named Liu T'ieh-yun. This was very quickly picked up and adopted as fact by various martial arts practitioners in China, not least those at Shaolin. See M. Shahar, *The Shaolin Monastery: History, Religion, and the Chinese Martial Arts*, 2008.

15   The British Museum has a most elegant bronze standing statue of Tara from the eighth century, who may have come from the mainland. She was found lying by the roadside between Trincomalee and Batticaloa in the 1890s, having been dumped there by a local monastery in

a clear-out of all Mahayana elements at a time when Theravada Buddhism in Ceylon was undergoing a major revival and cleansing itself of all non-Theravada teachings.

16 The main source for this claim seems to be an eleventh-century Tamil Buddhist grammarian named Buddhamitra, writing in the Introduction to his Tamil compendium of Tamil grammar *Virasoliyam*, compiled during the reign of Virarajendra Chola.

17 B. Jambulingam, *Buddhism in the Chola Country*, 2000.

CHAPTER 7: JUGGERNAUT

1 Henry Yule, *Cathay and the Way Thither*, Vol. I, 1866.

2 Andrew Stirling, *Asiatic Researches*, Vol. XV, 1818.

3 Stuart put his Hindu statuary on display to the public in his house in Calcutta but after his death in 1828 the collection was shipped to London in accordance with his instructions and sold in auction, most of it being bought by John Bridge, whose heirs sold it to the British Museum in 1872.

4 Recent discoveries of other overtly phallic early linga in South India, such as the 7-metre-high linga in the Ardhanarishvara temple in Indabettu, Karnataka, identified by Professor T. Murugeshi of MSRS College in 2012, suggest that this type of linga was the original form, subsequently stylised and desexualised.

5 See, for example, T. A. Gopinatha Rao, *Elements of Hindu Iconography*, Vol 1, 1919.

6 Horace Wilson, the first Orientalist to translate the *Vishnu Purana* into English, concluded that it was a product of the eleventh century. Wendy Doniger suggests a date of 450 CE, which is older than most Indian historians accept.

7 Sringeri has subsequently been demoted in favour of Rameshwaram.

8 At Badrinath the weathered black stone *murti* said to represent Vishnu as Badrinarayan in the main temple shows Lord Vishnu in an unusual meditative *padmasana* pose. Since photography is forbidden and the statue always draped in vestments and garlands, it is impossible to make out what actually lies underneath. According to the *Skanda Purana*, this *murti* is said to have been recovered by Adi Shankara himself from a nearby lake and enshrined by him in the temple he built for it.

9 P. B. Desai, 'No. 19 – More inscriptions at Aldar', *Epigraphia Indica* Vol. XXIX, pp. 140–4, 1951–2.

10 Quoted by S. Anand, 'Bodhi's Tamil afterglow', *Outlook* magazine, 19 July 2004.

11 N. Vasu, *The Modern Buddhism and its Followers in Orissa*, 1911, pp. 158–59.

12 Abhimanyu Dash, 'Invasions on the temple of Lord Jagannath, Puri', *Orissa Review*, July 2012.

13 Ibid.

14 George Turnour, 'Account of the tooth relic of Ceylon', *Journal of the Asiatic Society of Bengal*, Vol. VI, Part 2, 1837.

15 Its probable destruction at the hands of the Portuguese is told in Charles Allen, *The Buddha and the Sahibs*, 2002.

16 Alexander Cunningham, *The Bhilsa topes*, Ch. XXVII, 1853.

CHAPTER 8: CHOLAMANDALAM INTO COROMANDEL

1 *Itinerario de Ludouico de Varthema Bolognese nello Egypto, nella Surria, nella Arabia deserta & felice, nella Persia, nella India & Ethiopia*, 1510; R. A. Eden, *History of Travayle in the East and West Indies*, 1577.

2 Richard Burton, *Footsteps in East Africa*, 1856.

3 Marcus Vink, 'The World's oldest trade: Dutch slavery and slave trade in the Indian Ocean in the seventeenth century', *Journal of World History*, June 2003.

4 Taken from the architectural historian George Michell's excellent guide *Badami, Aihole, Pattadakal*, 2011.

5 Muhammad Habib, tr., *The Campaigns of Ala'u'd-din Khilji, being the Khaza'mul Futuh (Treasures of Victory) of Hazrat Amir Khusrau*, 1931.

6 It has been pointed out to me that both here at Chidambaram and at Madurai the temple structures, much of which pre-date these raids, show no signs of extensive damage. So a case of hyperbole or just good restoration?

7 Zia-ud-Din Barni, *Tarikh-i Shahi*, tr. Sir H. H. Elliot and John Downson, *The history of India, as told by its own historians*, Vol. II, 1867.

CHAPTER 9: MALAYA INTO MALALBAR

1 William Logan, *Malabar Manual*, 1887.

2 P. S. Menon, *A history of Travancore from its earliest times*, 1878.

3 Younger brother of the prominent British Christian Evangelical and abolitionist Zachary Macaulay, whose son Thomas Babington Macaulay would later inflict upon India his notorious *Minute on Education* and, for better or worse, the Indian Penal Code. See Charles Allen, *The Prisoner of Kathmandu: Brian Hodgson in Nepal 1820–43*, 2015.

4 For more on Buchanan-Hamilton see Charles Allen, *The Buddha and the Sahibs*, 2006; and *The Prisoner of Kathmandu*, 2015.

5 Francis Buchanan-Hamilton, *A journey from Madras through Mysore, Canara and Malabar*, Vol. 2, 1807.

6 When the distinguished administrator and writer K. M. Pannikar, himself a Nair born of a Nambudiri father, published his ethnographic study,

'Some Aspects of Nayar Life' in the *Journal of the Royal Anthropological Institute*, vol 48, in 1918, the custom was to all intents extinct.

7   B. Sobhhan, *Dewan Velu Thampi and the British*, 1978. See also *Travancore State Manual*.

8   Colin Macaulay, *Desultory notes on a cursory view of some papers extracted from the records of the East India House, which have been printed for the use of the Committee of the House of Commons, on the Travancore Petition*, by Lieutenant General Macaulay, 1832.

9   Lord Monson and G. L. Gower (eds), *Memoirs of George Elers, Captain of the 12th Regiment of Foot (1777–1842)*, 1903. See also Richard Cannon (ed.), *Historical record of the 12th, or the East Suffolk, Regiment of Foot, containing an account of the formation of the Regiment in 1685, and of its subsequent services to 1847*, 1848.

10 Quoted in P. S. Menon, *A history of Travancore from its earliest times*, 1878.

11 Col. John Munro in a letter to the Madras Government dated 7 March 1818, quoted in *Appendix to the report from the select committee of the House of Commons on the affairs of the East India Company*, 1832.

12 R. N. Yesudas, *Colonel John Munro in Travancore*, 1977; see also W. Hamilton, *A geographical, statistical and historical account of Hindostan and other adjacent countries*, 1820.

13 Travancore State was in no way exceptional in recognising slavery as an institution. In a note on slavery in his Madras Presidency Census Report of 1871, the Census Commissioner pointed out that throughout the Presidency 'the whole of the Pariah community without exception were the slaves of the superior castes' and that 'almost all the inferior agricultural tribes were in a similar position'. Fifteen forms of slavery were officially recognised under Hindu law, and Brahmins, categorically, could never be slaves. The EICo was the first government in India to ban the buying and selling of slaves in its territories and to punish those caught transporting slaves. However, that seemingly progressive action has to be set in context: the EICo had itself been involved in the East African slave trade for the best part of a century from 1693 onwards, chiefly in order to stock its pepper plantation at Benkulen in Sumatra with labour. While never as active as Portuguese or Dutch slavers, the British authorities in Madras took full advantage of two bouts of widespread famine and social disorder throughout the Deccan in 1782–4 and 1790–93 to buy up young children from destitute families, along with slaves from the local rulers of Tanjore and Madurai, for shipping east.

14 W. T. Ringeltaube to Col. John Munro, Quilon, 30 March 1818. Quoted in I. H. Hacker, *A hundred years in Travancore, 1806–1906: a history and description of the work done by The London Missionary Society in Travancore, South India during the past century*, 1908.

15 G. D'Arcy Wood, *Tambora: the Eruption that Changed the World*, 2014.
16 Quoted in Robin Jeffrey, *The Decline of Nayar Dominance: Society and Politics in Travancore 1847–1908*, 1976.
17 Swami Vivekananda, *The Complete Works of Swami Vivekananda*, Vol. I, from comments made during a public address in Madras in 1897.
18 Wikipedia, Padmanabhaswamy Vishnu temple – sources cited there and contemporary newspaper reports.

CHAPTER 10: TIPPOO'S TIGER

1 For example, the Philadelphia Museum of Art caption for image 199-148-401 says: 'This vision of Kamadhenu, the wish-granting cow of ancient Hindu legend, combines a white zebu cow with the crowned, frontal female face, colorful "eagle" wings, and peacock tail of Buraq, the animal that the prophet Muhammad rode to heaven on his night journey (Miraj). From at least the fifteenth century, Persian paintings showed Buraq with a horse's body, wings, and a woman's face; the peacock tail may have been an Indian addition. Popular portrayals of Kamadhenu in India today often show her in this Indo-Persian composite form; this may be one of the earliest images to merge the visual characteristics of the Hindu Kamadhenu with the Islamic Buraq.'
2 Sir W. W. Hunter, 'The Religions of India', *The Times*, 25 February 1888.
3 Sir Henry Elliot, *The History of India, as told by its own historians*, Vol. 2, 1870.
4 *The Travels of Ibn Batutah*, ed. Tim Mackintosh-Smith. It has been argued that the real name of the mountain range that divides Afghanistan is the Hindu Koh, or 'mountains of India', derived from the time when Brahminism and Buddhism flourished in what was then Indian Gandhara, and that Hindu Kush is a corruption. But that misses the point, which is that by Ibn Battuta's time the main pass over the Hindu Koh had become known as the Hindu Kush, a trail of tears for the hundreds of thousands of enslaved Indians transported over it.
5 Koran 47:4.
6 See, for example, Scott C. Levi, 'Hindus beyond the Hindu Kush: Indians in the central Asian slave trade', *Journal of the Royal Asiatic Society*, Vol. 12 (3), Nov. 2002. The Slave Dynasty took its name from the fact that its founder, Qutub-ud-Din Aibak, was a Turkic slave who rose to become military commander under Mahmud of Ghori.
7 Bearing in mind that under *zakat*, the fifth pillar of Islam, it was also obligatory on all Muslims to give alms according to their wealth. But of course one requirement was compulsory, the other rarely enforced.
8 Duarte Barbosa, *The book of Duarte Barbosa*, 1516; tr. H. E. J. Stanley, *A description of the coasts of East Africa and Malabar by Duarte Barbosa*, 1866.

9   'Slavery in India', *The Asiatic and Monthly Register*, Vol. XXVI, 1828. See also http://malabardays.blogspot.co.uk/2009/01/murdoch-brown-overseer-of-randattara.html

10   Richard B. Allen, *European Slave-trading in the Indian Ocean 1500–1850*, 2014.

11   Charles Allen, *God's Terrorists: the Wahhabi Cult and the Roots of Modern Jihad*, 2006.

12   According to Benjamin Rice's *Mysore Gazetteer*, Tipu destroyed eight thousand temples. Let us assume eight hundred as more realistic.

13   The invaluable contents of Tipu Sahib's library, consisting of some two thousand manuscripts acquired in the course of his father's and his own predations upon their neighbours, were divided between Cambridge and Oxford universities in Britain and the College of Fort William in Calcutta.

14   The full story is told in Charles Allen, op. cit.

15   Abdulla bin Swalih al Usaimeen, quoted in Muhammad Safi BA thesis paper 'The role of Sayyed Fazl Pookkaya Thangal in the anti-colonial movement in Malabar', undated.

16   M. T. Ansari, *Islam and Nationalism in India: South Indian Contexts*, 2016.

17   R. C. Majumdar, *History of the Freedom Movement in India*, Vol. 3, 1988.

ENDNOTE: HISTORY AND ANTI-HISTORY

1   A delightful English translation by Kausalya and George L. Hart is accessible online as part of Project Madurai, which makes Tamil literary works freely available: www.projectmadurai.org/pm_etexts/utf8/pmuni0415_03.html

2   H. C. Clifford, *A Letter to the Editor of the Bombay Times, with Prefatory Remarks and an Appendix*, 1842.

3   Aswathi Thirunal Gouri Lakshmi Bayi, *Sree Padmanabha Swamy Temple*, 1998.

4   Nancy Gardner Cassels, *Social Legislation of the East India Company: Public Justice versus Public Instruction*, 2010.

5   For example, by the ninth century England had produced such histories as Gildas's *De Excidio et Conquestu Britanniae*, the *Anglo-Saxon Chronicles* and the Venerable Bede's *Historia ecclesiastica gentis Anglorum*.

6   Robert Caldwell, *A political and general history of the district of Tinnevelly*, 1881.

7   Roberto Calasso, *Ardor*, 2014, tr. Richard Dixon.

8   G. P. Deshpande, *Dialectics of Defeat: Problems of Culture in Post-Colonial India*, 2006.

9   See his 'Letter to the Hindus of Madras', Sep. 1894, in *Letters of Swami Vivekananda*, 2002.

10   Swami Vivekananda to Swami Ramakrishnananda, Chicago, 19 March

1894, in *Letters of Swami Vivekananda*, 2002.

11   Swami Vivekananda to Alasinga Perumal, from New York, 29 Sep. and 19 Nov. 1894, in *Letters of Swami Vivekananda*, 2002.

12   Swami Vivekananda, *Letters*, Vol. 4.

13   For a fuller understanding of Vivekananda's rebranding of Hinduism, and the Vedic science of yoga, see Meera Nanda, *Science in Saffron*, 2016.

14   G. G. Joseph, *The Crest of the Peacock: The Non-European Roots of Mathematics*, 2000.

15   Quoted in Anita Diehl. *E. V. Ramaswami Naicker-Periar: a Study of the Influence of a Personality in Contemporary South India*, 1977.

16   Max Müller, *Biographical essays*, 1884.

17   Quoted in Dr Zareer Masani, 'The saffron censorship that governs India', in the *Independent*, 26 March 2015.

18   V. D. Savarkar, *Samagra Savarkar vangmaya*, Vol. 3, 1927.

19   M. S. Golwalkar, *Bunch of Thoughts*, 1942. But see William Dalrymple, Koenraad Elst, Arundhati Roy and many others.

20   S. R. Goel, *How I Became a Hindu*, 1982, rev. 1993.

21   Raj Sharma, *The Caste System: a Report*, c. 2008.

22   A roll of honour from nineteenth-century Germany alone would have to include, in addition to those already named, such luminaries as Peter von Bolen, Otto von Böhtlink, Paul Deussen, Martin Haug, Alfred Hillebrandt, Franz Kielhorn, Heinrich Lüders, Gustav Oppert, Richard Pischel, Rudolf von Roth, Lucian Scherman, Leopold von Schroeder, Adolf Stenzler, Albrecht Weber and Ernst Windisch. This tradition of German Indology has continued to the present day, thanks to the ongoing scholarship of such modern academics as Professors Oscar von Hinüber, Klaus Klostermaier, Herman Kulke, Lothar Lutze, Annette Schmiedchen, Heinrich von Stietencron, Michael Witzel and the leading authority on Ashokan edicts and sites, Harry Falk.

23   Max Müller, 'Lecture 1. What can India teach us?' *Gifford Lectures*, 1883. When that great Indian reformer Swami Vivekananda met Professor Müller in Oxford in 1894 he was moved to describe the meeting as a 'revelation', going on to declare: 'His long and arduous task of exciting interest, overriding opposition and contempt, and at last creating a respect for the thoughts of the sages of ancient India – the trees, the flowers, the calmness, and the clear sky – all these sent me back in imagination to the glorious days of ancient India, the days of our *brahmarshis* and *rajarshis*, the days of the great *vanaprasthas*, the days of *Arundhatis* and *Vasishthas*. It was neither the philologist nor the scholar that I saw, but a soul that is every day realizing its oneness with the universe.' (Swami Nikhilananda, *Vivekananda: A Biography*, 1953.)

24   Swami Giri's *Myth of the Aryan invasion* is an online publication, not to be confused with *The Myth of the Aryan Invasion of India* written by

another US convert to Hinduism, the prolific author David Frawley whose books include *In Search of the Cradle of Civilisation* (1995) which also rejects the Aryan Invasion Theory.

25 Mahesh Sharma, quoted in an interview published in the *Indian Express* on 11 September 2015.

26 I happen to disagree with quite a few of the judgements that Professor Thapar has made in the course of what now amounts to a huge body of published work extending over half a century, particularly with regard to Muslim iconoclasm, but I fully acknowledge that those conclusions were arrived at on the basis of thorough research and not ideology, which is what differentiates her and her colleagues from their opponents.

27 Romila Thapar, *The Past and Prejudice*, 1975, originally broadcast on All-India Radio as three lectures in January 1972.

28 Romila Thapar, 'Hindutva and history: why do Hindutva ideologues keep flogging a dead horse?', *Frontline*, Vol. 17, Issue 20, 30 Sep–13 Oct 2000. More recently still, the distinguished economist and Nobel Laureate Dr Amartya Sen has written at length about the emergence of the Hindutva phenomenon and the dangers posed by its rewriting of Indian history in *The Argumentative Indian: Writings on Indian Culture, History and Identity*, published in 2005.

29 Wendy Doniger, *The Hindus: An Alternative History*, 2009. Quoted in her Introduction, p.17.

30 James W. Laine, *Shivaji: Hindu King in Islamic India*, 2003.

31 Editorial, 'Resurrecting the author', *The Hindu*, 7 July 2016.

32 Anand Ranganthan, 'The death of nationalism: Who killed Dabholkar, Pansare and Kalburgi', *Newslaundry*, 14 September 2015.

33 Attributed to the US senator and sociologist Daniel Moynihan.

34 It also has some admirable media proprietors, such as the owners of Chennai's family-run *The Hindu* newspaper, the most widely read English-language daily in South India, and its fortnightly magazine *Frontline*. Founded in Madras in 1878 by six Tamil lawyers and law students to counter what they saw as the bias of the Anglo-Indian press of the time, *The Hindu* continues to maintain that same tradition of standing up to the orthodoxy of the day and giving space to the unorthodox. *Newslaundry* is another such news organisation that comes to mind.

PICTURE CREDITS

Every effort has been made to trace copyright holders and to obtain their permission for the use of copyright material. The publisher would be grateful if notified of any corrections that should be incorporated in future reprints or editions of this book.

Cover and page vi: © the Trustees of the British Museum.
Page xiii: James Forbes, *Oriental Memoirs*, 1813.

INTRODUCTION

Page xvi: Churchill, *Collection of Voyages and Travels*, 1744.
Page 1: © British Library London, UK/Bridgeman Images.

CHAPTER 1

Page 16: E. Thurston, *Castes and Tribes of Southern India*, 1909.
Page 17: © British Library London, UK/Bridgeman Images.
Page 21: © British Library London, UK/Bridgeman Images.
Page 24: (top) Photo courtesy of Dr Shanti Pappu, 'Prehistoric antiquities and personal lives: the untold story of Robert Bruce Foote', *Man and Environment*, XXXIII (1), Sharma Centre for Heritage Education, 2008; (right) *The Foote Collection of Indian Prehistoric and Protohistoric Antiquities*, Madras Government Museum, 1916; (bottom) Both photos courtesy of Siddeshwar

Prasad, *Journeys across Karnataka*.

Page 30: (left) © Victoria and Albert Museum, London; (right) © the Trustees of the British Museum.

Page 32: (left) © the Trustees of The British Museum; (right) E. Thurston, *Castes and Tribes of Southern India*, 1909.

Page 41: Author's photos.

CHAPTER 2

Page 44: Author's photo.

Page 45: A. Cunningham, *Archaeological Survey Report for the Year 1872–3*.

Page 49: (left) National Museum, Delhi; (right) National Museum, Islamabad.

Page 52: Author's photos.

Page 62: (left) A. H. Longhurst, *The Buddhist Antiquities of Nagarjunakonda*, 1930; (right) Author's photo.

Page 64: © Victoria and Albert Museum, London.

Page 68: (left) Photo courtesy of the late Professor Bivar. A. D. H. Bivar, *Catalogue of the Western Asiatic Seals of the British Museum*, 1969; (right) © Victoria and Albert Museum, London.

CHAPTER 3

Page 74: © the Trustees of the British Museum.

Page 75: Author's photo.

Page 78: Photo courtesy of the Director, SOAS.

Page 86: Photos courtesy of Christa and Günter Neuenhofer.

Page 95: (above) Photo courtesy of Nigal Kalathil; (right) Los Angeles Country Museum.

Page 100: (left) India Post; (right) Wikimedia Commons.

CHAPTER 4

Page 104: B. L. Rice, *Mysore and Coorg from the Inscriptions*, 1909.

Page 105: © British Library London, UK/Bridgeman Images.

Page 108: Photo courtesy of Christa and Günter Neuenhofer.

Page 110: (top) Photo courtesy of Saraswathy Amma and Sharat

Sunder Rajeev; (bottom) Photo courtesy of Jibu K. Rajan.

Page 113: © British Library London, UK/Bridgeman Images.

Page 120: (top) B. L. Rice, *Inscriptions at Sravana Belgola*, 1889;
(bottom) Author's photo.

Page 123: Author's photos.

Page 125: E. Haeckel, '*Hypothetical sketch of the monophyletic origin
etc*', 1876.

Page 135: Author's photos.

Page 140: Photos courtesy of Iravatham Mahadevan.

CHAPTER 5

Page 142: J. Burgess, *Amaravati Report*, 1882.

Page 143: Author's photo.

Page 149: (left) Photo courtesy of Harry Falk; (right) G. Bühler, *ASI
Report*, 1883; (bottom) Photo courtesy of Richard Davies.

Page 153: (left) © British Library London, UK/Bridgeman Images;
(right) Photo courtesy of Aditya Patankar.

Page 160: J. Fergusson, *Rock-cut Cave Temples of India*, 1842.

Page 166: (top left) Author's photo; (top right) National
Archaeological Museum, Naples; (left) Ashmolean Museum,
Oxford.

CHAPTER 6

Page 168: Photo courtesy of Christian Luczanits.

Page 169: Author's photos.

Page 176: Both © British Library London, UK/Bridgeman Images.

Page 178: Wikimedia Commons.

Page 182: (left) © the Trustees of the British Museum; (right)
Author's drawing.

Page 190: Photos courtesy of Christian Luczanits.

Page 196: Author's photo.

Page 199: © Victoria and Albert Museum, London.

Page 201: (left) Chennai Museum; (right) Photo courtesy of Dr B.
Jambulingam.

CHAPTER 7

Page 204: © the Trustees of the British Museum.

Page 205: © British Library London, UK/Bridgeman Images.

Page 207: © Victoria and Albert Museum, London.

Page 209: (left) G. P. Pillai, *Representative Indians*, 1897; (right) J. Fergusson, *Picturesque Illustrations of Ancient Architecture in Hindostan*, 1848.

Page 211: Author's drawing.

Page 212 (left) Photo by I. K. Sharma, courtesy of the ASI; (right) Drawing courtesy of Joe Cribb.

Page 223: Unidentified Victorian engraving, c. 1860.

Page 226: A. Cunningham, *The Bhilsa Topes*, 1853.

CHAPTER 8

Page 228: H. Moll, 1715.

Page 229: P. Bestius, *Tabularum geographicarum contractarum*, 1606.

Page 238: W. Schouten, *Oost-Indische Voyagie*, 1676.

Page 243: (left) Freer Gallery of Art, Washington; (right) Author's photo.

Page 245: Chidambaram engraving, c. 1870.

Page 247: (top left) © the Trustees of the British Museum; (top right) © British Library London, UK/Bridgeman Images; (bottom) © the Trustees of the British Museum.

Page 253: Photo courtesy of Rangarajan Anguswamy and Leiden University.

Page 256: (top) © British Library London, UK/Bridgeman Images; (bottom) Author's photo.

CHAPTER 9

Page 260: Abbé Prevost, *Histoire General de Voyages*, 1746.

Page 261: J. Forbes, *Oriental Memoirs*, 1813.

Page 264: (left) Royal Asiatic Society; (right) *Illustrated Guide to the South India Railway*, 1913.

Page 267: Author's photo.

Page 271: © British Library London, UK/Bridgeman Images.

Page 274: Author's photo.

Page 276: (left) © British Library London, UK/Bridgeman Images; (right) P. S. Menon, *A History of Travancore from its Earliest Times*, 1878.

Page 284: © the Trustees of the British Museum.

Page 289: Both P. S. Menon, *A History of Travancore from its Earliest Times*, 1878.

Page 297: (left) India postage; (right) Courtesy of Ajay S. Sekher.

CHAPTER 10

Page 302: © the Trustees of the British Museum.

Page 303: Author's photo, courtesy of Cheraman Juma Masjid Museum.

Page 306: (left) © the Trustees of the British Museum; (right) Private Collection/Archives Charmet/Bridgeman Images.

Page 313: (top) © Granger-Bridgeman Images; (bottom) © British Library London, UK/Bridgeman Images.

Page 320: (top left) India Museum catalogue, pre 1861; (top right and bottom): Author's photos.

Page 325: Wikimedia Commons.

Page 327: © Victoria and Albert Museum, London.

Page 331: © Bettmann/Getty Images.

ENDNOTE

Page 334: © British Library London, UK/Bridgeman Images.

Page 335: © Victoria and Albert Museum, London.

Page 338: © R. Ashok/*The Hindu* newspaper.

Page 350: Private collection.

Page 354: Both India Postage.

Page 357: © the Trustees of the British Museum.

Page 368: Photo courtesy of Anand Ranganathan and *Newslaundry*.

INDEX